DEADLINE!

DEADLINE!

HOW PREMIER ORGANIZATIONS
WIN THE RACE AGAINST TIME

DAN CARRISON

AMACOM
American Management Association
New York • Atlanta • Brussels • Buenos Aires • Chicago • London • Mexico City
San Francisco • Shanghai • Tokyo • Toronto • Washington, D.C.

Special discounts on bulk quantities of AMACOM books are available to corporations, professional associations, and other organizations. For details, contact Special Sales Department, AMACOM, a division of American Management Association, 1601 Broadway, New York, NY 10019.
Tel.: 212-903-8316. Fax: 212-903-8083.
Web site: www.amacombooks.org

This publication is designed to provide accurate and authoritative information in regard to the subject matter covered. It is sold with the understanding that the publisher is not engaged in rendering legal, accounting, or other professional service. If legal advice or other expert assistance is required, the services of a competent professional person should be sought.

Library of Congress Cataloging-in-Publication Data

Carrison, Dan.
      Deadline! : how premier organizations win the race against time / Dan Carrison.
          p.   cm.
      Includes index.
      ISBN 0-8144-0726-9 (hardcover)
      1. Time management—United States—Case studies.   2. Deadlines—United States—Case studies.   I. Title.
  HD69.T54 C37 2003
  658.4'04—dc21   2002006055

Printing number

10   9   8   7   6   5   4   3   2   1

To my wife, Loan, and my son, James.

CONTENTS

PREFACE

The secrets of deadline management are best revealed through the lips of the executives, managers, and team members who actually met the challenge. In selecting which deadlines to profile in this book, my most important consideration was the availability of those who actually did the work. Of only slightly less importance was the company's willingness to *share* its deadline management philosophy with the rest of the business community, which would include, of course, its own competitors. Determined to reveal new techniques within each chapter, I sought a wide variety of challenges to profile, from a variety of industries—ending up with an NFL stadium, a nationwide film distribution system, a mission to Mars, a kidnapping, a futuristic jetliner, and a relief effort in the aftermath of the "perfect storm."

I discovered early in the selection process that not every company wants a writer running loose within its facilities, with the intent of publishing its managerial secrets. The six organizations that agreed to be profiled had no qualms about opening their doors to the public. This was due, in part, to the natural confidence of senior management and to the advocacy of key contacts within each organization, who "sold" the benefits of the book project to all who would be participating. Any writer hoping to gain access to an organization needs a champion—someone who enthusiastically embraces the concept of the book and who willingly runs interference, sets up and enforces the interview schedules, arranges for transportation to the actual job sites, and facilitates all of the follow-up questioning with patience and good humor.

I was very fortunate to have six champions: Terry Kuflik of Turner Construction Company, Robert Mintz at Airborne Express, JPL's Mary Hardin, Laura Bosley at the FBI, Debbie Heathers at Boeing, and Conoco's Margo Williams Handy. Thanks to their advocacy, the nearly one hundred hours of interviews with some very busy people went like clockwork. Thanks to their occasional protection from well-intentioned edits, the reader will find realistic, unvarnished business narratives in the pages that follow—not press releases.

During the seventy interviews, I was struck time and again by the professional capacity of the executives, managers, and team members who had accepted these seemingly overwhelming challenges and who had triumphed—sometimes against all odds. I met no "empty suits." These men and women were extremely impressive. Their organizations are lucky to have them. I only hope I have done justice to their remarkable achievements.

I was delighted to find that the techniques used to conquer the monstrous deadlines profiled herein could help me meet my own less dramatic deadlines, not the least of which was the completion of this book.

MAKING THE
IMPOSSIBLE HAPPEN

◆　◆　◆

If there is a universal response in the workplace to the sometimes unrealistic deadlines imposed upon us by upper management, or by our customer, it is probably best expressed in the ubiquitous cartoon image of a group of employees holding their sides in paroxysms of laughter, asking the hysterical question, "You want it *when?*" This cartoon is usually on the "inside" of a business, out of the sight of the customer and the CEO, where irreverent pinups are permitted to serve as stress relievers for those of us who, in reality, cannot laugh away even a preposterous deadline. As much as we would love to tell those whom we serve, "Poor planning on your part does not constitute an emergency on my part," we hear our own lips finally saying "Yes," as our heads nod affirmatively, as if bowing to the will of Providence.

And in the blink of an eye, we are suddenly saddled with a time-consuming challenge without the sufficient time to do it. The possibility (pointed out by our managers) that we will be heroes upon the successful completion of the mission doesn't help the sinking feeling in our stomach. The much more likely outcome, we say to ourselves, will be that nobody is going to be a hero because the job cannot be done; in fact, it can scarcely be *begun* before we simply run out of time.

Many of us accept the challenge of a business deadline in precisely the half-hearted way we might accept an athletic challenge from a

3

much more robust associate. We intend to go through the motions, like a good sport, fully expecting to fail and counting on the understanding of our peers, who cannot blame us for being unable to succeed against such overwhelming odds. We might even hope for a margin of victory in our failure, for having had the courage to take on such a task. So we roll up our sleeves and get to work, while scrupulously documenting all of our actions and all of the reasons why the deadline could not be met. The more intrepid may attack the deadline with full force, convinced that the way to win a race against time is simply to run as fast as possible—only to discover that the pace cannot be sustained for long, and that frenetic enthusiasm can create more problems than it can resolve.

In the following pages, the reader will find that some very serious deadlines have been met by cheerful, self-controlled team members, who consider themselves lucky to have been part of company history in the making. This is not to suggest these deadlines were without suspense, and even moments of despair. But all of the seventy or so "deadline busters" I interviewed for this book have a well-balanced, good-natured relationship with recurring pressure. The assignment of a deadline does not make them overly anxious, nor does it transform them into workplace demons, driven by time. All have learned from personal experience, or from seasoned team members, that seemingly impossible deadlines can be wholeheartedly accepted, systematically controlled, and successfully met. For the less experienced, these time-critical challenges proved to be rites of passage—and, for the company veteran, yet another hard-won victory.

The reader will benefit, as I have, from the experiences of the "giant killers" profiled in this book. The deadlines are varied: a new NFL football stadium that seemed doomed from the start; the ongoing distribution of America's movies to theaters nationwide, within a two-hour window; the 2001 mission to Mars—successful in spite of the historical fact that two-thirds of all Mars missions have failed; an actual kidnapping case (literally a "drop-dead" deadline); the design and delivery of the 777 wide-body jet airliner; and an intensive corporate relief effort in the aftermath of a "perfect storm." The organizations are varied: Turner Construction Company, Airborne Express, Jet Propulsion Labs and Lockheed Martin, the Federal Bureau of Investigation, the Boeing Company, and Conoco. Yet all of the deadline-management principles that emerged from the crucibles of these projects will serve the reader well—whatever the deadline, whatever the industry.

A serious deadline is a kind of crisis, one that can even affect your career within the organizations you serve. If you have not yet experienced a time-critical overwhelming task, you will. And there will be people within the workplace who will be counting on you, which is, in some sense, their way of isolating you as the responsible member. Fortunately, the procedures developed by the individuals and teams in these suspenseful and dramatic business case studies will help you not only tame the monster when it appears, but look forward to the next deadline to be handed down from top management, or from the customer.

Among numerous, practical deadline-management techniques, the reader will learn how to:

- Prepare a deadline template for future deadlines

- Begin before the starter's gun, and without the expected conditions

- Create a deadline-oriented corporate culture, in which your people eat deadlines for breakfast

- Make it easier for your customers to make *their* deadlines

- Mold your "free spirits" into a confident deadline team

- Move "slower" and be "faster" in the long run

- Stay in "the driver's seat" during even the most critical deadlines ain a state of deadline readiness

◆ Celebrate problems within an open, sharing, team environment

◆ Think beyond the deadline

There is nothing like a successfully met deadline to showcase your capacity to deal with anything that comes along. For those who wish to become the "go to" person in their company when deadlines appear on the horizon like looming waves—or those who simply wish to control their fear when time-critical challenges are assigned, or inherited from former associates who couldn't deal with the anxiety—*Deadline! How Premier Organizations Win the Race Against Time* will prove an invaluable and inexhaustible resource.

TURNER CONSTRUCTION COMPANY MAKES THE ROCKY MOUNTAINS THUNDER

*"On paper, this project seemed
doomed to fail."*
—CHRIS BRETTELL, PROJECT MANAGER, BRONCOS

"This job had a lot of hair on it."
—ROD MICHALKA, SENIOR VP,
TURNER CONSTRUCTION COMPANY

*The new $400 million Broncos stadium has
come in under time and under budget. Beating
both the schedule and the budget is
unprecedented in the sporting arena industry.*
—FACT

◆ ◆ ◆

All major construction projects have their share of headaches and must be driven against time, but sports entertainment arenas and stadiums present difficulties and risks not found in other buildings of similar cost, not the least of which is the intense public scrutiny. "An NFL stadium is like the town cathedral of the Renaissance," says architect Terry Miller, who led the design effort, "it's a community icon." The cathedral analogy seems most appropriate, although to suggest that NFL football is a "religion" in the city of Denver is to elevate the term "religion" above its normal modern day significance. Unless one uses the word with a more ancient context in mind, such as in the time of the Crusades, Broncos football is *more* than a religion in Denver; it is an all-consuming passion. Indeed, if the reverse were true—if matters of religion were attended to with the fervor reserved for NFL football—the geographical coordinates of the city of Denver would be a direct link to Heaven; feet would not long remain in contact with the ground.

As it is, the city is an earthly paradise of football fandom. And that can put an enormous pressure on the builder. For most of us, the anxiety we experience when confronted with a serious deadline usually manifests itself as an image of our unhappy customer. That image may sometimes haunt us through the daily struggle to bring the project in on time. But that is only one customer, in a big world. If there is a refuge from the prospect of failure, it may be in the consolation that it is highly unlikely we will be confronting that *particular* customer in the future. But in the case of failing to deliver an NFL stadium on time, there are hundreds of thousands of customers—the hometown fans— all ready to point you out in the street as you drive the company truck, as the living embodiment of the Grinch who stole Christmas. Failure might mean not only losing your job, but also having to move out of town.

The funding mechanisms and approval processes are also more complex for sports entertainment projects. When building a stadium, the general contractor must deal not only with the individual owner, but also with state, county, and city authorities, all of whom represent a stake in the endeavor, and all of whom have the power to slow it down or bring it to a dead stop. The fiscal consequences of failure to meet the deadline are also greater with sporting facilities. If, for example, a builder is late in delivering an office building to its owner, thus delaying the tenants from moving in, he or she can grudgingly pick up the tab for a month's lost rent. But if a *stadium* does not open on game day—after 60,000 tickets have been sold (at, say, an average of one hundred dollars apiece), along with television rights, advertising, and anticipated profits from innumerable associated activities—picking up the tab for just that *one Sunday* would be an impossibility.

THE DEADLINE

Well aware of the inherent risks in building any sporting arena, Turner Construction Company contracted to deliver to the citizens of Denver a brand new NFL stadium by August 2001. Had this been a normal stadium project, the three-year timeline would have been aggressive enough. But unique to this particular undertaking were unprecedented challenges, some of which came as complete surprises.

- ◆ The timeline soon shrank to 27 months before construction could even *begin* (for reasons that we will explore).

◆ The project was to be a "design-build" job, which meant that it was to be designed as it was being built by a joint venture of builder and architect—the first *ever* stadium to be approached in such a radical manner.

◆ It had *two* contractual owners to appease, sometimes with different objectives.

◆ The labor force was mixed, union and nonunion, often a volatile combination.

◆ The ownership of the very land on which the stadium was to be built had not yet been transferred; only a third of the parcels were actually accessible on start day. That is like asking a contractor to begin building one-third of a house!

◆ Furthermore, it would be impossible to "clear the decks" and begin work even on the available land; the new stadium was to be erected literally in the shadows of two existing stadiums: venerable Mile High Stadium, which the city would not yet allow to be demolished, and McNichols Sports Arena, where the Denver Nuggets and Colorado Avalanche played, not scheduled for demolition until a year and a half into the project.

Additional minicrises occurred during the building of this stadium, including a precast concrete shortage, the inability of the original steel contractor to fabricate the enormous structures required, an endangered species of field mouse encountered on-site, and a design review board of local architects and city fathers who, in the middle of the project, suddenly demanded significant changes. It is positively amazing that this $400 million NFL flagship (officially named INVESCO Field) came in not only under time, but under budget, as well. The "under budget" aspect should be emphasized. Most stadiums, without encountering any of the above-mentioned obstacles, either open late or open unfinished, with months of "weekday" finishing touches remaining between games. Those arenas that have been brought in on time, in the literal sense, almost always conclude in the panic mode, running three frenzied shifts per day and usually costing millions of dollars over the guaranteed maximum price. To hand the owner the keys to a completely finished stadium *ahead of schedule and millions of dollars under budget* is unprecedented in the industry. How this was accomplished will be of interest to all who must win the race against time, in any business.

PARTNER WITH "YOUR ADVERSARY"

It is not surprising that, for a project of this magnitude, America's largest builder was chosen. Turner Construction Company, headquartered in New York, builds more than fifteen hundred projects a year across the nation and abroad, totaling, in 2001, $6.3 billion in value of construction. An equally prominent architectural firm was chosen: HNTB, the designer of Oakland Arena, Oakland Stadium, Qualcomm Park, Giants Stadium, Arrowhead Stadium, the Pontiac Coliseum, Kemper Silverdome, the RCA Dome, and the Ballpark in Arlington.

The organizations were selected a week apart, and both were pleased at the prospect of working with each other. But within weeks, it became obvious to them that their working relationship would be even closer than anticipated. "We realized," remembers Rod Michalka, senior vice president of Turner, "that, if we were to meet this aggressive timeline of thirty-six months, the traditional way wasn't going to cut it."

The "traditional way" puts the builder and the architect in an adversarial relationship. The architect is hired by the owner to design, and to protect, his or her vision. That design is ultimately put "out to bid"; general contractors then compete to arrive at the most cost-effective proposal to make the owner's vision a reality. The architect remains an advocate for the owner throughout the project, keeping a watchful eye on the contractor, so that all is done according to plan. The contractor, for his or her part, has every incentive to find errors and omissions in the drawings, so that more money for the corrections can be legitimately requested. This venerable arrangement, for all of its potential for finger pointing, has served the industry well over the generations. The only problem is, it takes a lot of time. The design alone could take a year and a half, followed by more than two years of construction—and that's assuming everything goes just right. Both Turner and HNTB could see that making the August 2001 deadline mandated by the owner using this tried and true method would be very doubtful. But, by building the stadium *as it was being designed*, the team could trim six to eight months off the timeline.

There is a sense of momentum in the very phrase *design-build;* while the contractor is completing Step 1, the architect is busily designing Step 2. The relationship requires a great deal of trust, as well as competence, between both entities. If there is a mistake, the builder cannot ask for more money, because the builder, not the owner, is responsible for the architect. The risk, then, is generally entirely on the builder, which explains why the design-build approach is rare on very large projects. Even rarer is the voluntary assumption of risk by the architect. Terry Miller, senior vice president of HNTB, was quite prepared to bet on the competence of his design team. "At first, we offered to assume 50 percent of the risk; but it really came down to who had the most control of the project—and that was Turner. So we agreed to assume 20 percent of the risk." The design-build team had now become a joint venture—the first ever on a project of this magnitude.

At the behest of Turner, FMI, a consulting firm for the construction industry, had been brought in to facilitate partnering sessions between Turner and HNTB management. Some on both sides were skeptical, fearing that these sessions, a few of which were scheduled to be at "retreats," would amount to nothing more than group hugs and campfire renditions of "Kumbaya." But the doubters were pleasantly surprised. The sessions were open, honest, and frank. In fact, they were so productive that it was decided to invite the owners themselves. Lance Nichols, leading the on-site design team, remembers the retreats well:

 They turned out to be very helpful, mainly because we learned each other's objectives. Turner's hot buttons were: schedule, safety, controlling costs. Mine were: a great-looking product, good quality, and a great referral for another stadium. The Broncos had one thing on their mind, and that was NFL football. The District had to think beyond football, to soccer and other community events. We realized that all of us were flying at different altitudes.

The recognition of one another's objectives would facilitate all future dealings within the decision-making group. Motives would be more understandable, and more predictable, reducing the chances of being at odds with one another without knowing the underlying cause. Key figures in the project would know where the other was "coming from." It was clear, too, at the end of these sessions, that, if the deadline were to be met, the owners would have to step down from the customer pedestal and become part of the delivery process.

Partnering with a traditional adversary can be both a liberating and disquieting prospect. On the one hand, it would be a great relief to have a former opponent as an ally; the battles typically fought would have already been won. No longer must you prepare to confront, or tiptoe around, your adversary; you're both on the same side. But new concerns arise. Accustomed to making unilateral decisions, you must now give a vote to your new partner in the enterprise. Company secrets, such as profit levels and customer "management" techniques, are now laid bare to somebody who may be an adversary once again, on a future project. If the venture does not go well, the relationship may end in bitterness, or in court. Later, like former lovers meeting at a social gathering, both of you may wonder what is being said behind your back. You would have been better off as simple adversaries. Conversely, if the project goes well, expectations will have been raised for partnering on the *next* project—an option, to be sure, but one that you would rather contemplate from a position of command. There will be more profit-sharing with a partner. True, less risk will be borne alone, but that, in itself, entitles your new partner to have a voice in matters you may consider none of their "business."

PARTNERING WITH A TRADITIONAL ADVERSARY CAN BE BOTH LIBERATING AND DISQUIETING.

The best justification for partnering with an adversary, of course, is the time that will be saved on a fast track project—if, that is, both parties feel equally driven to meet the deadline. The mutual assumption of risk will assure common cause and create a mandate for openness and trust. To the degree that mandate is followed, your relationship with your adversary will change irreversibly. Even if you find yourselves on the other side of the table on a future project, the insights gained into each other's character, business practices, and business concerns, will make for a better understanding of the other's position. Business is not, simply, "all about the numbers"; most of us would prefer to work with people we like and trust, especially if they are in an adversarial role.

DON'T WAIT FOR THE STARTER'S PISTOL

The team had been assembled; all that was wanting was the taxpayer's permission to build a new stadium, and that was by no means a safe assumption. Many proposed stadiums have been voted down in recent years; San Francisco lost a new stadium at 48 percent of the vote, and the Cardinals stadium referendum was defeated *twice*. The proposed new Broncos stadium did have something going for it, however: It was, in a sense, already paid for. The sales tax that had been instituted by the voters a few years earlier, in order to pay for Coors Field baseball stadium, was not slated to expire until 2016. But Coors Field had been paid off early, in 1999. The taxpayer was being asked to voluntarily allow this tax to continue, thereby financing the new NFL stadium. If this was approved, the residents of Denver would be getting two stadiums out of a tax originally designed to finance one.

The referendum, however, would not be held for months. Turner and HNTB could not afford to wait for the election results. In order to meet their deadline, they had to proceed *without* the authorization of the voters, up to the eve of the election, and then abide by the will of the people. Should the stadium proposal be defeated, the design-build team would be out of pocket for the cost of months of design and preconstruction mobilization.

"We simply had to take the chance," recalls Rod Michalka. "But at the same time, we had to minimize the risk. So I went shopping for insurance." One can only imagine the initial reaction of an insurance agent when confronted with Michalka's request to insure the design-build team's efforts should the stadium be voted down. The answer to the obvious question, "Why not simply wait until the voter has spoken before proceeding?" and the answer, "that the interim before the election was time too valuable to waste," may have raised an eyebrow, as well, for somebody unaccustomed to dealing with major deadlines. "It was not an easy sell. We went to Lloyds of London first. They did a lot of research into stadium referendums of other cities that had been defeated. They were also very concerned about the possibility that quarterback John Elway would retire, or that the Broncos might have a losing record up to the eve of the vote that would detract from the community's passion. You've got to remember: It's not as if the Denver fans were clamoring for a new stadium; they *loved* the old one."

Mile High Stadium, for all of its faults, was an NFL shrine. It had a glorious history and was normally packed to the gills. The proposed $400 million stadium, although twice the square footage, would have a total of only *two more seats*—reflecting the complex ratio of seats-to-demand that owners prefer—so it wasn't as if the fans were being offered a thousand more opportunities to witness a live game. There were a lot of very vocal Broncos supporters who saw few advantages in the new stadium for the average fan. The offer of twice as many executive suites is hardly compelling to a working person who could barely afford tickets in the old stadium. Yes, there would be more bathrooms and concession booths, but the promise of creature comforts does not sway the rugged individualist, and that's how Denver folks see themselves. The fact that the proposed new stadium was to be uncovered, at an altitude where it can snow any month of the year, and most certainly throughout football season, is a tacit recognition of the hardiness of the Broncos fans. Cowboys don't

HAD THEY WAITED FOR THE STARTER'S PISTOL, THE STADIUM WOULD NEVER HAVE BEEN COMPLETED ON TIME.

need domes to keep out the rain and snow, and they don't need fancy new stadiums with corporate names.

It was very, very possible that the people of Denver would, like those in San Francisco and St. Louis, reject the proposed new stadium. Nevertheless, the design-build team worked—in effect, without permission—up until the eve of the vote. HNTB put its resources into creating a design for the voters to approve, while Turner continued developing the construction timelines and affordable budget guidelines, with the full understanding that these months of work would be at risk. If the proposed stadium were to be rejected by the voters, the insurance policy would help ease the pain, but nobody could reimburse the design-build team for the cost of the policy—a whopping $1 million. Yet, in retrospect, it is clear to all that, had they waited for the starter's pistol, the stadium would never have been completed on time.

Waiting for official sanction before one begins a project seems a reasonable enough precaution. Negotiations over contractual terms have, after all, been stalemated or have fallen apart, and last-minute changes to the scope of work could certainly nullify the preparations we may have made. And, indeed, it seems the habit of a lifetime to wait until it's "official" before we begin most activities—be it a term paper, a New Year's resolution, a change of behavior (such as quitting smoking right after the *diagnosis* of emphysema, rather than after repeated warnings over the decades), or a project strongly rumored to be imminent. Not only do we wait for the announcement from on high, we wait further, often until the very last minute—perhaps for the proper send-off, or for others to climb onboard—before we begin.

Turner's example of starting without the official sanction of the citizens of Denver was definitely risky, but it was not reckless; even without the insurance policy, their decision to begin immediately made practical business sense. *Not* to have begun would have incurred much more risk. Not all organizations are so aggressive, however; a great many of us would not consider proceeding without proper authority. The bigger the contract the more cautious we become; it will not become an order until it has the blessing of senior management, and the credit department, and the legal division, etc. We fear that, by beginning work without the unqualified backing of our own organization, and that of the customer, we might be seen, at best, as naively enthusiastic; at worst, as irresponsibly obsessed. Yet, what is there, really, to lose? As long as the preparation is on our side of the fence, the risk is limited. Turner, after all, did not start digging at the site; their activities were internal, and the odds were good enough for an insurance company to indemnify the preparations being made.

Perhaps our deadlines will not require Lloyds of London, but most of them will require forward management. Just as a nation need not wait until an actual declaration of war in order to take steps to defend itself, an organization is sometimes entitled to move first and let the project catch up. In the unlikely event of the last-minute cancellation of the project, our activities can be defined as a very realistic drill, which should not be discounted. The next deadline will be better managed, due to the lessons learned in our preparations for the one that got away.

DON'T WAIT FOR THE EXPECTED CONDITIONS

During the first half of the football season preceding the referendum vote, the Broncos had no stauncher fans than the Turner executives in New York, who followed the team's progress obsessively. Elway had, to the delight of all, signed up for another year, and the Broncos—the previous year's Super Bowl champions—were undefeated by the time of the special election. The referendum authorizing the new football stadium passed by 57 percent to 43 percent. Although a comfortable margin, one wonders how close the vote might have been if all the pieces to the puzzle not been in place—if Elway hadn't committed to another season, or if the team had had a losing record. In any event, nobody could have been happier with the victory than the design-build team. After much back-slapping and toasts into the night to innumerable football players, past and present, Turner was poised, shovel in hand, to begin construction the very next day.

"That's when we found out from the city," grimaces Emil Konrath, the Turner veteran chosen to bring this enormous project in on time, "that we weren't going to get all of our land at once." In fact, access to nearly three-quarters of the property on which the stadium was to be built was being denied by the city. The design-build team, which had quite naturally anticipated complete control of all of the site—how else could you build a stadium?—was shocked. They were told the land issues would be settled in the "near future," but the clock had begun ticking. While their start date continued to move, in the wrong direction, the one constant that never moved was the end date.

There were a number of reasons for the delay in the availability of the land, none of them of much consolation to a design-build team ready to "blow and go." For one, the city had not yet completed the necessary transactions with the various owners of several land parcels and did not seem to be in any particular hurry to do so. Secondly, McNichols Arena, home to the Denver Nuggets and the Colorado Avalanche, had been contracted, unbeknownst to Turner, for a number of concerts and events well into the winter. Turner had planned to demolish the thirty-year-old arena months earlier; it was in the way; now they had to live with it and work around it. And thirdly, Turner learned that venerable Mile High Stadium, also in the way and slated for early demolition, was to remain standing as a safety net, should they fail to meet the August 2001 opening date.

So Turner found itself denied the very land it needed to build the new stadium the traditional way, as an oval spiraling up, and, to the extent to which it *could* build, it must do so in the claustrophobic proximity of not one, but two, existing stadiums.

That is when Emil Konrath had a general contractor's equivalent of *satori*, the moment of enlightenment said to come to Buddhist monks who have mediated long and hard. Not exactly the monkish type, Konrath stared at the problem long and hard, calling up his nearly three decades of bare-knuckle high-rise construction experience with Turner. Then, the answer came to him. HNTB's Lance Nichols remembers the drama of Konrath's solution. "Instead of building the stadium the way all stadiums have been built for the last one hundred years—as one complete, recognizable oval, coming out of the ground, level by level—it occurred to Emil that the stadium could be looked upon as *eight interconnected five-story buildings*. When he pointed this out to us, we suddenly realized we didn't have to build the whole thing, level by level; we could build it by sections, going all the way to the top. We only had the land for three out of the eight sections available to us, but we could at least start there."

Konrath's solution was like baking a pie one complete, perfect, succulent slice at a time. No stadium had ever been constructed in such a fashion; but, then again, no contractor had ever been denied access to three-quarters of the site on start day. Many months later, the land parcels would eventually be transferred, and permission would be granted to demolish McNichols Arena. If the design-build team had waited for that day to begin construction—*and no one could have blamed them* for insisting on possession of all the site—they never would have made the deadline. "The problem is," says Emil, "that even if you have a legitimate reason for not delivering on time, and God knows we had a good reason, all people would remember would be that Turner didn't deliver. I couldn't allow that to happen. If we were going to make the deadline, we had to start *somewhere*, we just couldn't wait."

KONRATH'S SOLUTION WAS LIKE BAKING A PIE ONE COMPLETE, PERFECT, SUCCULENT SLICE AT A TIME.

It is said that the subcontinent Greenland is so named because its discoverer, Eric the Red, wanted to attract settlers from his homeland. The hardy Viking men and women who were lured by the visions of verdant pastures found themselves confronted with a frozen wasteland, and, no doubt, a fast-talking Eric the Red. Anybody who has been in business for a few years has experienced the sensation of landing on similar shores—perhaps a sales territory that did not quite live up to the loving descriptions of management, or a "key account" that turned out to be run by the CEO from hell. At such times we find ourselves nodding our heads in agreement with the inner voice that warned us not to sell the house and relocate or take on the new challenge of key account manager.

Sometimes, the unexpected conditions are trivial: Business cards have not yet been ordered for us, and the company car, with the cell phone in the glove compartment, won't be available for a few weeks. And sometimes, the lack is more serious, such as desperately needed equipment on back order, or a change in management that has not yet produced our new manager. Or, perhaps we are developing a market plan for entering uncharted territory that just needs "a little more" research. In all cases, we are tempted to wait until we feel confidently ready to begin—driving the company car, business cards in our pocket, on the cell phone, updating our new manager on the arrival

THERE ARE OCCA-SIONS WHEN ONE HAS TO CHEAT—NOT THE CUSTOMER—BUT TIME, ITSELF.

of the needed equipment, and implementing a foolproof business plan that will turn the CEO from hell into a pussycat and terraform the forbidding sales territory into fertile orchards that grow contracts on trees.

Turner knew that critical deadlines cannot wait for everything to be "just right"; and that if one *does* wait, the deadline may be jeopardized. There are occasions when one has to cheat—not the customer—but Time, itself. It would be interesting to know if Turner would again build a stadium as if it were a series of interconnected high-rise buildings when it didn't have to (that is, when all the land was immediately available). But even if it had not discovered the solution for normal conditions, it certainly has created an action plan, should the incredible restrictions encountered on that project ever be encountered again. The kind of aggression exhibited by Turner is usually possible, oddly enough, from "conservative" companies, which do not demand, in the interests of fair play, intervention from the courts, or sympathy from the customer. Turner had every right to stamp its feet and appeal to higher authorities; instead, it accepted its conditions, but not its fate.

PUT ALL DECISION MAKERS UNDER ONE ROOF

Given the speed required to meet the deadline, Turner was determined to do things differently in a number of ways, one of which was to consolidate the decision makers. Normally, construction sites are characterized by "trailer cities"—a kind of Cannery Row of portable trailers and storage bins that take up a fair amount of the job site. While the important subcontractors are on-site, conspicuously missing are the architects and, of course, the owners, who can be found in their downtown offices. Turner insisted on putting designated members from the alliance of four—the Football District, the Broncos, HNTB, and Turner itself—under one roof, on the job site. Having so many partners, each protecting its own interests, in such close proximity, may have initially raised the specter of too many cooks spoiling the broth. But the environment proved to be a secret weapon.

Under usual conditions, the flow of information between contractor and architect, and architect to owner, and back again through the architect to the contractor, can take weeks, for each and every issue that arises. With the decision makers on-site, only a step across the hall from each other, the process is accelerated to warp speed. In the case of the Broncos stadium, potentially worrisome issues were often put to rest in minutes. Rather than trying to describe a situation to one another over the phone, the team members could simply step outside and *look* at the problem, and, with the subcontractors at their side, resolve it.

Not every issue requires the attention of the decision makers; there were decisions made daily in the field by supervisors who were, in turn, empowered to take control of their areas of concern. But inevitably issues rose to the surface, to be dealt with by the owner's representatives and the Turner-HNTB partnership. Meetings were often in session; it was unlikely, however, that a troublesome issue had a long life. "One thing that made this team different, at least from my experience," says Broncos project manager Chris Brettell, "is the way we went into meetings. We walked in with one goal, and that was to come out of it with an answer, not another 'tabled' question. And we'd stay in that room until we got it."

Of course, the system would not work without the decision-making authority being transferred from corporate headquarters to those closest to the task, on the actual job site. The representatives of the District, Broncos, HNTB, and Turner did not have to defer to higher authority, although that higher authority did exist. Each of the four respective representatives was empowered to make a command decision on behalf of his organization—not only empowered, but *urged* to make up his mind quickly. "There's a good decision and a bad decision," says Tim Romani, executive director of the Metropolitan Football District, "but the worst decision of all is indecision. Even if you make a bad decision in a timely manner, you'll have time to correct it. But if you wait too long, and *then* make a bad decision, there will be no time to recover. It's a double kill."

If there is anything to the caveat about having too many cooks spoiling the broth, it is certainly more likely if there are scores of assistant cooks banging about in the kitchen. Although somewhat compartmentalized, each of the on-site decision makers had considerable staffs; accordingly, there were lots of people under that roof. To avoid delay or confusion, the builders, designers, and owner's representatives found it best to funnel all information through one designated person on each team, and not to bother anyone else with it. As long as that rule was obeyed, the needless duplication of effort was avoided.

Apart from the critical determination to make this a design-build venture, the assembling of the decision makers under one roof proved to be the single most valuable technique for making the ambitious deadline of August 2001. For those of us who do not have a twenty-acre site to house all decision makers, the concept is still very practical. It is not out of the question to move a few desks around within our limited work space, in order to create a command center from which to manage our deadline, with empowered representatives—from the customer, as well as from any vendors involved—temporarily occupying a desk in an area dedicated to the project. The inconvenience for all will be compensated for by the speed at which the deadline is met and the pace of the bonding that will occur between all who struggle together to get the job done. Such an experience can be the stuff of reunions.

NEVER CREATE YOUR TIMELINE IN A VACUUM

Every deadline, big and small, requires a map. How one is going to get to the end state, and in what order, must be plotted out on a piece of paper, not etched in stone. The Turner timeline is a living document, reflecting unavoidable changes in course over the many months. Certainly, the design-build team would have preferred a straight, uneventful journey. But it was prepared to react with flexibility to circumstances outside its control. Its schedules were designed to adapt. The only thing that never changed was the delivery date to the customer; that *had* been etched in stone.

Developing a logical sequence of events for all that must be accomplished, in order to construct a one-of-a-kind NFL stadium, must be something like trying to imagine a million dollars in a single stack of one-dollar bills; the mind rebels, it cannot build up the image for long. Of course, Randy Mendenhall, Turner's scheduling guru, had a computer to retain the more than 7,000 activities that had to be mapped out logically. Nevertheless, he had to develop each schedule, one by one, each with its own set of internal monitoring mechanisms.

Mendenhall speaks in a deceptively slow, Midwestern drawl, which may be his way of managing his own emotions in such a fast-paced environment. When asked how he could coordinate the thousands of tasks that had to be completed before opening day, he laughs. "That wasn't the hard part; the hard part is always getting all the trades to buy in. They want to know if the schedule is realistic. *Can* it be done? I have to convince them it can, and then I have to enforce it." It would have served no purpose for Mendenhall to dream up a timeline that ended in August 2001, just to please Turner management; it would soon be exposed as a floating abstraction, a castle in the sky that could not be built as scheduled. So he involved the major subcontractors in all of his planning. "I try to get as much input as I can from those who will actually be performing the work." There is no conflict of objectives; everyone on the project wants to finish it as soon as possible. The quicker they get it done, the more money they make.

Mendenhall's timelines are really made up of minischedules, separated by milestones that represent significant "drop-dead" deadlines within the overall project. If the milestone is jeopardized, Mendenhall calls for battle stations; all of the subsequent tasks down the line are, by implication, also threatened. A recovery schedule must be developed to regain the original pace. One of the ways to enforce the schedule is to take advantage of every opportunity to move ahead. Mendenhall, accordingly, never counts on the identical opportunity being there the next day. "I grew up on a farm; the weather changed so fast that, when there was a clear spell to get something done, we rushed into it. It's that same way on a job site; for all you know you may be about to experience the worst winter in thirty years. You'd better make good use of every day you have."

Tim Romani likens milestones to incremental racing times. "A marathon runner needs to know his times for eight miles, twelve miles, etc. If he waits only for the final, finishing time, he'll never be able to manage his own race. It's the same thing with us." Mendenhall agrees and adds that schedules also perform a self-diagnostic function. "You have to have a schedule in order to find out where the problem is. Then, once you understand *why* you're not where you thought you would be, you can begin to recover." Between monitoring the status of milestones on the timeline and recovering where necessary, Mendenhall's day is rivaled only by that of an air traffic controller. "You can't let this get to you," he drawls, gesturing to the critical path charts that cover the four walls of his office. "I've seen a lot of good people that it got to." Some of the individuals he refers to no doubt developed their schedules in a vacuum.

Every business deadline, regardless of the industry, has some sort of schedule. Like sales or production quotas, they are sometimes the result of an airy business math, which divides the final goal, mandated by the customer or board of directors, into twelve-month chunks—and there's your target. Those who have to actually do the work may not be consulted, for fear of introducing objections that could jeopardize the end date; and that end date represents management's inviolable commitment to the customer. Management may even feel a bit embarrassed for caving in so quickly to the demands of the customer and now makes its own demands with a toughness that would have better served the company in earlier negotiations. The rank and file, then, is brusquely presented with a schedule, which is also enforced, like a law the police may not believe in but are compelled by grim duty to follow to the letter.

An unrealistic schedule creates cynicism within the team tasked to keep pace. Certainly, a team that does not believe it can do the job will, in all likelihood, fail; and it doesn't take the whole group to feel that way in order to jeopardize the schedule. Just a few members, whose work must be done before others can follow, can cause a ripple effect that will be very hard to contain later. If the team, moreover, senses that its leader is not a believer and is just bravely going through the motions, the deadline will not be met. By soliciting the input, and the commitments, from those who will perform the work, management not only has a more realistic schedule, it has also made it difficult for anyone to come back at a later date and object to the timeline. If the promised end date initially seems overly ambitious, a brainstorming session is in order, in which all who will be involved can explore creative solutions to meet the customer's mandate. Instead of a half-hearted collection of individuals, haunted by an impending failure, management will have mobilized a team bent on victory.

INVOLVE THOSE WHO CAN INHIBIT YOU EARLY IN THE PROCESS

Turner had finally been given permission to bury McNichols Arena in the parking lot of the new stadium. But, though welcome and long overdue, the actual demolition of McNichols Arena could have caused a delay in itself. Normally, all work would cease while everybody stepped back and watched the sturdy concrete structure, riddled with reinforcing steel, slowly taken down. The process could have caused weeks of delay. But Turner, typically aggressive, kept working on the new stadium, alongside one end of McNichols, while the other end of McNichols was being demolished. This way, crews could work (in complete safety) nearly up to the last minute of McNichols's demolition.

Nonetheless, there was a delay associated with the demolition. The Denver Fire Department, seeing a golden opportunity, requested permission to practice disaster response drills in the rubble of the old stadium. Although time was at a premium, Turner shut down its demolition operation and even helped fund the drills. At one time, there were nearly one thousand disaster response personnel on-site. Months later, with the national experience of the attack on the World Trade Center behind them, builders might consider such a gesture to the Fire Department a civic duty. But in spring 2001, this invitation was fairly unprecedented. It cost Turner two precious weeks.

"Why did we do it? It was good PR," explains Emil. "We made friends with an agency that could have held us up for a lot longer than two weeks, believe me. We don't get our certificate of occupancy until the Fire Department is happy. I'd much rather have them on our side." Accordingly, Project Manager Charlie Thornton set aside one day a week to deal proactively with any agency that could possibly have an influence on the schedule—and there were scores of them. "I made myself available to every city, state, or county agency that expressed an interest in the project, and I did it with a smile," he grins. "With one phone call, some unhappy bureaucrat—or a college professor who suspects we're digging into an ancient Indian burial ground—could have held us up for weeks. I kept them happy." Thornton's cooperative attitude is genuine; although a busy and preoccupied project manager, he is friendly and accommodating. By giving the project a friendly face, Turner was able to keep the community agencies and delegations on its side.

When a local academic study discovered evidence near the job site of an endangered species of mouse (officially, "Preble's meadow jumping mouse"), Thornton was all smiles and cooperation. While no doubt inwardly concerned at the prospect of an injunction halting construction, he personally invited the Department of Fish and Game experts for their judgment—and prayed. It turned out well for both Mother Nature and the new stadium; the federal department ruled that there was no adverse environmental impact. Had Charlie Thornton's attitude been obstructive, the verdict probably would have been the same, but perhaps a bit more prolonged. People have a habit of mirroring the demeanor of their counterpart; from day one, Thornton's proactive friendliness disarmed many a city councilman and state delegate who may have harbored resentment over the referendum results.

Turner's penchant for bringing people "on board" early in the process applies also to its own key subcontractors. Roger Webb of Baker Concrete, a major player in the project with a $50 million contract, was asked to "office" on-site fully six months before he would be pouring concrete. "For nearly half a year, I attended design meetings and gave my input; no contractor had ever asked me to stay so close to a project before I was actually needed. It turned out to be a good thing, too; we were able to save the owner a chunk of change." Webb was to have a brainstorm of his own.

Every stadium built to date has a mixture of precast concrete forms (structures that have been formed off-site and trucked in) and cast-in-place concrete structures, which are, as the term implies, poured "wet" into forms that are removed when the concrete dries. But the traditional method was not going to work under then-current conditions. Webb could see that, without the other land parcels being accessible, it was going to be difficult to erect the enormous precast structures, not to mention *store* those that would be needed on the future parcels. He started thinking about a method to pour concrete in place that could cover spans normally supported by precast structures. By welding together small four-foot panels, he was able to demonstrate to Turner that poured-in-place concrete was a viable option, one that could save the owner time and money.

Turner's policy of bringing key subcontractors on board before they're needed is in stark contrast to the "just-in-time" mentality of many businesses, which do not want to bring resources into play until the last possible minute, because resources, whether inventory or personnel, cost money. Had Turner brought Roger Webb on to the job site the day his work was to literally begin, as most general contractors do, the owner never would have benefited from his time- and money-saving innovation.

It was not always possible, however, to involve those who could exert a disproportionate influence on the project—especially during the months before the election, when there was no official sanction, and, therefore, no budget to pay everybody for their efforts. And, while the design-build team had plenty of enthusiasm, it was difficult to instill a similar *élan* into the bureaucrats and citizenry boards of Denver, made up of local professionals, until the project had been authorized and funded. Months later, Turner and HNTB were to be stunned by the emergence of a committee with the power to bring the job to a standstill. The city's Design Review Advisory Committee (DRAC) was composed of local architects, designers, and art historians. While Turner and HNTB knew that, somewhere along the line, they would have to go through the "formality" of a design review, no one could have guessed the degree to which it would become involved in the design of the new stadium. HNTB, the premier sports architecture firm in the nation, was suddenly being told that some significant changes had to be made.

The problem was, the design was 60 percent complete, creating perhaps the most distinctive NFL stadium to date. At the owner's insistence, the famous horseshoe shape of old Mile High Stadium had been incorporated into the new one, with the upper seating bowl simultaneously forming the shape of a giant saddle, appropriate for a team called the Broncos. As this was a design-build project, Turner had not been waiting around for a complete set of finished plans. The drawings for the foundation and structural steel had been released, so the work had begun. The caissons—enormous shafts drilled into the earth and filled with reinforced steel and concrete—had been poured, based on the loading calculations of the HNTB design. Structural steel had been put in place, similarly dedicated to a certain load. It was not possible, at this stage of the game, to make changes to the core without gravely altering both the schedule and the budget. In the words of HNTB's Terry Miller, "The train had left the station. The time for making significant structural changes had passed."

The design review committee interpreted the Turner-HNTB stance as resistive and uncompromising. HNTB no doubt felt it was being second guessed by "locals" whose suggestions betrayed an unfamiliarity with the complexities of a 76,000-seat, 1.7 million-square-foot stadium. In it's defense, DRAC members believed they had a fiduciary obligation to make sure the citizens of Denver would get a stadium that would be regarded as a thing of beauty for the next fifty years. Many on the committee thought the HNTB design could be improved upon. Furthermore, they had the power to insist on changes—the committee wielded the authority to influence the timing of Turner's receipt of the building permits. It could literally stop Turner in its tracks.

After a number of sometimes contentious meetings, Emil Konrath, using a mixture of diplomacy and the authority of a veteran builder, persuaded the committee that the core of the stadium was nonnegotiable. The foundation and the structural steel were in the ground, engineered to a specific load, and could not be altered. The committee could, however, suggest changes to the exterior of the stadium. This was no little sacrifice on the part of HNTB; to an architect, the exterior of the building is *what you see*. Thousands of hours of hard work and creativity had gone into a design it was justifiably proud of; to allow a third party not only to question its design but also to "improve" on it had to be a bitter pill. In the end, the DRAC crisis passed. The committee had exerted its influence and did make some changes to the exterior skin of the building, costing Turner time and the owners an additional $10 million. But the stadium was still a beautiful thing to behold. If Turner had to do it over again, it probably would have spent more time courting and cultivating the local architects.

PUSH, BUT PROTECT

Within a few strides from the job site, a fourteen-floor Red Lion Hotel overlooks the stadium. Conveniently, there is a bar at the top. It was not uncommon in the evenings to find a number of tradesmen from the project below, relaxing after their twelve-hour day. After introducing myself, I was invited to join a table of field supervisors, who looked over their mugs at me with suspicious glances. I explained that I was writing a case study of their project and asked if they could think of the single most important reason for such an enormous undertaking coming in under budget and ahead of time. Without hesitation, the name "Emil" erupted on the heels of raucous laughter. It took a moment for the supervisors, all of whom reported to Emil Konrath, to come up with a suitable term for his unique leadership style. "Driven management" was the consensus, and "Hell on wheels" the footnote.

Konrath does not deny the characterization. Throughout his career, he has earned a reputation in the industry for being a passionate advocate for Turner, and for the customer. Owners like him; they sense someone who is willing to fight for their interests. "I push hard. You have to keep the sense of urgency alive every day. So I'm always charging around the project. But," he winks, "I make sure there is somebody on the site to watch over the people I push, and to hold them back a little, if necessary."

Konrath himself embodied "the push," while safety director Mark Hargett was delegated to protect those inspired by Emil from their own enthusiasm." "Most safety violations," says Hargett, "are committed with the best of intentions—somebody trying to be a hero. Take a masonry guy, building a wall. He is well aware of the schedule and aware of the other guys down the line—painters, plasterers, electricians, and carpenters—who are depending upon *him* to keep on track. If he falls behind, so does everybody else after him. Sometimes this guy is willing to take a chance with his own safety, just to make up a little time."

Apart from the human concerns of life, limb, and family, a job-site accident can dramatically slow the pace of the project; a fatality can have a devastating effect on the morale of the entire crew. Few workforces recover from a job-site fatality and go on to meet the project deadline. So, although Hargett occasionally had to take a stand that seemed to hinder the momentum of eager subcontractors, such as insisting a heavier crane be brought on-site for a given task (which can take a precious week), his proactive vigilance in the long run saved the project from countless lost days.

Although not all deadlines require a safety director, they do require a similar guardian to protect enthusiastic "corporate soldiers" from themselves. Deadlines create a crisis environment; under pressure we are all apt to risk, if not our own safety, our better judgment. Even paperwork mistakes, made in the final hours of a very long day, can cost a task team precious time. Emil's leadership style of pushing—and of delegating someone to push back occasionally—is worth emulating on any time-critical project. Many managers assume that it is human nature to be easy on oneself and that all employees require motivation. But deadlines, while they bring out the best in us, can also bring out the worst: anxiety, fatigue, irritability, and disharmony at home. There may be times when a "push" is the last thing required, and when the manager should exercise great care in adding to the already sufficient burden carried by the team. Overtime hours should be monitored and occasional weekends "enforced," so that the team members, like athletes preparing for a great effort, are properly rested. Pizza parties might follow schedule review meetings, so that team members don't walk out of the room grimly obsessed; and when overtime is required, it is presented as a temporary challenge, rather than as a way of life. A smiling and confident manager, as well, can set the example, personifying a team that is "on track," cheerfully determined, and bent on success.

UNDER PRESSURE WE ARE ALL APT TO RISK OUR BETTER JUDGMENT.

BURN YOUR BOATS

When Caesar invaded England, he assembled his army on the beach to watch the very boats on which it arrived burn to ashes. It was Caesar's graphic way of saying that there was no way home; the only option was victory. The Roman emperor, unlike Turner, was not hampered by a historical equivalent of the city of Denver.

The city of Denver was, quite understandably, suspicious of the claims of contractors and architects. It had been intimately involved in the spectacular Denver International Airport project, which became almost a national byword for waste and overruns. In the end, DIA was tens of millions of dollars over budget, and very late. Now, another contractor was full of promises and, worse, asking for a demonstration of the city's trust: Turner wanted permission to demolish venerable Mile High Stadium a year before its replacement was due to be completed.

Even though Turner could prove that the new stadium was actually ahead of schedule, the very idea that the Broncos might not have a facility in Denver for even one Sunday, should Turner fail for whatever reason to deliver, was abhorrent to the city. And, actually, the city had every incentive to keep Mile High as long as it could. Should Turner fail to have the new stadium ready for football on August 1, the first few NFL games would be played at Mile High, with all proceeds going to the city, while, when the new stadium hosted the games, the proceeds would go to the Broncos. Perhaps not surprisingly, permission to demolish Mile High months ahead of schedule was denied.

Not only could Turner not burn its boat, it couldn't escape its presence. The work for the new stadium took place literally in the shadow of the old. Mile High loomed over the job site, as if to reassure the community, and the workers at the site, that home games would be played in Denver, even if worse came to worse. Rather than being in any way buoyed by the physical manifestation of a safety net, the Turner team was frustrated and determined to eradicate, to the best of its ability, the notion that Mile High Stadium still existed in the event of an emergency. By imparting a sense of urgency to its subcontractors, who became obsessed with meeting the schedule on a daily basis, and by *never once suggesting that the old stadium was an alternative* to opening August 1, 2001, Turner was able to eliminate Mile High as a factor to be considered "just in case." The blocking-out process was so complete in the minds of some that, when I questioned them about the old stadium, their expressions seemed momentarily to ask, "Stadium? What stadium?"

Turner had to suffer the presence of the older stadium for a contingency it would not allow itself to seriously contemplate. A "back-up plan" is supposed to help one reach the deadline, in the event of a failure along the way. Considering the future use of the older stadium would not be an alternate path, any more than a draft of the terms of surrender is a "back-up plan" for victory. Unable to burn its very large "boat," the Turner team simply blocked it out of consciousness.

The very idea of cutting off all means of retreat is frightening to most of us, who have been schooled to "keep our options open." Having no "fall-back position" is the equivalent to having our back to the wall. Yet, this is precisely the feeling the wise deadline manager will cultivate. If the team is allowed to think in terms of options short of complete victory—if, for example, it believes that *substantial* completion of the project will be grudgingly accepted by the customer, in a year of economic downturn—then there will be few late nights at the office. The proper attitude can be encouraged simply by cutting off all directions except forward. The team should be aware that there will be no personnel reassignments until the deadline is met, and, for that matter, no vacations scheduled during the final, critical weeks. Team meetings should never be allowed to become forums in which to revisit past issues; the discussions must be focused on tomorrow. The manager must do everything possible to sustain a sense of momentum, by reviewing the weekly progress made and forecasting the team's position in the weeks to come, securing, in the process, commitments from every member to keep pace with the schedule. At no time should there be discussions of the remotest possibility of not meeting the deadline, or speculation that the customer might be withholding unrevealed margins of time, or might be secretly satisfied with less than a completed project.

THE PROPER ATTITUDE CAN BE ENCOURAGED SIMPLY BY CUTTING OFF ALL DIRECTIONS EXCEPT FORWARD.

MAKE THE DEADLINE A PRESTIGIOUS PROJECT

Enforcing safety regulations, or rules of conduct, on such a high profile project is perhaps easier than on other, less prominent, sites simply because nobody wanted to be thrown off the job. The new Broncos stadium represented a once in a lifetime opportunity for the local tradespeople, all of whom are Broncos fans. More prestigious than even Denver International Airport (which will not have an NFL blimp hovering over it every Sunday, broadcasting its pictures all over the nation), the stadium would become a point of reference for all who were involved in its creation.

"If you look closely," says Bob Sternberg, one of Turner's senior site managers, "very closely, because it's so discreet, you will find an initial etched in stone here, and a name there, where only its owner can find it, to show his buddies, or his kids. Everyone on this job is proud to have worked on it. Years from now, as they watch the games here or at home, they can say, 'Yeah, I did that.' So, why spend your day building a warehouse by the railroad tracks, when you can be on the most famous project in the city?"

It is safe to say that, in many companies, deadlines are treated something like top secret projects. The task teams meet behind closed doors; the goals of the deadline are not broadcast to the rest of the office staff, perhaps out of a superstitious fear that widespread awareness may compromise its chances of success. Only afterwards are victorious team members highlighted in the company newsletter, as if only now the story can be told. But a deadline challenge, properly presented, should be the buzz of the workplace; those chosen to be a part of it should count themselves lucky. And if, in fact, many employees are relieved *not* to be part of an endeavor that has the anxious eye of management on it, preferring anonymity to association with a pet project that may very well fail, management simply hasn't presented the opportunity well.

By making the deadline a prestigious project, even those in the organization who are not associated with it walk a little taller and may boast to friends and family of the challenge the company has taken on. It is frankly amazing how many employees of a large organization may not be aware of the great adventures embarked on by their own associates down the hall. The more aware the rank and file is of the company's great challenges, the more supportive it can be; great ideas often do appear in the Suggestion Box, but not if the deadline is pursued in secret. When employees know that something really important is "in the works," they tend to be less vulnerable to competitive job offers and more likely to buy company stock, and perhaps the stock of the customer being served. A prestigious project makes everyone within the organization more aware of the customer and less likely to unwittingly offend the customer; the cozy relations between the executives of both parties can be undone by the actions of those far removed from the conference rooms—receptionist, delivery driver, or customer service technician—who may not even know of the critical undertaking in progress.

Properly presented, a major deadline is both an adventure and a rite of passage within the organization. It is the chance of a career to associate oneself with a team of special individuals who stepped forward at a time of crisis. Some who shied away from the project will volunteer for the next, sorry to have missed the chance to have been a part of a widely recognized endeavor. A prestigious deadline imparts a sense of history—because many projects hearken back to previous undertakings—and a sense of history in the making. No manager should underestimate the lure of a publicly declared challenge; there are those in every organization who yearn for something meaningful in the workplace, or, at the very least, a dynamic change of routine.

SETTLE CONFLICTS IMMEDIATELY

One of the deadline-management tools that came out of the partnering sessions facilitated by FMI was the "stand and deliver" session. On a regular basis, task teams were required to update management with a formal presentation. What prevented these presentations from becoming "dog and pony shows" was the degree of interaction. Project managers did not sit back with folded arms while nervous field supervisors reported; they were actively involved. More often than not, the "presentation" evolved into an earnest dialog.

"We asked," says Lance Nichols, "'What can we do to help you?' And, conversely, 'What are we doing to hinder you?'"

The ball frequently ended up on management's side of the court. In either case, action items were assigned, accountability accepted. These sessions greatly helped this complex project keep pace with the ambitious schedule. While management was being made aware of issues that, if unresolved, could jeopardize the deadline, the task team members had an opportunity to make their case for more support. Furthermore, they had a chance to distinguish themselves, in front of management, from the more than one thousand warriors on the job. More than one tradesman, supervisor, and subcontractor caught the eye of management during the stand and deliver sessions.

One session in particular serves as an example to all who must manage teams committed to making a deadline. In the absence of Emil Konrath, who had an appointment, a key contractor "stood and delivered" a shocking announcement: After a careful analysis of the schedule and of the remaining work to be done, the contractor projected a finish date for its own trade months *beyond* the sacred, immutable end date of August 2001. As one can imagine, the room erupted into earnest and heated discussion. In an effort to calm things down, the person presiding over the meeting called for a two-week "cooling-off" period, in which the contractor would reexamine his projections. A follow up meeting was accordingly scheduled.

> "**I'LL TELL YOU HOW TO SETTLE CONFLICTS: YOU SETTLE THEM IMMEDIATELY.**"

In recalling the situation, Konrath's lips tighten. "A few minutes after I heard about the meeting I missed—and now that I think about it, my not being there may have had something to do with that announcement—I was banging on the trailer door of that contractor. As it turned out, he didn't need two weeks at all; I gave him two *hours* to reconsider, and guess what? He was suddenly 'on schedule' again." Konrath smiles at the notion of a "cooling-off" period. "I know there are management books out there about conflict resolution, and how to patiently bring everybody back on course and pulling in the same direction. But on a job like this, every minute is precious. Do you think I'm going to let somebody hold up all the subsequent trades for two whole weeks?" Konrath leans forward. "I'll tell you how to settle conflicts: You settle them immediately."

Emil, incidentally, is perhaps five foot six and 160 pounds. In his late fifties, his hair is graying, and he has the world-weary and wise face of a general who is in no hurry to go to war. He is, in fact, rather distinguished. Yet, he banged on the door of an upset contractor twenty-five years his junior, not because he is physically intimidating but because he felt compelled to rise to the defense of his project. His was an effort to protect something he cared about, not simply to impose his will, and he went alone into a situation that had not yet had sufficient time to defuse. From a purely human relations standpoint, he chose exactly the wrong moment to oppose a rebellious team member bent on gaining either more time or more money—a contractor who, after his public declaration, could little afford to lose face. Yet, from the perspective of a deadline manager, Konrath did the right, and courageous, thing.

One certainly cannot blame the "stand and deliver" session facilitator for declaring a cooling-off period; our experience tells us that the passage of a week or two often gentles the soul. Usually two men who were on the verge of coming to blows will later regret the incident and yearn for a face-saving way to reconcile. Mediators, in fact, often fulfill the role of a parent or teacher, in an adult reenactment of a childhood playground incident, by coaxing the two parties into the renewed friendship each privately desires but cannot be the first to express. If Human Resources is made aware of a clash of wills among employees, it will schedule just such a meeting or two and probably resolve the issue to the satisfaction of both parties. But the time spent placating the offended egos of team members is time lost to the deadline, and, for people like Emil Konrath, the deadline comes first.

Equally wise managers will make it clear to their teams that, like all great enterprises, the deadline is bigger than those who serve it, and that every member must occasionally subjugate personal likes and dislikes, at least until the project is over. Deadlines are just as much a test of maturity as they are of one's ability to manage resources and time. But participating in a great deadline can also be a liberating experience. Priorities temporarily rearranged seldom return to their previous ascendancy. We may find, after the victory celebration, that service—to the company, to the community, and to loved ones—is more fulfilling than being served.

It may be, in retrospect, a good thing that Emil Konrath missed that meeting and was compelled to deal with the contractor one on one. Settling conflicts immediately is certainly good deadline management advice, but settling them privately is best for all concerned. Emil, of course, is an experienced executive and may have listened to the contractor's provocative announcement and simply tabled the issue until a follow-up session, later that day. But he is also a human being, and there is some speculation that, had he been in the room, the acoustical football stadium would have echoed his response. By dealing with the issue "off-line," without an audience (or, perhaps one should say, without "witnesses"), he was able to resolve the problem in such a way that the contractor could comfortably go to work the next day, albeit with a revised schedule and a bruised ego, without feeling too terribly self-conscious among fellow workers.

LIVE IN TOMORROW

As the nation's largest builder, Turner exercises great power on a project. But, for all its might, Turner is, like every general contractor, paradoxically dependent on its subcontractors to fulfill their commitments. Turner based its Guaranteed Maximum Price to the owners of the new stadium largely on the bids provided by its "subs," all contractually bound to their original proposals. But if the subcontractor fails to perform, the eventual cost to the builder, who must now hire a replacement and recover the pace of all the subsequent subcontractors, can be out of all proportion to the original bid. Smart builders, therefore, are not seduced by low bids and would much rather negotiate with a truly qualified, known entity. Having done that, even smarter builders have a back-up plan, or resource, should the qualified sub have a problem.

One of the endearing qualities of old Mile High Stadium was, quite simply, the noise it made. Broncos fans discovered that by stamping their feet in unison in the more recently added portions of the stadium—made out of steel, in an otherwise concrete stadium—an enormous sound could be produced, eventually dubbed by the sports media as "Rocky Mountain Thunder." The deafening reverberations are, of course, intimidating to the visiting football teams, as are the signs, near the visitor's bench, declaring the 5,000-foot altitude and announcing the availability of oxygen.

The HNTB designers had promised the community that the new stadium would retain the Rocky Mountain Thunder—and then some. Whereas the seating area in Mile High Stadium was perhaps only 20 percent steel, the seating areas of the new stadium would be made up *entirely* of steel. "It was like building a battleship," says Terry Miller. He adds, with a nearly mischievous grin, "the noise will be deafening. My only concern is that somebody down in the concession area will have to order a hot dog in sign language. But that's a risk the owner is willing to take. This will be the noisiest stadium in the world."

To build a stadium that has been compared to a beautiful, giant erector set, steel forms had to be bent, or welded, into place. Since welding steel takes more time than "bending" steel in huge off-site machines called "brakes," Turner chose a steel fabricator with the longest brake—fully sixty feet in length. From the beginning, however, the Turner inspectors spotted problems. The bends were slightly off. Enormous steel forms had to be sent back to the fabricator. "Before we knew it," remembers Chris Brettell, "we were weeks behind and sweating bullets."

Unable to live with the slow pace of the original fabricator, and unwilling to depend solely on locally based contractors, Turner contacted Angeles Steel in Los Angeles, a premier fabricator, with a slightly smaller brake. Unbeknownst to Angeles Steel, Turner had placed it on a short list of companies to be considered in the event of a failure on the part of the chosen subcontractor. Already busy, Angeles Steel nonetheless instituted a double shift to accommodate the sudden 25 percent increase to the year's production plan. Working twenty hours a day for ten months, the company eventually fabricated and delivered two million pounds of steel. The 60,000 fans drumming their feet on the steel floor have no idea of the heroics that were necessary to recover the pace of the project timeline, but the Turner team will long remember the contribution of Angeles Steel.

Having a contingency plan can reduce many of the anxieties associated with a deadline. Much of our stress hangs on the question that so often wakes us up in the middle of the night during a critical project: "What if?" "What if" questions can torment us throughout a job. "What if the people we depend on stumble?" "What if the shipment arrives late?" etc., etc. Perhaps even Turner veterans like Rod Michalka and Emil Konrath occasionally wake up in the middle of the night. But, it is very likely, they simply remind themselves there is a back-up plan for that particular nagging possibility, then go peacefully back to sleep. This is not to suggest that Turner could have created a back-up plan for every contingency on a project of this size; even the best construction managers in the business are not omniscient. Turner's decision to build the new stadium as an integration of high-rise buildings, for example, was not a "back-up plan"; it was an inspiration in reaction to completely unprecedented and unforeseeable circumstances.

Sometimes, the best one can do is cast a vigilant eye toward the future, while maintaining the best of relationships with those met over the years of a long career, who may be able to help in the event of an emergency. When asked if there was a Turner Way for handling time-critical challenges, Emil Konrath frowned and thought for a moment. "In this business, most companies I've seen are struggling, sometimes heroically, with Today. But, on my team, there are only a small number of people concerned with Today—and they are the field supervisors. Everybody else I want thinking about Tomorrow—just how far into Tomorrow depends upon their responsibilities. I would say that's the Turner Way: planning hard, and living in Tomorrow, so that potential problems are defused."

SHARE THE SAVINGS

There is a perception among those of us outside the construction industry that builders will, if allowed, drag a job out as long as possible, generating change orders at a higher profit level than their original bid. Actually, builders make the most money by finishing as early as they can.

Most deadlines have budgets, which can be broken down into days and months. If it is costing a construction company like Turner, say, $200,000 each month it is on the job, then, by finishing a month early, it has saved $200,000. If they have a "sharings clause" in the contract, as is the case with this stadium, then customer and builder alike benefit from a project finished early. Turner's share of the savings is then further distributed in the form of bonus checks to all of its associates involved on the project. Everyone, consequently, is motivated by this additional incentive to *beat* the schedule; an early-finish bonus actually discourages the seeking of change orders that could prolong the project.

To the degree possible, the Turner example of "spreading the wealth" among its associates responsible for meeting the deadline should be emulated by any organization taking on a time-critical challenge. All the motivational speeches in the world do not have the impact of a well-deserved bonus check. If raises in salary are the ways in which a company normally acknowledges excellence, then a bonus check under the "abnormal" crisis state of a deadline is most appropriate. A pat on the back for sustained efforts beyond the call of duty is insufficient reward, if the employee suspects that management has benefited financially from his or her sacrifice. In fact, it is crucial from an enlistment standpoint for the *next* challenge, that bonuses be awarded to all involved in the successfully met deadline. Nothing can damage morale more than unshared recognition. If a manager accepts a bonus for the efforts of his or her team when the team itself is not given a bonus, the sense of triumphant exhilaration will be short lived indeed, replaced with resentment, bitterness, and cynicism. Not only will the next deadline have few volunteers, but experienced "deadline busters" may have left the organization for one that rewards its people more equitably.

NOTHING CAN DAMAGE MORALE MORE THAN UNSHARED RECOGNITION.

Management must realize that the eyes of the rank and file are always watching, searching for a confirmation of its worst suspicions. "Management" is already seen by many as an exclusive club—immune to the consequences of failure, and the first to take credit for the efforts of the unrecognized. Notable corporate failures, such as Enron and Global Crossing, in which executives seemed to profit while the 401(k) plans of the employees were irrevocably diminished, only strengthened the impression for many that management somehow always prevails, and that the rank and file is the last to know. By sharing the savings of a successfully met deadline with all of those originally tasked, management offers a tremendous incentive, while perpetuating a team eager for the next time-critical challenge. It also casts itself in the role of a working partner with the team, prepared to share the fruits of victory and also prepared to suffer the consequences of not meeting the deadline.

NEVER ACCEPT A "MISSION IMPOSSIBLE"

There is something in the challenge inherent in every deadline that makes us want to swallow the lump in our throat and accept. Much of our compulsion must be in our upbringing: Certainly none of our fictional or Hollywood role models would hesitate to accept a dangerous mission. Although the recorded instructions in the *Mission Impossible* films and television series bear the caveat "should you choose to accept," what self-respecting superhero would decline? In fact, the very impossibility of the challenge seems to be a prerequisite for even approaching the hero, as if other "missions *possible*," are relegated to the more mundane 9-to-5 working stiffs.

Another factor that paves the way for our acceptance is that deadlines are rarely presented to us as negotiable propositions. Our customers, or our superiors, lay the challenge out before us, asking, in effect, "are you competent enough to take this on?" Presented in those terms, our only option, other than acceptance, is to admit incompetence. We feel somehow that if a deadline can simply be expressed, it can be met by the right person—and we like to think of ourselves as the right individual.

What struck me most during the interviews of the seemingly fearless professionals charged with the responsibility of bringing this awesome stadium in on time was a universal willingness to walk away from a truly impossible deadline. "Even the most competent people in the world will fail in an environment in which they can't win," believes Tim Romani, executive director for the Metropolitan Football Stadium District. "And, quite frankly, when I heard that the opening date for the project was scheduled for August 2001, I said, 'No thanks.' 2002 made a lot more sense."

Romani, having just brought in the Pepsi Center—Denver's new NBA and NHL arena—had every reason to question the feasibility of the 2001 deadline. Every sporting facility construction project requires the blessing of numerous city agencies; he had worked with the city of Denver for the last three long years on the Pepsi Center and appreciated how painfully slow the bureaucracies can move. The new Broncos stadium was not only a much bigger project, it would also involve many more agencies: those of the city, additional state delegations, *and* agencies from the surrounding six counties that made up the Metropolitan Football District. "When I became convinced that actual human beings could make the opening date—not imaginary subcontractors on a spreadsheet—I agreed to run the project for the District. Otherwise, what good would it do me to take on a job that I knew had a great chance of failing? If the stadium didn't come in on time, I'd never be able to explain *why* to the next owner in need of a stadium, because I would never get the chance."

A free agent like Tim Romani, who has built a reputation for bringing sports entertainment facilities in on time, must think in terms of his résumé, but so must a "company person." The seasoned execs at Turner were prepared to decline, or to negotiate, an unreasonable deadline. They were well aware that the reasons for a failure to deliver on time, whether it be an earthquake, labor strike, or the worst winter in thirty years, are soon forgotten by the small world of thirty-two NFL team owners. The owners would remember only that Turner did not "come through" on the new Broncos stadium. And, in that case, there might never be another.

When deadlines are handed to us, not from our customer but from our own management, it is even more difficult to decline a mission impossible and go to work the next day comfortable about our future with the company. Saying "No thank you" to an assignment is an exercise of an option that doesn't exist; the challenge isn't being offered, it is politely mandated. Even moments spent *considering* the challenge seem inappropriate; soldiers do not ponder the orders of an officer, as if they have a choice in the matter. Corporate soldiers, likewise, have no option but to accept the challenge briskly as it is presented by management; it's OK, however, to sleep on the terms. Being an employee does not prevent us from countering with our own suggestions for the timeline, budget, or required resources. We can say, in so many words, "Thank you for entrusting me with this challenge; of course I accept. I do, however, want to think more deeply about what I will need to bring this to the successful conclusion we all desire."

"We only have two resources," says Romani, "time and money. If you are asked to bring in a thirty-month project in twenty-four months, you will never hold the budget. If you are given an inadequate budget, you most certainly go overtime. I would advise anyone to consider both, and, if you're not happy with what you're being offered, counter with your own timeline or budget." Most customers, or managers, will see the light if the case is made reasonably. They want, above all, to meet that deadline successfully.

EMBRACE THE DEADLINE

For many, the announcement of a business "deadline" spoils a heretofore splendid relationship with the company. Suddenly, all is changed; the customary smiles are gone. One finds oneself forced into a race against time. Even the most industrious employees—who have daily met their obligations in an undeclared deadline—can be intimidated by the heightened awareness of their activities. Tried and true work habits can suddenly seem insufficient for one "officially" tasked with beating the clock. There is no more time for the enjoyment of the job; the challenge is just to get it done as quickly as possible. Some of us suffer the presence of a deadline as we would toothache, knowing that it cannot last forever. "Soon," we tell ourselves, "all this nonsense will be over; management will find something else to occupy its attention, and we can get back to work, in peaceful anonymity."

But Tim Romani believes that a deadline, rather than simply being borne, should be welcomed from the start. "Most people's last day of work is pretty much like the first, it's simply the final day of the same routine. Here it's different. Our last day is a time of celebration; it's the antithesis of the first day. It's a time of joy. Once you realize that, you also realize that the deadline is your friend, because it takes you as quickly as possible to that moment of joy. That's why I embrace the deadline. If you live in fear of it, you might as well go sell insurance."

"IF YOU LIVE IN FEAR OF THE DEADLINE, YOU MIGHT AS WELL GO SELL INSURANCE."

With apologies to insurance salespeople (it was an insurance policy, after all, that made the prereferendum design work possible), Romani's advice is eloquent. Deadlines, indeed, lead us toward a time of celebration and of triumph; they constitute the highlights of our careers. It is at these times of celebration, incidentally, that the fellow employees who once counted themselves lucky not to be part of the high visibility project now wish they had been involved. To its credit, Turner Construction has few timid souls. By creating a deadline-oriented corporate environment—in which the cream of the industry eagerly awaits assignment to prestigious, high-profile projects—Turner has developed the most sought after construction management teams in the business.

CHECKLIST OF DEADLINE MANAGEMENT TECHNIQUES FROM THE CRUCIBLE OF THIS PROJECT

- ❏ In the interests of time, partner with your adversary.
- ❏ Encourage your customer to be part of the delivery process. Make it "we," not "they."

❏ Start where you can; don't wait to "clear the decks."

❏ Put all decision makers, or their empowered delegates, under one roof for the duration of the deadline.

❏ Decentralize the command structure. Let those closest to the task make the decisions.

❏ Make everybody a believer in the schedule. No one anywhere should give the impression that the deadline could slip.

❏ Be intense. Take advantage of every opportunity NOW (because it may not present itself again).

❏ Understand *why* you're off schedule before you develop a recovery schedule.

❏ Involve agencies, review boards, gatekeepers, etc., early in the process.

❏ Bring your other project allies "on board" before they're actually needed.

❏ Appoint a protective counterpart to "driven management."

❏ Burn your boats, like Caesar. Show your team there is no alternative to victory.

❏ Make the deadline a high-profile project, so that everybody involved, from the top down, is proud to be part of it.

❏ Settle conflicts immediately; don't allow a cooling-off period.

❏ Include a "sharing clause" in your contract, then share the savings among your team members when the deadline is beaten ahead of time.

❏ Delegate team members to anticipate future problems. *Who has been there before!*

❏ If it is truly a "mission impossible," don't accept it. Either present a more realistic schedule or walk away.

❏ Embrace the deadline!

AIRBORNE EXPRESS ACCEPTS THE TECHNICOLOR CHALLENGE

"UPS and FedEx wouldn't have anything to do with this project. And even now—after we've shown Hollywood and the world it can be done—they would still back away."
—JOY WILLIAMS, ACCOUNT EXECUTIVE, AIRBORNE

"We thought it was all over our first real day on the job. We had put a lot of time and money into this project and hadn't seen one dime come back. Then, when we had our first chance to show our stuff, disaster struck."
—KEN McCUMBER, SENIOR VP, SALES, AIRBORNE EXPRESS

"Of the more than 631,000 movies delivered and retrieved by Airborne Express to theaters across the nation in the year 2001, within a two-hour window, less than 100 caused a 'dark house.'"
—FACT

◆　◆　◆

For nearly a century, the movie theater has been a sanctuary from the tribulations of everyday life. No matter how sophisticated the television or home theater may become, the movie house will always be the true port of embarkation for our imaginations. Although a public room packed with spectators, nowhere else offers such a sense of eager isolation. The surrounding blackness cuts us off from our own worries and fears; sound from every direction fills the spaces between us. Our eyes are drawn to the light of a world we have temporarily ascended, where actors earnestly struggle with challenges that cannot harm us. We have escaped the daily grind and give little thought to the daily grind of others that makes our escape possible.

To the degree that we do think about the movie industry *as* an industry, we cannot imagine that those who create such magic work under conditions as mundane and as stressful as our own. Haven't we heard, time and again, that Hollywood types are "laid back" and that producers and directors are famously indulgent with their often flighty superstars? We read of productions going over budget, of temperamental stars walking off the set in a huff, and of obsessive directors shooting one scene dozens of times "just to get it right" regardless of cost, and we imagine that those lucky enough to be in "show business" work in a creative, flexible environment unfettered by the iron laws that bind most other industries.

But, in fact, the movie industry is one of the most unforgiving when it comes to making deadlines, from both a production and a distribution standpoint. A film is not a "blockbuster" because an ad in the paper says it is; only the viewing public can make that determination by its patronage. Getting the films out on time to the more than 35,000 movie screens across the nation is as important as the film production itself; a studio does not begin to recoup the hundreds of millions of dollars required to produce, and then to duplicate, and then to advertise a film until somebody buys a ticket. If a highly anticipated movie is not at the right place at the right time, both the theater and the studio lose not only the critical opening weekend revenue, but the confidence of the public—now distracted by competing films—as well.

For decades, one film distribution service monopolized the motion picture industry, having served the studios since the Golden Age of Hollywood. In an industry dominated by entrenched relationships, serious competition to National Film Service (NFS) seemed a remote possibility. NFS delivered the movies to America—*all* the movies. In the early 1990s, however, Technicolor—the film duplication lab whose logo is familiar to generations of moviegoers—decided to enter and revolutionize the film distribution business. In need of a reliable national shipping service, Technicolor approached UPS and FedEx with a vision so "out of the box" that the two industry giants declined to participate. What made Technicolor's radical concept a reality was Airborne Express, and even *it*—a global shipping and logistics carrier known in the business community for its willingness to consider special handling requests—had to be sold on the project by Technicolor. The deadlines were simply too extreme.

IN LESS THAN SEVEN YEARS, TECHNICOLOR AND AIRBORNE EXPRESS HAVE CAPTURED NEARLY 70 PERCENT OF THE MARKET.

Today, NFS is no longer in existence. In less than seven years, Technicolor and Airborne Express have captured nearly 70 percent of the market. The deadline-management techniques that came out of the crucible of this high-risk project will be of interest to all who must race against time.

THE DEADLINE

Technicolor wanted to bring film distribution into the twentieth century. While National Film Service used recipe cards to account for each film, Technicolor promised the studios to integrate inventory, tracking, and invoicing with a state-of-the-art online system. Although NFS had an infrastructure of thirty-two hubs scattered across the nation, Technicolor proposed only two mega distribution centers, east and west, for stricter logistical control. The high quality of Technicolor's prints often suffered because of rough handling, reflecting poorly, and undeservedly, on Technicolor. New snap-on reels were proposed, so that the prints would no longer have to be wound on the reels (as they were at NFS hubs), which exposed them to dust and unnecessary contact. Technicolor, being a lab, could also offer a rapid turnaround print refurbishment, so that the studios, who paid fifteen hundred dollars or more per duplication, could get the most play out of each print. To put those numbers in perspective, Buena Vista's *Pearl Harbor* required an estimated $15 million worth of prints, to be distributed across the nation.

Technicolor had the vision, but NFS, for all of its antiquated procedures, had the hubs, the trucks, and the drivers. Technicolor needed the infrastructure of a UPS or a FedEx to make its vision a reality. And that's exactly where it went.

The two Goliaths of the expedited shipping industry listened dutifully, as the Technicolor executives explained the delivery challenges unique to the motion picture industry. The meetings, however, did not last long. What the Hollywood execs were asking for was so fraught with exceptions to the procedures each company had painstakingly built up over the decades that not even these giants could accommodate the demands for special handling. Having tried No. 1 and 2, Technicolor turned to No. 3 in the air express industry—Airborne Express.

Being "No. 3," at least in terms of the billions of dollars of revenue each company earns annually, is, however, not a position that is true in all areas. Airborne Express was an industry leader in several important categories, which contributed to the eventual joint venture with Technicolor. Airborne was the first express carrier to own and operate its own airport, and one of the first to offer same-day, next-flight-out delivery service. It could also be argued that Airborne was more accustomed to *making* deadlines, by the nature of its customer base—very demanding, high-volume corporate accounts, with very little residential business. Airborne was also No. 1 when it came to flexibility. Being smaller than the giants, it was willing and able to accommodate special shipping arrangements with corporate America and had already contracted for special handling requests by organizations such as IBM, Compaq, American Express, Xerox, Wal-Mart, Prudential, and many others. In response to this project, Airborne would develop three more industry "firsts," now emulated by the two giants.

> **"THIS WAS A CHALLENGE ON SUCH A VAST SCALE THAT IT WAS BREATHTAKING. WE HAD TO SIT DOWN AND DECIDE IF WE COULD EVEN *DO IT*, MUCH LESS MAKE ANY MONEY AT IT."**

Although receptive to new ideas, the Airborne executives who heard Technicolor's proposal listened with folded arms. It would take six months of persuasion on the part of Technicolor, and careful systems analysis on the part of Airborne, before their historic agreement would be reached. "What they wanted," recalls Ken McCumber, Airborne senior vice president of sales, "was such a challenge, on such a vast scale, that it was breathtaking. We had to sit down and decide if we could even *do it*, much less make any money at it."

From a shipper's point of view, Technicolor was asking for the moon.

- ◆ Airborne at that time delivered before noon in the major cities, enjoying a four-hour delivery "window"; Technicolor was asking it to deliver simultaneously to thousands of theaters across the nation within a narrow *two-hour* window.

- ◆ Airborne was accustomed to delivering packages as soon as it received them; the studios demanded a "hold for release" policy, so that shipments could be withheld until a delinquent theater paid its film rental bill to the studio.

♦ Airborne rightfully expected to *complete* each scheduled delivery, but the studios reserved the right to make last-minute changes, diverting a shipment from theater A to theater B. Theaters, too, could cancel at the last minute, having opted to show a different film.

♦ Airborne asked its customers to fill out the address label for any given package, but the theater managers would not allow their employees to complete the return air bill.

♦ Airborne (like UPS or FedEx) was generally unaware of a delivery problem until the irate customer called. Technicolor demanded a proactive monitoring system, nonexistent in the industry, which would identify the shipments in danger of late delivery well before the deadline was reached, as well as the whereabouts of each one of the many thousands of film cans in the system at one time.

♦ Airborne had made its reputation by reliable delivery of packages weighing five pounds or less; they were now being asked to ship two bulky film cans (sometimes three), weighing twenty to thirty-five pounds apiece, simultaneously to thousands of theaters every week.

♦ Airborne was accustomed to scheduling a "pickup" after a phone call from the customer; Technicolor demanded a yet-to-be-devised automated, computerized, pickup system.

♦ Airborne shipped a lot of packages, not surprisingly, by air, but the heavy, unwieldy film cans would have to go by ground, requiring an expensive ramp up of its infrastructure.

♦ Airborne thought in terms of one deadline—the delivery to the end user—while Technicolor delineated three deadlines: (1) the delivery of prints from the Technicolor lab to two distribution centers yet to be built; (2) the simultaneous delivery of the film cans from the distribution centers to thousands of theaters across the nation; and (3) the on-time return of the print back to the distribution center.

◆ In order to get paid, Airborne would have to develop a complicated split billing system, to invoice Technicolor and the individual theater for the same shipment.

The Airborne executive steering committee had been presented with a concentric series of deadlines. The first one, developing the internal systems necessary to even begin the enterprise, would be followed by the never ending time-critical delivery and pickup cycle for an extremely demanding new customer base. Getting paid could be an accounting nightmare. Failure to deliver would be trumpeted throughout the movie industry by disgruntled theater managers, and by the competing film distribution service. There was no doubt, also, in the minds of the Airborne execs, that Technicolor would have the highest expectations of Airborne and would be a very exacting partner in the joint venture. Once committed to a long-term contract, Airborne would be locked into a service that could prove to be more of a servitude, taking years to pay for itself.

To complicate matters further, Technicolor had no distribution customers. The one studio willing to take the chance was Buena Vista, the famed Walt Disney studio. If the new service failed, Buena Vista would have no choice but to crawl back to National Film Service and face rejection or, at the very least, higher prices. Accordingly, Buena Vista would not sign on the dotted line unless and until Technicolor had an ironclad, long-term contract with a reliable carrier. There was no guarantee that other studios would follow suit. Airborne was being asked to make a leap of faith, and an expensive one at that—preliminary estimates had indicated that hundreds of thousands of dollars would be needed just to develop the internal tracking system necessary to begin deliveries. If Technicolor could not persuade other studios to come on board, Airborne would be bound by a five-year contract, serving one studio with a system designed for twenty. The resulting revenues would not even pay for the gas.

Technicolor, as well, faced critical deadlines and substantial risk. Part of its responsibility would be to create the two major distribution centers: one next to Airborne's main air and ground hub in Wilmington, Ohio; the other on the West Coast, in Ontario, California. It also had to develop, in concert with Airborne, an integrated system of communication for automated pickups, as well as a very detailed database for all of the theaters across the nation. Its initial investment would be in the millions. If only one studio could be sold, albeit a prestigious one, the distribution centers would become white elephants. Or, if Airborne Express proved not to be up to the challenge, Technicolor's credibility would be irreparably damaged. Whatever happened, Technicolor and Airborne would be in it together, bound by mutual risk, legal liability, and the haunting potential of a huge market.

BE AN ADVOCATE FOR THE "OTHER SIDE"

The first and most dramatic deadline was the agreement itself between Technicolor and Airborne. After no less than six months of negotiations, the Technicolor project champions and attorney flew to Seattle to get a signature from the Airborne execs. The pressure on both teams was considerable. Technicolor had an appointment the very next morning, back in Hollywood, with Buena Vista Studios to sign the film distribution contract, and of course the studio wouldn't sign until it saw that Airborne and Technicolor had consummated a long-term partnership. Furthermore, it was crunch time in Wilmington, Ohio: Technicolor had to sign a lease for its huge distribution center next to the Airborne hub before the property went to another interested party. Obviously, it couldn't sign a long-term lease without a long-term agreement with Airborne.

For their part, the Airborne execs were equally motivated to get an agreement. If negotiations fell through, the opportunity might be lost forever. Buena Vista, the one studio willing to be a pioneer, would lose confidence in Technicolor's ability to get a committed carrier and remain with venerable NFS. Also, the internal dissent within Airborne, from those who thought the project too risky, would be strengthened. The execs who could see the day, perhaps years down the line, when Airborne would "own" the entertainment industry, wanted a deal just as badly as their Technicolor counterparts. That deal may not have happened, were it not for the dual advocacy roles played by Airborne's (then) VP and GM of Airborne Logistics Services, Ken McCumber, and Technicolor's director of new business development, Loren Nielsen.

"I tried to give the Technicolor folks a heads-up," remembers Mc-Cumber, "as to what our senior management here would not budge on. I knew they were coming for a signature, and I wanted them to do all their due diligence before they got here. If they were surprised by any of our bedrock positions, they'd have to go back to the drawing board—and there wasn't time for that."

Despite the negotiations over the previous six months, critical issues had yet to be resolved. Tension palpably increased as the hours ticked by. As day turned into night, positions seemed only to harden. McCumber moved between the two armed camps in the conference room with the immunity of a war correspondent. By selling his own people internally and coaching the "opposition," he helped facilitate an agreement during a session that ended with the sunrise. Though an Airborne "company man," he was seen as a trusted champion of the project by his counterparts.

Loren Nielsen, Technicolor's lead negotiator throughout that long night, also had a dual advocacy role. While representing the interests of Technicolor, she was quick to show Airborne how it could make money by agreeing to partner in this project. "I did business plans for them on my laptop. I'd show them, in their own terms, how the dollars would flow. Yes, maybe one aspect of the pricing would look bad, because the theaters were already accustomed to paying very little for a delivery, but other activities—such as hauling the prints to the distribution centers—would be profitable enough to compensate. Overall, their business was going to grow. They were going to get more studios over the years and make money on the promotional products, as well. Some of the Airborne guys would cringe when I brought out the laptop," she laughs, "but I think showing them what they could expect down the road really helped make believers out of the execs who just couldn't 'see it.' Not only that, but sometimes I needed the computer models to show them that what *they* were asking for wouldn't work."

Loren remembers, "That night, Ken and I weren't on opposite sides of the table, representing our companies; we were on the side of the Project." Technicolor's attorney actually created the contract during the "all-nighter," making changes as each side compromised. A deal was finally struck. Exhausted himself, Mc-Cumber drove the red-eyed Technicolor people back to the hotel, to collect their unopened suitcases, and then on to the airport for the dawn flight back to Hollywood. Loren and her associates would meet with Buena Vista Studios within hours, a signed contract with Airborne in hand. Buena Vista would sign the agreement with Technicolor, and the same day the lease in Wilmington would be locked in—in large part due to advocacy of Ken McCumber and Loren Nielsen, who, while loyally representing their respective companies, became strong proponents for the other side. Had that night been an adversarial confrontation, it is unlikely the two companies would have come to an agreement.

> **"That night, Ken and I weren't on opposite sides of the table, representing our companies; we were on the side of the project."**

Generally, when we are called on to represent the interests of a customer to our own management, we do so without conflict or risk. We simply tell our superiors what it is the customer is looking for and then strategize to best meet those needs with our own products or services. Management's blessing is sought for routine pricing or billing concessions. But, if the customer requires unprecedented services rendered—such as an equipment lease, when management, having been burned in the past, is dead set against leasing—it takes courage to be his or her advocate. It also takes a strong business case to demonstrate persuasively the benefits of meeting the customer's requirements, despite, perhaps, past evidence to the contrary. The employee who becomes a strong advocate for the customer may raise a few important eyebrows in his or her own organization, but, if the case is strong, both sides will win. It will become apparent that the goals of both organizations were always in alignment, and that it took an individual with foresight and courage to make this mutually beneficial solution clear to all concerned. It should come as no surprise that Ken and Loren distinguished themselves in front of their own management, while helping make the case for the other side.

CREATE A CULTURE IN WHICH RISKS WILL BE TAKEN

As we have seen, Ken McCumber initially had some internal selling to do, to persuade executives in his own organization that this very bold venture on the part of Airborne, though fraught with liabilities, would eventually pay for itself many times over. If he had been proven wrong—if, for example, no other studios had joined Buena Vista, or if Buena Vista had wandered back to NFS—McCumber had much to lose: his credibility, perhaps his advancement within the organization, but not his job. "I'll say this for Airborne," he laughs, "they give you a chance to fail."

Glen Dufur, one of Airborne's Systems Development gurus, felt equally comfortable in the hot seat. Before the contract had been signed, Dufur had been asked to quickly come up with an estimate of the time and money needed to develop the internal systems necessary for proactive monitoring and automated communications with Technicolor's mainframe. As it turned out, his estimate had to be more than doubled. He may have sweated bullets over the challenges before him, but not over losing his job. "Management knows they're asking for something on the fly. If I were worried about the consequences of my best estimate, I could simply throw a lot of money at it and be safe. But then we'd never do anything around here, because I would have made the cost prohibitive."

The executives who ultimately signed on to this project did so knowing full well there were those within the organization opposed to it. Had the project failed, their names would have been forever associated with a major investment that had not panned out. If they had worried about the impact on their careers such a failure would have had, perhaps the joint venture with Technicolor never would have taken place.

Airborne cannot be characterized as a rich company, with slush funds of venture capital set aside for attempted market penetrations. On the contrary, it is a tightly run, no frills organization that *doesn't even advertise*. It is proud to be known as the "low-cost carrier" and conducts its business accordingly. But in what could be described as a parsimonious corporate culture that would not take losing money lightly, Airborne execs feel empowered to consider out-of-the-box business opportunities, without fear of being hammered by the organization should they fail.

This is not to suggest that performance standards are not high. Airborne is just as concerned with personal productivity as any profitable organization; nevertheless, its executives are encouraged to develop strong business cases for unusual opportunities. They are prepared to take risks. Ken McCumber, Airborne's vigorous senior VP of sales, has been with the company twenty-nine years at the time of this writing; Glen Dufur for eighteen years; Jim O'Donnell—the driving force behind the implementation of this program—for twenty-eight years; and Jerry Cameron—the VP of pricing (recently retired), who was perhaps the strongest negotiator with the Technicolor execs during the "all-nighter" in Seattle—for thirty years. Yet the careers of these "company men" could hardly be characterized as middle of the road; all have been associated with some very challenging opportunities for Airborne, some extremely profitable, others not so profitable. In many of these ventures, their counterparts in the partner companies are no longer with their organizations. Airborne's tolerance for risk taking can be seen by those left standing.

AN ORGANIZATION THAT "LETS YOU FAIL" WILL LIBERATE AND EMBOLDEN CREATIVE THINKING.

Perhaps some who read this will have heard an ambiguous set of messages passed down by their own senior management. When "risk taking" is encouraged, but "accountability" is aggressively enforced, discretion is usually the better part of valor. Few will think the lime-light of the launch of the intrepid venture is worth the third degree, behind closed doors, should the project fail. Many of us would serve such an organization cautiously, without the leaps of faith that can bridge gaps between our customers and bring in unprecedented business. If management is not prepared to take the risk, along with its representatives, and to share in the occasional and inevitable failure, there will be very few pioneers who remain with the organization. For their part, of course, the risk takers must never be cavalier and must never feel as if they are gambling with someone else's money. The company has entrusted them with resources that ultimately come out of every associate's pocket and has every right to expect the exercise of sound judgment. Clearly, an organization that "lets you fail" will liber-ate and embolden creative thinking on the part of its associates. In the case of Airborne Express, this tolerance by senior management has paid for itself again and again.

INVOLVE YOUR CUSTOMER WITH THE BETA TEST

The contract with Technicolor had been signed before Airborne had had a chance to prove itself, which is an indication of Technicolor's level of confidence. After many months of systems development, it was time for a series of internal tests, each one more demanding than the last. Initially, one hundred theaters were involved, followed by a test of two hundred, three hundred, and, finally, sixteen hundred theaters. Actual film cans were used, weighted to simulate the heavy print. To the cautious delight of all, the tests went rather well. After months of intense preparation, Airborne and Technicolor managers were ready to test with an actual movie release.

Thousands of prints of *Sister Act 2* were released into the system that winter, very possibly the worst time of the year for Airborne to begin so auspicious a project. Not only was the time of the year fraught with potential weather-related problems, it was also the holiday season,

Airborne's busiest time. There were problems almost immediately, weather related and otherwise. In the East and Midwest, line-haul trucks, carrying prints by the ton, became mired in snowdrifts. Even in comparatively moderate California, word came that the rear gate of one eighteen-wheeler had burst open in the Mojave desert; this being the first time that hundreds of the heavy, bulky cans had been stacked into one truck.

Joy Williams, Airborne's lead account manager for Technicolor, heard the news with horror. The driver, it was reported, believed he had retrieved all of the films but couldn't be sure because of the darkness. After getting the best fix she could on the location, Joy bought a flashlight and headed out from Hollywood into the desert. The thought of even one print, much less twenty or thirty, not making it to its respective theater was difficult enough to contemplate. The possibility of the prints being found by a stranger and ultimately appearing on the black market, costing Buena Vista—the one pioneer studio willing to trust Technicolor and Airborne—millions of dollars in lost profits, was enough to put this account manager in a very serious frame of mind.

"I simply *had* to find out if the driver was right and really had picked up all the cans." Williams, a petite businesswoman in suit and high heels, must have made a singular impression on the local desert wildlife, all alone, sweeping her flashlight to and fro on the desert floor—an ancient seabed beneath a clouded moon. "There were *things* out there—I could hear them moving," she recalls. "Pretty soon I was so scared and so worried about the prints that I started to cry. When I searched closer to the road, cars slowed down; people peered at me as they went by, their faces red in the taillights of the car in front of them. I know it sounds funny now, but I was really afraid somebody was going to scoop me up into their van."

Williams spent hours searching along the freeway, among the cacti and innumerable little shadows that seemed to move at the touch of her flashlight beam. Stopping at a roadside store, she bought a pair of sneakers ("All they had were lime green!") and a toothbrush. She checked into a truck stop motel for the remainder of the night and resumed her search with the dawn. She could find no film cans. As it turned out, the driver really had accounted for all of his spilled load. But Joy Williams had certainly demonstrated her commitment to the success of the project, as well as assured herself a place in the Airborne Hall of Fame of customer service war stories.

Her dedication to the first run of this all-important project was duplicated by many Airborne employees over the next couple of days, as they scrambled to get thousands of prints simultaneously to thousands of theaters on time. But, despite the heroics, there were dark houses and angry theater managers asking Buena Vista why they had entrusted the delivery of a much anticipated movie to a shipping company that had absolutely no actual experience in film distribution, while National Film Service, with a track record decades long, waited in the wings. News of the *Sister Act 2* debacle was trumpeted by NFS and their loyal studios, while Technicolor and Airborne representatives were called on the plush carpet of an irate Buena Vista Studios executive, who paced across the office floor with indignation. The one and only customer that had put its faith into this bold venture had been publicly embarrassed.

Airborne and Technicolor had learned a few hard lessons during this first insertion of many thousands of prints into their newly developed systems. But Ken McCumber and Joy Williams of Airborne, and Loren Nielsen of Technicolor, formed a united, if contrite, front before their customer. "There was no finger pointing," according to Joy, "maybe a little eye rolling, but we took it on the chin as a team." The joint venture had stumbled on their first outing, and had a way to go before Buena Vista Studios would become a believer. But, surely, even during the harangue, the Buena Vista exec must have realized that the parties at most risk were the very people being chewed out. Buena Vista, after all, could go back to National Film Service. They had, to their credit, been the first and only studio to enter these uncharted waters, but they had invested prestige, not actual time and money. Technicolor and Airborne, on the other hand, had each invested heavily in this high-risk venture, and were on the brink of finding themselves discredited in the very market they wished to enter. The delivery of the next movie, *Tombstone*, had to be a success.

Beta tests are usually associated with problems and, in fact, are designed to reveal problems so they can be corrected. For that reason, involving our customer in a beta test can be a very intimidating proposition. Just as actors do not want to be judged on the merits of their rehearsals, many companies would prefer to wait until "opening night" before their customer sees them in action. Accordingly, beta tests are often very confidential, internal events. Many of us would not feel comfortable having the customer witness the initial stumbles of a growing project, or, conversely, see how *easily* his or her expensive contract is being fulfilled. Either way, we may feel as if an advantage has been lost; the more the customer knows about us, the less authority we exercise. There is also a fear of our competition getting wind of developmental problems and perhaps spreading a whisper campaign that will find the ears of other customers and, perhaps, investors.

But there is much to recommend involving the customer in the beta test. His or her feedback, as problems are identified, is much more valuable at the early stages of the project, when corrections are comparatively cheaper. The customer may also feel an affinity with the developing product or service. Sometimes cynically referred to as the "puppy dog" close, early acquaintance with the project can have a very warming effect. An example might be that of an ATM manufacturer installing the future ATMs to be beta tested in the customer's cafeteria, where all can get to know the product; even the occasional glitches will be tolerated as they are corrected, due to customer feedback. And, certainly, the most cynical customer will admire the courage it took for us to expose a process that is normally hidden behind the doors of R&D.

CREATE A DEADLINE-ORIENTED CORPORATE CULTURE

All transportation companies have feet of clay. No matter how impressive the number of jets, trucks, and state-of-the-art hubs, the base of

Airborne Express, UPS, and FedEx is composed of part-time employees sorting packages on the graveyard shift and very busy drivers who are just as human and prone to error as the rest of us. Creating and sustaining over the years a sense of urgency within a rank and file beset by turnover is surely one of the greatest challenges a transportation company can face. If the drivers and sorters don't *care*, deadlines cannot be consistently met.

Airborne uses a top down/bottom up approach to impart a sense of urgency throughout its organization. Every wide release of a Technicolor print is heralded by all levels of management. Occasional E-mails from President and CEO Carl Donaway will go out to the branch managers to underscore the importance of each and every film delivery and to ally management at the highest level with the deadline. Senior management is also very much involved in the aftermath of the release, either to thank those involved for an error-free delivery or to investigate the reasons behind a "dark house." The "bottom up" managerial efforts begin at the grassroots level. At every one of Airborne's nearly 300 nationwide branches, Technicolor coordinators have been appointed by each station manager. Their job is to constantly remind—some say "nag"—each driver of the upcoming film delivery for the week. Coordinators receive no increase in salary, only in responsibility. But many an Airborne manager has thanked his or her lucky stars to have been appointed a Technicolor coordinator. Although failure is highly visible, so is success. Station managers pick their best people for the job and are usually vindicated.

One of the ways Airborne fires up the troops is by firing up their supervisors. Every single night at the huge sorting hubs, a preops meeting is held in which the supervisors, each with twenty-five sorters under their command, are briefed for their upcoming shifts. The high-priority shipments are identified, assignments are made, and high expectations are expressed. It is made perfectly clear that the orange film cans of a new wide release are never to be "bumped" because of a full truck; the theaters are counting on Airborne to deliver on time. What could be a routine job is not allowed to become routine. All are caught up in the sense of urgency, making the night fly by.

Airborne managers also motivate by personal example. It is not at all unusual to see the airline's top executives dressed in jeans and a work shirt, on the floor loading packages into the trucks on an especially busy night. During the holiday season, November through December, senior managers work shoulder to shoulder with the package handlers on the floor and at the loading docks. The effect is no less than that of a general joining his troops as they march into harm's way. Backs straighten, the pace quickens, and a team spirit swells throughout the group. "What is equally impressive, although the sorters don't see it," notes Dave Sikorski, manager of Ground Operations Support at the Wilmington hub, "is that the execs walk from a night on the sorting floor back to their offices and put in a full day without sleep. It's not like they're working the graveyard shift and taking the next day off to recover."

WHAT COULD BE A ROUTINE JOB IS NOT ALLOWED TO BECOME ROUTINE.

When there is turnover in driver personnel, the new driver will ride with a veteran, who will introduce him or her into the trials and tribulations of film distribution. The new driver soon learns that Airborne management has very high expectations of him or her personally; the job cannot be done without concentration. The driver learns immediately that he or she will be held accountable for a dark house. One training video portrays a disappointed audience sitting in a dark theater, the white screen showing only a text message in big bold print: "Ladies and Gentlemen, there will be no movie tonight because Airborne screwed up!" Although the new driver may laugh nervously at the hypothetical scenario, the point is well taken. Nobody wants to be the cause of a dark house.

It is not uncommon for a station manager to ask a new driver to repeat his or her theater delivery and pickup instructions aloud, so that both parties can be confident they are of the same mind. Sometimes, the simple act of repeating one's instructions, as in the military, reinforces the importance of the mission. We think to ourselves, "it *must* be important, why else am I being asked to repeat the instructions?" Airborne managers know that a new driver, in an effort to mimic the urgency of a situation, may rush off with the best of intentions, but perhaps without a clear idea of what is to be accomplished; that's why the repetition of orders is so important. And, just so that nothing is left to chance, the driver will be contacted throughout the day by his or her Technicolor coordinator until all on-time deliveries are made.

And, finally, the product itself imparts its own sense of urgency. "We don't have to be reminded that our mortgage payment has to be sent in on time," reasons Joy Williams, "It's the same thing when one of our drivers sees the orange can in the truck. He's been to the movies all his life, and he knows the film has simply *got* to be there. Everybody at Airborne knows how important those shipments are."

Even though the district field service managers have a spectacular delivery record, nothing is taken for granted by Airborne management. "We treat every new release as if it were our first," says Manager of National Accounts Field Services Jim O'Donnell. "The E-mails out to the station managers begin weeks before a major release; everybody is on the alert. The closer D-Day comes, the more we communicate. We cannot assume that everybody understands how important this is, even if they have been performing their jobs flawlessly for years. We never, ever, let up." The proof is in the pudding. In the year 2001, Airborne Express had fewer than one hundred "dark houses"—out of more than 631,000 deliveries and pickups. With its feet of clay, Airborne has a failure rate of only .000158 percent.

Once one is aware of Airborne's successes in leading its rank and file to such a standard of excellence, all excuses for the poor performance of one's own personnel sound rather feeble. There could not be a greater challenge than motivating part-time employees on the graveyard shift. Looking at the joint venture from a case study vantage point, a business student might have thought Airborne had accepted the Technicolor challenge of delivering thousands of films within a two-hour window consistently without the tools to meet it. Isn't it axiomatic that, in order to spur its rank and file to excellence, an organization must be prepared to "pay for it" in terms of ever competitive salaries, increased benefits, and perks? Yet Airborne package handlers, rushing to meet a deadline at two o'clock in the morning, are not particularly pampered; the work is hard, the conditions are Spartan. What they do receive in goodly amount, however, is the attention of their managers and supervisors, who, themselves, lead by personal example.

Just how important the personal attention of management can be is best exemplified in a famous workplace experiment, often cited in sociology textbooks. A group of factory assemblers volunteered to become guinea pigs in a broad, long-term test of various inducements on production. Music, for example, was piped into their isolated corner of the factory, and production, not surprisingly, increased. An additional coffee break was added, and production again increased. A bonus system was instituted, rewarding the assemblers for exceeding assigned quotas, and production went up. Predictably, additional perks spurred the productivity of the group. Then, one by one, these inducements were withdrawn, until conditions returned to the original state. Yet production continued to increase!

It became apparent to the behavioral scientists that these workers—heretofore strangers, now friends, cheerfully engaged in an adventurous experiment—would continue to crank out record numbers of assembled products, simply because of the attention being paid to them, and the sense of involvement with management on a significant project. Clearly, the personal attention of managers who care and who also share the burden and the accountability of a deadline can go a long way toward motivating the unlikeliest of workforces, including part-timers unloading crates and sorting packages in the wee hours of the morning.

CREATE A "ZERO ERRORS TOLERATED" MENTALITY

The strident E-mails of Jim O'Donnell have made more than a few Airborne employees tremble. Preceding every film release, his messages are fired into cyberspace with the impact of a national alert, to every one of Airborne's three hundred stations. There is no small talk in the communiqués, only the details of the upcoming delivery challenge. Terse sentences end with double punctuation marks, as if pounded out on the keyboard against time. The tone is official, unequivocal, and urgent; words like *must* and *shall* convey the impression of a military order to attack at dawn. Those in the organization who have not met Jim O'Donnell do not want to; surely, the man breathes fire.

On entering Jim's office for the first time, one feels a bit like Dorothy, or the Tin Man, fearfully peeking behind the ferocious mask of Oz, only to find a sweet-tempered and mild-mannered, smiling man in his fifties. But O'Donnell makes no bones about his "zero errors" mandate—both as a goal and as an enforceable policy—in fact, the enforcement is what makes the goal a realistic target, rather than a floating abstraction. He holds himself to the same high standard applied to Airborne's station managers. The zero error tolerance does not necessarily mean that the same employee will not be given the opportunity to repeat his or her mistake; few earnest Airborne employees are terminated for one dark house. But their error will be taken very, very seriously by management. There will be no doubt in the employee's mind after verbal and written counseling of the importance of an on-time film delivery. A zero error policy, then, means that "zero errors" will go unnoticed, no matter how small or inconsequential. In fact, Airborne managers are on the lookout for the small mistakes.

"I know it sounds petty at first," says Marilyn Wharton, the driving force behind Airborne's Technicolor Logistics Center, "but when you monitor the small mistakes, you find out that the driver who is 'almost late' with a film delivery was also almost late the week before with a hospital dialysis solution delivery. A profile develops of little problems here and there; we want to nip that in the bud before his behavior results in a dark house—because it will, sooner or later, trust me."

A managerial style that monitors the small mistakes may seem obsessive and somewhat anachronistic, in today's kinder and gentler workplace. Modern management often goes out of its way to assure its employees that there is no Big Brother looking over their shoulders and that mistakes can be valuable lessons. Many employees, coming from a sympathetic school system or from a family environment in which failure is accepted unconditionally do not like being spoken to in such unequivocal terms and may run, righteously indignant, to file a complaint with Human Resources. In many organizations, it takes something fairly major to even *qualify* as an error worth reprimanding. Most managers would be embarrassed to confront a subordinate with a triviality. But not Airborne managers. They recognize that most major errors do not occur spontaneously and out of context; the employee will likely have a history of inconsequential mistakes that, were it not for proactive management, would never appear on the "radar screen." Never confronted for the small errors, the employee builds up an implicit defense against management, relying upon a sea lawyer's version of "precedence." "Why," he or she can ask, "have you never mentioned this before?"

It is also very possible that an employee may be blissfully ignorant of his or her transgressions—and just as surprised as anyone else when his or her behavior has led inexorably to a dark house. In either case, Airborne managers are quick to point out even trivial mistakes to their subordinates, not in an authoritarian way, like a caricature out of a Dickens novel, immune from the consequences of failure, but as a fellow employee subject to the same high expectations from his or her own boss. Being called on the carpet for a small mistake is much more acceptable to the employee when he or she is shown the disastrous chain of events that could have resulted from that behavior.

THE "ZERO ERRORS TOLERATED" POLICY, WHEN EXPRESSED, SOUNDS IMPOSSIBLY AMBITIOUS; WHEN ENFORCED, IT BECOMES SUDDENLY REALIZABLE.

There is no contradiction, incidentally, between creating a culture in which risks will be taken, as discussed earlier, and insisting on flawless performance. One is the precursor of the other. A failed business venture on the part of an Airborne exec would not be an "error," but, rather, a calculated risk that *could* have brought in profitable business and may yet. On the other hand, stopping the delivery truck for a long lunch with one's girlfriend, during the critical two-hour delivery time frame for theaters, is very much an error. Management can be simultaneously tolerant of bold creative thinking that in one instance did not pan out and justifiably intolerant of careless execution of thoroughly understood duties. The "zero errors tolerated" policy, when expressed, sounds impossibly ambitious; when enforced, it becomes suddenly realizable. As corny as it sounds, there are a lot people working for Airborne who are determined not to make a mistake. That kind of aggressive spirit, to the degree to which it exists throughout an organization, can make a company very formidable indeed.

IDENTIFY "POINTS OF VISIBILITY"

Until the joint venture with Technicolor, Airborne, like UPS, FedEx, and all other air express companies, generally became aware of a delivery problem with a shipment when the customer called, asking where in the world it was. A service representative would then key in the customer's information, and the shipment would pop up on the terminal screen. If the customer was a corporate account, as most of Airborne's are, perhaps hundreds of shipments would appear on the screen. The service representative would then peck through the entries until the delivery in question could be identified. At that point, a search would begin to locate the shipment and to get it to its proper destination as speedily as possible.

Even with Airborne's prestigious 97 percent on-time delivery rate, the Technicolor execs could not live with a system that did not "know" of a problem until notified by the customer—in this case the theater manager. Their promise to the studios and to the theaters was to bring the film distribution business into the twentieth century. They would not emulate the pencil and paper tracking system of their competitor, NFS. Technicolor required a system that would alert Airborne to a delivery problem in enough time to correct the problem. All the theater would ever know was that the film arrived on time.

The studios were very interested in the concept of control for two reasons: the price of each print and the disproportionate cost of a lost print. A print may cost the studios one to three thousand dollars; that same print, if pirated, could cost the studios millions of dollars in lost revenue. Film piracy has become very, very big business. According to the Motion Picture Association of America, hundreds of thousands of illegally copied videocassettes cost American motion picture companies an estimated $3 billion a year worldwide.

Developing a system that would *proactively* monitor all film shipments everywhere fell to IT (information technology) expert Glen Dufur. He had no place to look for inspiration; while UPS and FedEx had robust tracking capabilities, neither had a proactive monitoring system. "We had to develop a system from scratch," recalls Dufur, "one that would screen out all shipments that were where they were supposed to be and then pop through the exceptions. We wanted to know which shipments were not appearing at one of the internal stops along the way, and we had to know it with enough lead time to recover. It was one of the hardest things we've ever done."

But Dufur's solution was ingeniously simple. Each film was to be encoded and then scanned on its circuitous path from lab to distribution center, to hub, to station(s), to delivery truck, to theater, and back again. The vast majority of cans that are identified at the right place at the right time go on their way unannounced through the Airborne system. Shipments that appear at the wrong place or are absent when expected "pop through" the operator's customer service terminal screen, alerting coordinators and customer service reps to the jeopardized delivery. Dufur and his team had spent thousands of hours creating what would become an industry "first"—a proactive monitoring system that identified a delivery problem *before* the customer knew about it, *and* in time to fix it. He had developed the ultimate deadline-management tool, and its concept applies to any industry, because *all* deadlines involve a passage through a sequence of events. If these events can be made highly visible checkpoints, there will be no doubt of the progress, or lack thereof, of any endeavor. Becoming aware of a problem long before it is recognized

THEY CREATED AN INDUSTRY "FIRST"—A PROACTIVE MONITORING SYSTEM THAT IDENTIFIED A PROBLEM *BEFORE* THE CUSTOMER KNEW ABOUT IT, *AND* IN TIME TO FIX IT.

by the customer *as* a problem is clearly preferable to the reverse. Conscientious proactive monitoring can give us the time we would have otherwise lost to recover.

APPOINT A SINGLE VOICE OF AUTHORITY

One of the greatest obstacles to making any deadline is miscommunication. A clear understanding of what is to be done is difficult enough between two individuals under normal conditions; throw in an extended family of strong-willed personalities from Airborne, Technicolor, the studios, and the theaters—all under the pressure of an impending dark house—and an Airborne driver could be caught in a riptide of conflicting requests. Many Airborne drivers have been on their routes for years; they are friends of their theater customers and are anxious to accommodate. They are also deferential to VIP customers like Technicolor and studios such as Dreamworks, Sony, MGM, or Universal Pictures. Airborne management knows full well that their drivers must, at times, be protected from their own eagerness to please. Though the drivers have discretion in many areas, when it come to film distribution there is only one point of authority—the Technicolor Logistics Center (TLC).

The TLC was created to oversee and control the entire nationwide film distribution network. The operators, with space-age equipment at their fingertips, know everything there is to know about a shipment, but sometimes all the driver needs to hear is the reassuring voice of authority amid a cacophony of customer requests. What may seem like a rather undemocratic way to do business has served Technicolor, the studios, and the theaters well. Airborne decided from the beginning that one rudder, not two or three, would stabilize the flow of simultaneous deliveries to more than 7,000 theaters a couple of times every month.

The single voice of authority concept would apply to many projects with multiple interacting managers; it relieves those who should not be forced into making a decision from having to make one. And, actually, it also works in the reverse case. In today's age of "management by personal intervention," many supervisors are not only un-afraid to make a "command decision," but eager to distinguish themselves by doing so. Having one implacable, centralized point of authority will prevent unnecessary heroics and confusion. This final arbiter, however, must have the benefit of all possible information. Like Airborne's Marilyn Wharton, seated at the center of a vast communication network, he or she should be nominally omniscient.

While we all may yearn, in the heat of a deadline, for a single voice of authority, perhaps to put an end to the democratic differences of opinion among team members or to expedite a time-consuming, internal approval process, few of us actually want to be that person. The great relief of consulting the guiding authority is not so much the direction given as the liability assumed and taken off of our shoulders. That doesn't necessarily make us cowardly; it frees us, rather, to pursue the deadline without distractions and conflicting orders. Having one's manager serving as a traffic cop is a tremendous relief, especially if the project is going well, tempting other managers to involve themselves during the final stages. With one individual serving as the final arbiter, the deadline team is turned loose to do what it does best. That single voice of authority may not even have to speak very often; sometimes only a few decisions establish a "right of way" for the team members that is acknowledged and accepted by the rest of their associates. Just as a military column, bidden by separate commanders, cannot march in conflicting directions, a deadline team must be an elite unit, unto its own, politely independent of all but one voice.

MAKE IT EASY FOR THE CUSTOMER TO MEET THE DEADLINE

From the outset it became clear to Airborne, accustomed to being in control of its own procedures, that the thousands of theaters across the nation would form an unusually demanding customer base. Theaters seemed to do business in an airy realm, not bound by the considerations usually extended between business parties; none of Airborne's "normal" customers, for example, would dream of demanding the right to make last-minute changes that would cancel or redirect the shipment. But surely the most surprising, not to say frustrating, characteristic of the exhibition industry members was their almost rebellious attitude when it came to doing any paperwork whatsoever. Not that one could blame them. The individual receiving the film could be a ticket taker, projectionist, or popcorn popper and could not be expected to do anything more than sign his or her name. When it came to returning the film to Technicolor, theater managers did not want to fill out the shipping label themselves or to ask their employees to do so. The return of the film cans to Technicolor, however, was not a leisurely shipment; the deadline to get a film back for refurbishment or redistribution was as critical as its initial delivery. Airborne had to find a way to expedite the return of the print, while involving the new customer base as little as possible. Glen Dufur's systems development group went to work and came up with an innovation so practical as to make the team wonder why they hadn't thought of it before. An industry "first," it is now emulated by other shipping companies.

"We invented an intelligent label," Dufur recalls with a smile, "one that is bar coded with not only the address of the destination, but the name of the film and account numbers for tracking and billing. The people at the theater have to do nothing; our driver simply peels off the top of the label upon delivery, revealing a second label beneath for the return trip, already filled out with all the accounting information, and ready to go. The instant that label is scanned by our driver at pickup, he sets up knowledge in our automated system that the shipment exists, that it's been picked up, and is on its way back to Technicolor or to another theater."

What began as an obstacle that could have jeopardized the timely return of the film compelled Airborne to come up with something new. By making it easy for the customer, Dufur had also made it significantly easier for Airborne; the intelligent label has become an inventory tracking and customer invoicing tool that Airborne cannot live without today.

Making life easier for the customer is, of course, not always easy at all. Every company has a finite number of services and understandably prefers to remain in the realm of the practical. After all, we don't offer to provide day care for the customers or to do their grocery shopping; why should we raise their expectations by suggesting we can provide services above and beyond the industry standard? While dutifully assuming the "listening pose," we are more likely to be desperately thinking of ways to turn the conversation away from what the customer wants to what it is we offer. There is a natural and understandable fear of diminishing ourselves by opening a Pandora's box of customer wishes, only to have to explain why they cannot be met. Further, we do not want the customer wondering if there is another company out there who *can* grant these wishes. We do our best, therefore, to control the customer's imaginings and to diplomatically encourage him or her, in effect, "to get real."

Alternately, we may look on our customer as a doctor would a patient, honestly believing he or she doesn't know what's good for him or her. The customer may be aware of his or her own unique "symptoms," but not the cures available in the marketplace. As the industry experts (at least in terms of knowing what our competition is offering), we sometimes take an authoritarian stance and simply dictate the best course of treatment. The authoritarian position is especially tempting during a deadline, when there just isn't *time* to allow the customer to delay our own established practices. This is why customers are so delighted to finally meet somebody willing to develop a creative innovation that demonstrates an intimate working knowledge of their operations. The individual or organization that can truly make things easier for the customer will have so distinguished himself or herself from the competition that he or she will be looked on as a consultant, and a friend, from then on.

HANG ON TO YOUR COUNTERPART!

Glen Dufur and his team had to work very closely with Technicolor as the two organizations developed protocols for an automated communication system that facilitated deliveries, pickups, billing, and inventory tracking. The two IT teams also had to work together to develop a vast customer database of all the theaters in the country, as well as a split invoicing system. What proved to be a recurring obstacle to speedy development, however, had nothing to do with bits and bytes. "I kept losing my counterpart at Technicolor," Dufur remembers, throwing up his hands. "Just when the pace of things started to increase, there would be a change of IT directors over there. It was a pretty intense time, the hours were long, and for whatever reason, I would hear that the director I had been working with was no longer with the company. That meant I had to start all over, bringing his or her replacement up to speed. We had taken two steps forward, then one backward."

Dufur ended up working with three Technicolor IT directors, and he was not about to lose the third. It was in his own self-interest to do what he could from Seattle to see that his Hollywood counterpart kept his job. He found himself in the position of a counselor at times, giving the new director the benefit of his own insight into Technicolor management and its expectations. The two computer gurus swapped home phone numbers and talked about their newly born systems over the weekends, trying to come up with ways to debug initial problems. Whenever possible and appropriate, Dufur would put in a good word for his counterpart to Technicolor management, not to patronize him but perhaps to offset the modesty that characterizes so many systems analysts, who tend not to broadcast their own achievements. By being proactive in an area where he had no control (somebody else's company) he was able to help his counterpart succeed.

Dufur learned the hard way that losing an ally in the race against time could jeopardize his own chances of success. Whether we are working closely with an employee of our customer or associated vendor, we should never assume he or she will always be there for us. Sometimes, by doing our best to help our counterparts keep *their* jobs, we make ours easier. The deadline manager would do well to expand his or her definition of the "team" to include key counterparts among the customer, suppliers, local agencies, etc. Whenever possible, these honorary team members should be motivated, praised, recognized, and invited to milestone celebrations of the internal team. To the extent possible, one should become a kind of foster manager, thereby doubling the chances of a satisfied counterpart, or, if he or she reports to a less than sympathetic manager, at least creating a surrogate satisfaction that just may keep the counterpart involved, happy, employed, and eager to meet the deadline.

PROTECT YOUR PEOPLE FROM HAVING TO CHOOSE BETWEEN PRIORITIES

Airborne drivers, of course, have customers other than theater managers. Equally demanding customers are all along the drivers' routes—such as hospitals requiring deliveries of the most critical nature and corporate accounts that have extremely high expectations and proportionately low levels of patience. If drivers experiencing bad weather or traffic jams were to find themselves suddenly torn between two equally important delivery deadlines, it could be very difficult for them to choose. Left to their own discretion, drivers may be uncomfortable "complaining" about conflicting delivery times and may, with commendable but misplaced courage, push themselves beyond what is reasonable. Local station management does its very best to make sure their drivers are never put in impossible situations. "Every morning," says District Field Services Manager Dan O'Rourke, "I leaf through the delivery schedule of each driver. If I see a conflict, I won't leave it up to the driver to somehow resolve it; I'll shuffle the deliveries around with another van. Our drivers are good, but they can't be in two places at the same time."

It's that kind of Big Brother management that really does fulfill the positive, protective role of a big brother—and only management can do it. In the business magazines of today, there seems to be a great debate between the proponents of "hands-on" and "hands-off" management; the "hands-off" managers being the ones who delegate authority in order to cultivate the leadership qualities within their subordinates. Allowing drivers in the above case to choose between equally important priorities would not be an example, however, of "hands-off" management in any positive sense; it would be, rather, an abdication of leadership on the part of the supervising manager, who would have put the drivers in a position to take the heat, but not in a position to schedule their routes to possibly avoid the complication. The drivers would have been thrust into a "management position" for perhaps two agonizing minutes. This would not be a delegation of authority, as much as a delegation of responsibility that cannot be morally transferred.

ONE IS NOT "PREPARED FOR MANAGEMENT" BY BEING USED AS A SHIELD AGAINST THE WRATH OF THE CUSTOMER.

One is not "prepared for management" by being used as a shield against the wrath of the customer, by a manager without the foresight to avoid the issue or the courage to step out in front. Certainly, the ordeal of a deadline is a tremendous leadership training ground, with ample opportunities for personal and professional growth. But the team leader must do whatever possible to protect his or her members from distractions and obstacles that would only put them in a position to fail.

NEVER IDENTIFY A HIGHER PRIORITY WITHIN YOUR HIGH-PRIORITY SET

It could be argued that, while all the films to be delivered constitute a high priority, there are some deliveries that are more "important" than others. Special screenings, for example, are highly publicized events, most often attended by movie critics, the press, and theater owners. Some screenings are held for studio execs, producers/directors, film stars, business execs, and politicians. With the paparazzi-like media coverage of screen idols and movers and shakers stepping out of their limousines, special screenings can have the aura of mini Academy Awards ceremonies. A failed delivery of the very movie to be screened would be a public relations disaster for Airborne.

Equally important, though less public, is the film that must be quickly shipped back to Technicolor to be reprocessed and sent out to new theaters. One of the selling points of the Technicolor service to the studios was the ability to bring a film back to life within a twenty-four-hour turnaround period, if the quality had suffered from too many showings. Film duplication is not inexpensive; the studios are very interested in getting the most high-quality "play" possible out of a print, rather than paying to replace it. But the lab refurbishment must be quick enough to return the film into circulation while it is still a major attraction. One could certainly argue that the film to be restored in the lab and then recirculated, is a more "important" shipment than the film that has run its course and is being returned to Technicolor for storage.

Airborne, however, makes no distinction between the special screening delivery, or the refurbishment return, and the vast majority of its other film shipments. To make use of special couriers for a special screening, for example, would express a lack of confidence in a system already designed for high-priority deliveries. It would be saying to the sorters and the drivers, in effect, that "Yes, all the film cans are critical, but these shipments are really, *really* critical." It is a testimonial to the confidence of Airborne management in its own ability to perform that no such instructions are ever given. The driver cannot distinguish a special screenings film can from another; they are all "high priority."

The effect on the rank and file must always be a consideration when one is tempted to raise the bar arbitrarily. Successfully met deadlines require high morale. For a team that already considers itself elite to be told, in effect, that there is yet another level of responsibility that it is not to be trusted with could be very counterproductive. The customer, as well, would be troubled to learn that the highest level of service he or she has been paying for and depending on is deemed inadequate by his or her provider for truly critical missions. What would Technicolor have thought about the reliability of Airborne's service, for example, if Airborne had made special arrangements for a particular shipment, when *all* shipments were, in the opinion of Technicolor, equally critical? By resisting the temptation to provide an extra level of security for special screenings, Airborne was making a statement about its existing standard of excellence that must have been reassuring to its own rank and file and to Technicolor, alike.

The urge to add ever higher priorities above an already established threshold is sometimes succumbed to when management attempts to reward or recognize its associates for achievements beyond the norm. Many companies have an equivalent of a President's Club or a Silver Circle, which honors their top performers in Sales, Customer Service, etc. Recognized throughout the organization as the apex of performance recognition, membership is coveted and proudly displayed by those who have entered these exclusive circles. But when a company, in a misguided attempt to spur performance to even greater heights, creates yet another plateau of recognition—some kind of super duper Silver Circle—it diminishes the honor previously bestowed. As of the date of this writing, Congress has refrained from "updating" its 200-year-old standard for heroism, the Medal of Honor, with another category for the really, *really* brave. And the Baseball Hall of Fame has not opened a modern annex, entitled the Baseball Hall of Even More Fame; to do so would bring into question the achievements of the earlier recipients. Yet some companies blithely institute their own versions of these ludicrous examples. A better way to recognize higher performance would be to simply increase the bonus. Everyone knows that Babe Ruth made less money than Mark McGwire; nevertheless, the Hall of Fame, like Heaven, is populated with equals. One of the fastest ways management can lower morale is by diminishing past performance, in an effort to inspire current productivity.

BEWARE OF "LETDOWN" AFTER A MAJOR SUCCESS

Unlike many corporate one-time shipping assignments, the film distribution business has no end. Thousands of Technicolor prints are released into the Airborne system every week. One wide release is followed by another; they come in waves. Some nationally anticipated films, however, are more demanding than others. Summer blockbusters, such as *The Mummy Returns* and holiday smash hits like *The Grinch Who Stole Christmas* seem to arrive in ever-increasing record numbers, during a time of year that is already busy with other shipments. Some films, too, come late into the Airborne system, perhaps because a director takes longer than expected to approve a final cut or because Technicolor is especially challenged by the sheer volume of duplications ordered, as in the case of the three-can *Pearl Harbor*. There are also big spikes in demand between Thanksgiving and Christmas. At times like these, Airborne package sorters, station managers, and drivers must rise to the occasion.

The problem with occasional heroics is that there is the potential of an emotional collapse after the successful completion of the critical mission. With another wide release perhaps only days away, Airborne managers are especially alert to the condition of their teams after grueling, error-free deliveries. "Sometimes I'm torn between patting everyone on the back," says John Kaffka, national account manager for Sky Courier, Airborne's expedited delivery wing, "and simply treating the great job they did like any other day. If I make too big a deal about it, they may slide into a resting mode as a reward, but there's no time to rest." Sometimes, when there *is* time to rest—when, for example, there is more than a week between film deliveries—Kaffka keeps his people in the Technicolor mindset. "I put them on paperwork assignments having to do with Technicolor, and I continually brief them on the upcoming releases. I want to keep them always mentally in the game and ready."

Jim O'Donnell remembers that, after the challenge of distributing the massive wide release of Dreamworks' *Gladiator*, Airborne's next shipment, Disney's *Dinosaur*, was a good two weeks away. Fearing a letdown, he both praised and cautioned. "After congratulating everybody for a job well done, I reminded all our station managers that there are still a few big studios out there we haven't got. One major breakdown will result in horrendous negative press about us and about the program. We can never let our people relax."

The reverse case was true after the delivery of Dreamworks' *Shrek*. After a flawless distribution of several thousand prints, the Airborne infrastructure was immediately hit by *Pearl Harbor*. Like soldiers who, exhausted after a great victory, are suddenly challenged again, Airborne personnel had to dig deep for "back-to-back" error-free deliveries. That they were able to accomplish this is a testimonial to Airborne's management and to the kinds of personalities who tend to remain with the company. "We try to select people who perform better under recurring pressure," says John Kaffka. "Those that don't seem to thrive on the stress we transfer into a more placid department."

There are occupations in which "deadlines" are so frequent that the term no longer differentiates one project from another. Those who work on a newspaper or for a television station, air traffic controllers, and Alaskan crab fishermen become so accustomed to unrelieved pressure that their subconscious minds accept the frenetic pace of the workday as the norm. Veterans of extremely stressful occupations often move through their shifts with a calm that seems unnatural under the circumstances, just as some patients who must endure chronic pain develop a smooth and set facial "mask" from years of rigid emotional control.

It is a tremendous managerial challenge to find the balance between spurring the performance of already stressed employees and preventing burnout. Certainly, managers should make full use of the naturally occurring *esprit de corps* among team members who face unusual challenges. Perhaps these "deadline busters" should never be allowed to look on their jobs as the norm, nor at themselves as anything less than special. Members of elite military units, such as the Green Berets, do not "burn out" from the constant readiness exercises performed; their ability to endure the stress is proudly displayed and is acknowledged by fellow soldiers who voluntarily stand at attention as they pass. The manager who celebrates the distinctive characteristics of those who have what it takes to work in the "pressure cooker," day after day, will help to promote a robust, cheerful, and sustainable ethic within a team that eats deadlines for breakfast.

DEVELOP A PARALLEL PLAN

Airborne entered into its contract with Technicolor with one or two assumptions yet to be verified. One was that most theaters would be ready to accept a delivery when an Airborne driver was somewhere in the zip code. But once Technicolor had developed its considerable database of theaters—with the points of contact and hours of acceptable delivery—it became frightfully apparent that more than 1,100 theaters had delivery windows that were open when no Airborne driver was anywhere near them! The Airborne operations managers penciled out the cost to remedy the situation by hiring additional drivers, contracting outside carriers, and paying for special deliveries. The price tag came to a staggering $1.5 million in costs *annually*. The figures hit the Airborne execs like a brick, especially because this new realization came less than one year into a project that everyone knew would not turn a profit for a projected three years. With the additional annual "hit" of $1.5 million, the film distribution gamble might never break even, much less make money.

This came as a big blow to the champions of the project, who had, after all, "sold" upper management on an idea previously rejected by UPS and FedEx. After a serious review, it became clear to all that the contractually mandated prices could not be raised, while the additional expenses could not be profitably borne. "That's when we asked for the keys," remembers Jim O'Donnell. "We went to Technicolor for their permission to approach the 1,100 high-cost theaters and, if they couldn't change the delivery/pickup times, to ask for the keys to the door, or for permission to deliver to an alternate site (such as an adjacent business), so the driver could deliver the film cans when he was in the area, even if there was no one at work in the theater." Eventually, most of the theater managers agreed to some sort of accommodation, and a fiscal crisis was averted.

Developing a parallel path to the ultimate goal is an approach long favored by Loren Nielsen, who was Technicolor's director of new business development at the birth of the joint venture. "There's always more than one way to get to your destination. Maybe there's a preferred method, but if too many obstacles appear, you've got to find a way around them." Airborne's two-way label is another example of "getting around" the unprecedented obstacle of a customer base that did not want to be bothered with the paperwork of a return air bill. But surely the most revolutionary parallel path will be the delivery of films in digital form. Even as Airborne drivers wheel in the bulky film cans that make up a full-length movie, the organization prepares for the day when DVD-like disks will be handed over to the manager, to be "played" in a computer rather than on a projector. Issues such as resolution (film is still sharper) and protocols that must be standardized and accepted throughout the industry, as well as the all-important issue of protection against film piracy, must be resolved, but Airborne is already working with Technicolor to develop a parallel plan.

The development of a parallel plan involves a balancing act between a number of contradictions. If developed in secret, the manager forfeits the benefits of brainstorming contributions from the team members. If developed openly, one runs the risk of letting steam out of the effort currently expended; the team may begin to look over its shoulder, like a pitcher noticing activity in the bull pen. A parallel plan can be announced at precisely the wrong moment—just when a little extra "umph" would have pushed the original plan toward victory. Furthermore, parallel plans, if developed arbitrarily, are themselves subject to rescue, with yet more alternative strategies.

> A PARALLEL PLAN CAN BE ANNOUNCED AT PRECISELY THE WRONG MOMENT—JUST WHEN A LITTLE EXTRA "UMPH" WOULD HAVE PUSHED THE ORIGINAL PLAN TOWARD VICTORY.

Sooner or later, the team has to commit all of its energies and, come what may, get the job done. Surely, a sustained "do or die" attitude is preferable, from a deadline-management perspective, to a will too easily broken. A dispirited team leader, forever in search of alternative solutions, will never develop the momentum to roll through the inevitable obstacles encountered on every project, and may not find a way around them in time to meet the deadline.

How does one know when a parallel path is required, as opposed to extra effort thrown behind the original plan? Most likely, if one is in the heat of battle, he or she does not have the objectivity to make that judgment. The line between commendable determination and obstinacy is best defined by a manager who has been able to maintain a practical, yet dispassionate, equilibrium. If it looks as if the team is not facing facts, because of its emotional investment into the current strategy, then it is time to reevaluate that strategy. If Technicolor, for example, were to resist the implication of today's digital revolution, because of its massive investment into the infrastructure required to distribute hundreds of thousands of fifty-pound cans of film (as opposed to DVD disks, which weigh ounces), it would obviously miss out on future revenue—just as IBM once did by underestimating the potential of the personal computer.

DEADLINES BRING OUT YOUR BEST

When asked if he would do things differently, given the chance to "relive" the initial marathon negotiation session with Technicolor, Jerry Cameron had to think a moment. He seemed mildly surprised at his own answer. "Probably not. It was a long and stressful night—no doubt about that—but, looking back, I think those pressures brought out the best in all of us. Maybe it was a good thing we didn't get any sleep."

Who among us has not felt similar emotions, recalling a college term paper that kept us up all night or a critical project that held us in the office while the rest of the world slept? There always seems to be a moment of clarity, just on the near side of fatigue; we find ourselves unnaturally alert during the hours our primitive ancestors feared. Our minds in overdrive, we have caught up with Time and for the moment seem to be its master; when we remember our actions, the scene seems to be in slow motion. The sensation cannot last long; we soon return to our mortal selves. But it is certainly true that some of our best work will be under the spell of a deadline.

Eight years after that long night, Airborne and Technicolor have proven themselves to such an extent that twenty-two motion picture studios, big and small, have become loyal customers, accounting for nearly 70 percent of the film distribution market. These studios also account for the majority of the promotional market—trailers (previews), posters, three-dimensional displays, and assorted drink cups, bumper stickers, Pokeman trading cards, and other giveaways—a business boon anticipated and harvested by Airborne. As contracts with competing shippers expire, the few remaining studios that have yet to become customers will no doubt look very favorably on Airborne's spectacular on-time delivery rate. Before long, Airborne could effectively serve a very large segment of the market, less than a decade after Technicolor approached it with a concept so radical that UPS and FedEx had backed away.

CHECKLIST OF DEADLINE MANAGEMENT TECHNIQUES FROM THE CRUCIBLE OF THIS PROJECT

❑ While loyally representing your own organization, be an advocate for the "other side."

❑ Create a corporate culture in which risks will be taken.

❑ Involve the customer in the beta test.

❑ Create a deadline-oriented corporate culture.

❑ Instill a "zero errors tolerated" mentality.

❑ Identify "points of visibility" throughout your processes.

❑ Appoint a single voice of authority.

❑ Make it easy for the customer to make the deadline.

❑ Hang on to your counterpart in another organization.

❑ Protect your own people from having to choose between priorities.

❑ Never identify an even higher priority within your "high-priority" set.

❑ Proactively prevent a "let down" after a major success.

❑ Develop a parallel plan.

❑ Remember—deadlines bring out your best.

C H A P T E R   T H R E E

MISSION TO MARS—THE
2001 *ODYSSEY* ORBITER

*"With two failures behind us, some people
were saying this would be 'strike three' for JPL
and Lockheed Martin."*
—ROGER GIBBS, SPACECRAFT MANAGER

*"Our launch window was one second. If the
weather was bad, or the solar conditions were
wrong, or if a hundred other factors weren't
just right, we'd have to wait another Martian
year—twenty-six months."*
—DAVID SPENCER, MISSION MANAGER

*"A failure is hardest on the team that fails; it's
next hardest on the team that follows, which
now has to correct what may be—or may not
be—the cause of that failure."*
—GEORGE PACE, PROJECT MANAGER

◆ ◆ ◆

John Carter, the creation of Edgar Rice Burroughs, traveled to Mars through the author's fanciful method of "astral projection." Carter would stand in his garden at night, face turned up to the red planet, spread his arms, and will his consciousness across the void to a world that somehow had simultaneously produced grotesque, humanoid monsters and very earthlike and alluring damsels in distress. Sword in hand, Carter would aid the cause of justice on Mars, eventually awakening—exhausted and yearning to return—in the familiar surroundings of nineteenth-century America.

Jet Propulsion Lab's Roger Gibbs, spacecraft manager of the 2001 Mars *Odyssey* project, would surely smile at the notion of astral projection; nevertheless, there is a little bit of John Carter in Gibbs and in most of his team members, who were weaned on math, science fiction, and homemade rockets. It is no accident that the 2001 *Odyssey* mission was named after the famous sci-fi novel by Arthur C. Clark, *2001: A Space Odyssey*, or that the first space shuttle was christened after *Star Trek*'s *Enterprise*, or that the *Odyssey* control center is amply stocked with Mars candy bars.

In fact, what distinguishes many of the people behind this mission to Mars is a barely disguised adolescent energy. The *Odyssey* team members at NASA's Jet Propulsion Laboratory (JPL) cannot discuss their mission dispassionately. The conversations may begin dispassionately, in the obtuse language of the field, but once animated, the rocket scientists' serious demeanors give way to intermittent images of high school whiz kids finally given the opportunity by the principal to do something really crazy. The impression passes, but never quite completely. And, while business magazines may advise their readers to think of themselves as free agents, never fully giving body and soul to the organizations they serve, these men and women cannot hide their devotion to their work. For the most part, they are all doing what they've wanted to do since the ninth grade Science Fair. In terms of a lifetime career choice, they have all married their high school sweethearts.

Their partner on this project is Lockheed Martin Space Systems, which provided the *Odyssey* spacecraft, as well as their capacity to integrate into that craft the payload of scientific instruments provided by JPL. Although both organizations have had a close and friendly relationship over the decades, the times have called for an even closer one. "In the early days of the space program," remembers JPL veteran Glenn Cunningham, "we looked on companies like Lockheed as contractors; we told them what to do and sent a few of our people over there to make sure they did it right. More recently, our timelines were greatly reduced by NASA. The less time we had, the closer our relationship with Lockheed Martin had to become. To do these projects fast, you really need to develop a very trusting relationship with a partner, not a contractor."

Although JPL has designed and built plenty of space missions by itself, having a partner for the nuts and bolts introduces new considerations. If the JPL engineers and managers can be characterized as visionary, perhaps their Lockheed Martin counterparts can be looked on as slightly more practical and cautionary. While the big thinkers at JPL design the mission, the aerospace contractor must help make it happen—and make a profit for itself on top of that. If the engineers at JPL are trying to "push the envelope" of technology, their partner, while no doubt adventurous, is probably wondering who is going to pay for the additional R&D necessary to expand the capabilities of an already specified and manufactured device. Together, the two organizations complement each other, creating a mission plan that is both daring and doable.

The *Odyssey* project represents a redemption of sorts for both organizations. Not one but two Mars missions ended as failures in 1999. The Mars *Climate Orbiter* dipped too deeply into the planet's atmosphere, while a software glitch on the Mars *Polar Lander* spacecraft cut its rocket-assisted descent prematurely. Both of these missions, scheduled to reach Mars in the same year, were one of a kind and decades in the making; both failures were met with an unpublicized denial on the part of loyal team members, who kept at their consoles for weeks searching for a sign of the spacecraft's survival. Should there have been *three* failures in a row, the JPL team members, as well as their counterparts at Lockheed Martin, could very well have lost the support of NASA and of the American taxpayer. And it's not as if there is no competition in the field; Applied Physics at Johns Hopkins University, the Goddard Space Flight Center, Ames Research Center, Langley Research Center, the Naval Research Lab, and the Air Force itself all lobby for the funding and the opportunity to develop a NASA mission. The prestige of JPL, their aerospace contractor, and perhaps the very jobs of the *Odyssey* team members, were dependent on a successful mission.

The odds of a successful mission to Mars, when one considers the overall history of attempts, are not all that great. Over the past four decades, no less than thirty missions have been sent to the red planet, mainly by the United States and old Soviet Union, whose space program, one is apt to forget after its economic collapse, had some extremely impressive triumphs. Two-thirds of these combined missions ended in failure. Three out of the last four most recent missions to Mars failed. The risks are incomparable. No wilderness on Earth, including those of the vast oceans, represents an environment as hostile as outer space. And no project could have a more implacable "customer." The deadlines with Mother Nature are simply nonnegotiable.

THE DEADLINE

Until quite recently, interplanetary space projects were once-in-a-decade events. The projects had ten-year timelines and, even at that, were sometimes unable to meet the critical alignment of Earth, planets, and Sun that represents the one true horoscope for a spacecraft's mission. When Dan Goldin took over as head of NASA, the deadlines suddenly accelerated to warp speed. Rather than have one big, expensive interplanetary mission every decade, Goldin mandated that there would be *several* smaller, less costly missions instead. His famous "faster, better, cheaper" mantra meant more science, more headlines, more taxpayer interest, and, in the views of some in the media, more failures. But perhaps the number of missions needs to be greater before one can make that judgment. After all, Mars *Observer* was a ten-year project, and it failed. In 1997, Mars *Global Surveyor*—essentially the identical mission, but under a *twenty-seven-month* deadline, with a greatly reduced budget—was highly successful.

From that mission onward, interplanetary space projects have been fast track. But the two following missions were highly publicized failures. There were those within the aerospace industry predicting "strike three" for JPL. It was now up to the Mars *Odyssey* 2001 orbiter to put JPL and Lockheed Martin back on course as the most successful organizations in the short but dramatic history of space exploration. George Pace, the former spacecraft manager of both the *Observer* and *Surveyor* missions, was given the reins of the *Odyssey* project; he had less than three years to get a package of science instruments into orbit around Mars, at a total distance to be traveled of 286 million miles.

THERE WERE TWENTY DAYS IN WHICH *ODYSSEY* COULD TAKE ADVANTAGE OF THE IMPLACABLE LAWS OF PHYSICS THAT NORMALLY GUARD AGAINST INTERPLANETARY EXPLORATION.

If an enormous spaceship with unlimited power existed, NASA could send it to Mars whenever it wanted. But, for all the flaming glory of liftoff, in which the powerful rocket almost seems to be pushing Earth itself away, the capacities of modern science in a showdown against Nature are so very limited. In order to launch a low-energy probe like *Odyssey*, you have to catch Mother Nature with her back turned. There were twenty days in April 2001 in which *Odyssey* could take advantage of the implacable laws of physics that normally guard against interplanetary exploration; each day had two one-second "windows." Everything had to be just right—weather, equipment, solar phenomenon, and earthbound readiness at stations all over the globe—or the launch would have had to be delayed for another twenty-six months. It should be noted that such a delay could be very hazardous to the fiscal health of the mission. Anything can happen to a space project, in terms of Congressional funding, during a two-year period of earthbound inactivity, ranging from budget cuts to a total scrapping of the mission (and subsequent integration into another project). *Odyssey* would be a lot safer in outer space. The launch deadline simply had to be met.

During the not uneventful cruise phase, there were four alterations in course that were extremely time critical; a mistake on any one of them could have required a disproportionately costly correction down the line, in terms of precious propellant. The next major deadline occurred at the end of the seven-month cruise. The spacecraft had *one* chance to insert itself into the atmosphere of the planet, in order to slow down with every orbit, or it would simply fly by, out into the solar system and beyond (which is what the original "flyby" missions were designed to do, earlier in America's space program). Once in the Martian atmosphere, the spacecraft has a finite period of time to slow itself down, by using its long solar panel as nonaerodynamic "wings"—not to fly, but to create drag—so as to bleed off energy. This very maneuver almost ripped a solar panel off *Surveyor*, which would have doomed the mission. Every trip around the planet slows the spacecraft and brings it closer to the surface, which means closer to collision. At the exact, proper time, rockets fire to lift the craft higher and into a stable orbit. But, if at the end of 110 days the spacecraft is *not* in a stable orbit, and not at the proper orientation to the sun (for its solar cells to work), it must cut power and circle the planet without performing any science for another Martian year.

The phrase "rocket science" represents the top of the scale by which we laypeople measure the difficulty of a problem. What other profession is so frequently invoked, in such a positive manner, in everyday parlance? When we say something "is *not* rocket science," we are putting the problem in perspective; we are saying it may be difficult, but nonetheless manageable; it doesn't require a rocket scientist. When the problem *is* "rocket science," we as a nation step back and watch the professionals with the earphones at Mission Control try to win the race against time.

At times like these, we may wonder if "rocket scientists" handle deadlines differently from their counterparts in business. Let's find out.

BE WILLING TO SUBJUGATE YOUR PERSONALITY IN THE INTEREST OF THE DEADLINE

Others profiled in this book have indicated a willingness to walk away from a "mission impossible." George Pace, in his forty-year career at JPL, has played a variation of this theme. Rather than making a dramatic personal statement over a serious disagreement with management, he bides his time and lets the *organization* eventually wander away from its original stance. "Though the mills of God grind slowly," he quotes with an always ready laugh, "yet they grind exceeding small."

The original budget handed to him for the *Odyssey* mission was, from his experience, inadequate at slightly more than $200 million. Although he voiced his concerns, NASA stood firm; the budget was simply nonnegotiable. Rather than stalk off the set in righteous indignation, Pace went about assembling his team, fairly confident that the dynamics of the situation would eventually shift. And, indeed, over the first year of the project curious things began to happen. Other centers within NASA, seeing an opportunity to incorporate one of their own experiments into the mission, lobbied forcefully to be included in the project. New experiments were added, which meant, considering the limited load capacities of the spacecraft, that a few original experiments had to be deleted. The budget waxed and waned with each modification, but, in the long run, mostly waxed. Then came the two Mars failures in 1999. NASA managers, now fearing yet another failure, were suddenly asking Pace why he had "skimped" on the budget. More money was immediately allocated. Slightly more than a year after receiving his original inadequate budget, *Odyssey* was now generously funded. "If I had made a scene back then," he recalls, grinning, "I never would have had a chance to impact this mission."

Pace had developed his patience through previous experiences with the space agency. After the failure of the Mars *Observer* mission in 1993, in which he had been spacecraft manager, Pace went through an organizational mission postmortem that implicitly assigned the cause of the failure to his management. Although privately convinced he would never be given the opportunity to lead another high-profile interplanetary project again, he remained with JPL. The mills of God ground on. A new project, Mars *Global Surveyor*, came down the pike. Project Manager Glenn Cunningham insisted on Pace's assignment as spacecraft manager once again. "He was, simply, the best person for the job." George Pace recalls, "A lot of people had interviewed for that job, but Glenn just outwaited management." *Surveyor* turned out to be a spectacularly successful mission and circles the planet to this day, sending back information vital to all future Mars missions.

Perhaps the experience of dealing with very large entities, like planets in motion, helped Pace and Cunningham deal with the irresistible forces of upper management. If they had dramatically taken a stand, it is very likely that they would have lost their battles. But the inertia of upper management in most organizations eventually moves on, making a "matador defense" much more sensible than outright confrontation. The NASA execs soon became distracted with other issues; Cunningham and Pace had prevailed without heroics, demonstrating that even under the pressure of a deadline, it is possible to play a "waiting game" to one's advantage.

Their experience is well worth noting, especially in the contemporary milieu, which seems to stress the role of a strong personality in business success. Forceful and charismatic corporate leaders boldly stare at us from the covers of business magazines. From television and magazine profiles of the very successful, we are given the impression that the meek do *not* inherit the earth, and that the larger the organization, the more necessary it is to assert oneself in order to avoid the curse of anonymity. If we disagree with management, we sometimes feel compelled to take a stand—maybe even a "last stand," in an Alamo of our own choosing. Or, perhaps feeling unappreciated, we want to put our employer to the test: "their way" or "our way." George Pace's long career argues against dramatic confrontation. He saw that, in the case of *Odyssey*'s inadequate budget, resistance on his part would only jeopardize the deadline. In the interests of the mission, he subjugated, not asserted, his personality. "Rather than make a scene," he advises, "let the hand play out. You usually end up with what you need."

BUILD MARGIN INTO YOUR TIMELINE

In developing a schedule, there are temptations that must be resisted, not the least of which is the attempt to account for every precious minute of time and every penny of budget. Schedules are the playground of the "hands-on" manager, who believes a perfect process can be created, one that will, if everyone does their part, click like clockwork toward the deadline. One might expect that rocket scientists, of all professionals, might be particularly obsessive in their planning, but they are actually firm believers in cutting the project a little slack.

When General Motors comes out with a new automobile, there is very little guesswork (from a production standpoint) involved. The new car has millions of predecessors, all based on the same chassis, the identical engine, etc. A space mission, however, is a one-of-a-kind operation; as such, there *is* some educated "guesswork," in the sense that it is impossible to estimate the exact requirements of the mission. "We always make allowances for time, power, and mass," says John Casani, the dean of JPL space project managers. "You've got to build in some margin, and you want it to be frangible, so that mass margin can be converted into power margin, etc." Glenn Cunningham adds,

"Everything is so restrained on a space mission: mass, power, time, budget. There is very little resiliency, other than the resiliency you put into the job originally."

While most earthbound endeavors can benefit serendipitously from the friendly environment, gaining perhaps a little more time, or saving a little money, a spacecraft, once launched, is not going to happen on more resources along the way. There is no "tailwind" to take advantage of in the vacuum of space and no replenishment of propellant en route. On the contrary, there is a gauntlet of hazards between Earth and Mars—meteor showers, solar storms, disturbances in the planet's atmosphere—that must be taken into account. Project planners must allow for the unexpected, and they do that with margin.

George Pace took the concept of margin and built it into the schedule itself, reserving fifty-five funded but "uncommitted" days before the launch date, to be doled out as necessary to the teams requiring just a little more time. "You've got to be careful," cautions Pace, "because margin, once discovered by the teams, is no longer margin; they will claim it for themselves and maybe relax a tiny bit, knowing that there are fifty-five *more* days than originally thought. You have to hand it out with discretion." Ed Euler, veteran Lockheed Martin project manager, adds, "The best way to stop your people from mentally adding the margin to their end date and then relaxing a bit is to hold them hard to their original commitments."

John Casani remembers another method of managing margin used on his *Cassini* project, one suggested to him by an economics professor over a couple of beers.

His thought was, you don't want to hold any margin close to the vest. You give it all out in the beginning, equally to the teams—margins of time, dollars, power, mass, etc.—and you let everybody know that there is no more margin; they've got it all. Then you create a *marketplace* in which the team members can negotiate with each other for more margin if they need it. A team leader that needed a couple of extra kilograms for a science instrument might go to another team leader and offer to swap some of his data bandwidth for the little extra weight (or dollars, or power, or whatever his particular margin was at the time). It took the load completely off the project manager, and it put the decision making down into the arena where decisions *should* be made—by the scientists themselves. Sometimes it took quite a bit of convincing for someone to surrender margin, but, when all was said and done, they all wanted the mission to succeed. So the team members worked it out among themselves; after all, they were doing the work and knew best what was needed and what could be spared.

With either method—that of doling out margin or surrendering all of it up front—the creation and administration of margin is a very useful deadline management tool. Ironically, many business managers would be in *too much of a hurry* to factor the "luxury" of a margin into their schedules, while others may not see even the possibility of finding a little extra time or money in an already critically tight deadline. Casani, Pace, and Cunningham, the three most experienced space mission project managers to be found, would argue that margin is a necessity, not a fudge factor. By *Odyssey*'s launch date, Pace had used up all but a few hours of his margin. They would also advise that margin exists in the tightest of deadlines, and that the use of it should be considered a *planned contingency*. During the cruise phase of the *Odyssey* orbiter, for example, there are five planned maneuvers, but only four maneuvers to be accomplished: The fifth is a "backup," or margin for one of the four that may have failed. Why would a "backup" be *scheduled*, if it may never be needed? "We found on the last mission," recalls Roger Gibbs, "that if we don't make room in the schedule for a recovery maneuver, we won't have time to do it."

MARGIN EXISTS IN THE TIGHTEST OF DEADLINES, AND THE USE OF IT SHOULD BE CONSIDERED A *PLANNED CONTINGENCY*.

If a business project is broken down into the business equivalents of time, mass, power, etc., possibilities will be identified in each category that can be converted into margin. Can the products needed be purchased from different vendors and at different prices? Is the timeline altered if an alternative path is taken? How will a midnight shift affect the budget, if it brings the end date closer? There are so many possible combinations of solutions to the completion of every project that margin can be extracted from at least some and then allocated to those entrusted with the success of the mission. The important lesson to be learned from JPL is that one must plan to *use* the margin. If, for example, there is a possibility that a midwinter shipment could be delayed by foul weather, it is not enough to toss a few extra days into the equation in case they are needed. One must actually plan on using the time, because, if it does snow, there will be a lot to do in order to compensate for the slowdown. If it turns out that the margin wasn't needed, after all, so much the better; one is now *ahead* of schedule, rather than simply not being late.

OFFER "AWARD-BASED INCENTIVES"

It is doubtful that there exits in all of industry a more straightforward deadline enforcement tool than the "award-based" incentive program. When JPL partners with an aerospace contractor, the contracts are usually "cost plus." The base contract is to reimburse the contractor's cost for the project, the numbers being fairly easy to verify. The "plus" represents the profit, which is capped at an agreed-on percentage (usually somewhere around 15 percent), and which is metered out in the form of awards for performance against agreed-on standards. For example, Lockheed Martin would get a percentage of the profit awarded to it for keeping to the schedule, a percentage award for the integration of the payload, a percentage for flawless operation of the science instruments, and so on. Over the course of the mission, the awards pile up, and the contractor puts the money in the bank. What makes this system so straightforward and perhaps in a way so pitiless is that *Lockheed Martin must give it all back if the spacecraft fails.*

George Pace remembers, after the failure of Mars *Observer*, finding a check in the mail for $18 million. Even though the aerospace contractor had worked its heart out on that project, for ten long years, and even though the actual cause for the failure was never satisfactorily determined, it returned every penny of the progressive awards payments. If that doesn't sound crazy enough, Lockheed Martin agreed to the *same terms* on the following mission, Mars *Global Surveyor*. Fortunately, on that project it was able to keep the money. It is important to note that the execs and attorneys at Lockheed Martin certainly could have gotten into a finger-pointing match with JPL over culpability, but that is where the partnership aspect comes into play. "It wasn't JPL's mission," recalls aerospace veteran Ed Euler, "or Lockheed Martin's mission; it was *our* mission, collectively."

One can imagine the response in the general business community to these unforgiving terms: If the deadline is not met, all of the progressive profit payments must be returned. At first pass, the system sounds so unfair. A contractor or vendor could perform heroics and still have to return the money. But, in the case of the failed Mars *Observer* mission, it's not as if JPL profited from the failure, while holding the contractor accountable. Both entities suffered, Lockheed Martin monetarily, and JPL, a nonprofit extension of Caltech, in terms of prestige. And prestige is extremely important when NASA is considering which organization, out of many competitors, should be offered the next space mission.

It is not at all out of the question to apply a similar system to the business deadline on an organizational, vendor-to-vendor basis, and perhaps even on a personal basis. A company, of course, could not expect its employees to literally return the progressive bonus payments associated with a time-critical project, but the bonuses could be held in escrow until the deadline was met. Each team member responsible for the successful meeting of the deadline would get regular statements of the accumulation of his or her performance-based dollars. Should the deadline *not* be met, those bonuses would be withdrawn. It may seem cruel, but the bonuses were, after all, shares of *projected* profit, to be garnered by the company after a happy conclusion of the project. If the deadline were not to be realized, neither would the anticipated profit be realized. And if the forfeitures were scrupulously applied to each and every individual who had received an "awards" bonus in his or her account—managers and executives, alike—the consequences of failure would be grudgingly accepted. Certainly, the prospect of handing one's bonus back to the company would motivate many a team member to make that deadline.

MODEL YOUR TEAM AFTER YOUR COUNTERPART

When it comes to interaction with the rest of humanity, government agencies are notorious for insisting on procedures of their own making. The government has a form for every possible transaction, including, no doubt, a form to request a new procedure to deal with the unanticipated. Since JPL must report to NASA, it, too, has its requirements, and an aerospace contractor hoping to do business with JPL must comply. George Pace could see at a glance that forcing a partner to do things "the JPL way" could eat up a lot of time. Since Lockheed Martin was doing such a large part of the work, Pace decided to make it as easy as possible for the aerospace contractor to deal with the lab. "I modeled my team after their team," he explains. "We tend to have a lot of subsystem managers, but they tend to consolidate their subsystems under fewer managers. So I consolidated my subsystems and had a JPL counterpart for each of their system managers."

The acceleration of business between the two entities was very noticeable. "We really appreciated the one-on-one interfaces," recalls Lockheed Martin's Ed Euler. "Our team leaders could talk directly to theirs. George also tried to use our documentation formats whenever possible, and, if he couldn't, he would find the closest JPL form to ours." This willingness to *change*, in the best interests of the mission, is also, says Euler, exhibited by the huge aerospace contractor in its dealings with other customers. "Whenever possible, we try to do things the customer's way." Since JPL was a customer of Lockheed Martin, one might wonder why it was JPL that went out of its way to match the other's method of doing business. "They were *doing the work*," says Pace, "they were building the spacecraft to our specifications, under a demanding deadline, and we wanted to make it as easy for them to do that as possible. Besides, those folks have been very successful over the years, doing things their way. Why make them change on a such a short schedule?"

In the business community, every organization is justifiably protective of its own procedures. We like to do things "by the book" because company policy often represents lessons learned the hard way, institutionalized into the company manual to protect employees from making the same mistake twice. In our dealings with other business partners, we want to use, whenever possible, *our* contract documents, *our* billing procedures, *our* change orders. The prospect of using *theirs* makes management understandably nervous. But deadlines are, by definition, nervous times; attempts to disguise the disquieting nature of a deadline with "business as usual" trappings will only jeopardize the race against time.

MOLD YOUR "FREE SPIRITS" INTO A TEAM

Deadlines worth hundreds of millions of dollars are generally entrusted to teams and, more likely, teams of teams. The manager of a mission to Mars has team-building challenges like any other manager in the business community. Perhaps there are challenges—having to do with some of the personalities who must be managed—that are even greater. A team of rocket scientists is different from a team of corporate "soldiers." A corporate team member, for example, fully understands the pressure his or her boss is under to constantly apprise upper management of the team's progress; so, reports, projections, forecasts, etc., are filled out without objection. A rocket scientist does *not* understand and has little patience with any activity that has nothing to do with the work at hand. Corporate team members bow to the will of management because they want to be managers themselves one day. Rocket scientists engaged on a critical project generally have no ambition other than to be left alone. They can, furthermore, be slightly eccentric and maybe even antisocial, in terms of business etiquette.

HOW DOES ONE GET SO MANY FREE SPIRITS TO CONFORM TO ORGANIZATIONAL REQUIREMENTS?

There is yet another difference: The corporate team member, with apologies to all, is, quite frankly, often easier to replace. The scientists at JPL, on the other hand, are the best in the world; it's not as if the mission manager, frustrated with a team member, can pick up the phone and ask Human Resources to send in another genius. So the manager finds him or herself in a classic predicament: How does one get so many free spirits to conform to organizational requirements, when their very nonconformity, in the intellectual sense, is what makes them such valuable problem solvers?

Aerospace engineers are not necessarily easily handled. The popular image of a kindly distracted professor, lost in abstract thought, who cannot remember to comb his hair and who needs an occasional nudge to refocus his wandering brilliance, does *not* describe all JPL scientists. "Frankly, there are a lot of big egos in the space business," says Glenn Cunningham, who has managed his share of strong personalities, "probably because the work is unique. As a project manager, I tried to give them as much latitude as I could. I'd say: 'Here's your schedule and your budget; within these boundaries you're pretty much on your own, but tell me once a week what's going on.'" Roger Gibbs adds, "If a free spirit is a technical heavyweight, you can put up with a lot. If he or she isn't, you don't have to. They have to be worth the care and feeding." But Gibbs, too, gives his people plenty of . . . well . . . space. "I don't tell them how high to jump—I just want them to know what we as a team need from them, and how their product fits in. Trying to dictate a method of operation doesn't work."

"The first thing I do with a prickly personality," confides George Pace, "is find areas of agreement. I build on those areas, so that we can develop at least some kind of relationship. *Then* I'm able to broach the topic of disagreement and show the person—who is usually thinking only of the technical aspects—that sometimes there are political aspects that have to be considered." More than anything else, Pace wanted his "free spirits" to function as a team. "Being a team," he explains, "means not letting other teammates fail; it means meeting your commitments because others are depending on you to, and it means sharing the credit. If you can get your people to think and work like this, they can overcome any obstacle."

Every business has its share of free spirits and prickly personalities, perhaps in the form of a freewheeling sales star who continually bends the rules, or an irreplaceable computer guru who prefers solitude to team pep talks. Under normal conditions they represent a management challenge; placed under the crisis conditions of a deadline, they can make or break the team. The JPL "care and feeding" management principles would work well with the individualists in any organization. Simple techniques such as using their own strong egos as a management tool—or giving them a wide berth, but with strict accountability—can turn the most unconventional employee into a committed ally. Just as these legendary aerospace organizations are willing to make internal changes to speed up dealings with the customer or with its partner, JPL/Lockheed Martin managers are also less apt to impose their will on creative subordinates and are more likely to change their *own* ways in the interests of meeting the deadline. Rather than beat their people over the head to get status reports on a timely basis, for example, they might send somebody from Administration down into the labs to gather status from the lips of the rocket scientists, but not their busy hands.

RECOGNIZE THAT EMOTIONAL LIABILITY IS A BY-PRODUCT OF DEDICATION

Although rocket scientists may present unique management challenges, they also, as a body and individually, put forth prodigious effort, bordering on the self-sacrificial, which in turn presents its own managerial challenges, like protecting one's people from overworking. "Aerospace folks are a rare breed," says Ed Euler. "They'll work ungodly hours to get the job done and not even put in for overtime, for fear that management may worry about them burning out. It's not uncommon to see a person who is on the midnight shift show up at 10:00 A.M. to watch an orbit correction maneuver. We have to tell them to go home, and if they say they can't sleep, we tell them go home anyway and lie on the couch with their eyes closed."

Roger Gibbs is continually monitoring the work habits of his team to see who may be in danger of becoming obsessive. "From a managerial standpoint," he adds, "we try to set a schedule that won't work anybody into a frenzy." The only burnout Gibbs wants to see is from the rocket itself; a team member collapsing at a moment of crisis would only jeopardize the mission. His protective management style is at odds with those who prefer the business equivalent of revered football coach Vince Lombardi, who was famous for "bringing out the best" in his players by relentlessly pushing for perfection. But, if engendering loyalty is a metric of successful management, then Gibbs is right up there.

When the *Odyssey* mission lost its Lander and then its Rover—due to budgetary cuts and to the sudden (and understandable) "risk averse" attitude on the part of upper management—Roger Gibbs felt deeply the sweet pain of a manager fortunate enough to lead a team that would do anything for him. In an effort to convince upper management, stung by the two failures in 1999, that *Odyssey*'s planned experiments at the surface of the planet *would* work, Gibbs asked his team to go the extra mile by painstakingly answering all of the technical objections raised by NASA's board of review. Twice the team responded to the concerns of the board, each carefully prepared response requiring months of extra effort. When the decision to cancel the landing portion of the mission—and to focus solely on the orbiting scientific experiments—was clear, Roger's sense of obligation to his own people was profoundly humbling. "I have a team," he says with obvious reciprocity, "that will crawl over glass for me."

The loss of two highly anticipated phases of the mission came as a blow to the *Odyssey* team. Morale had to be restored; personnel once dedicated to the Lander and the Rover experiments had to be redeployed. It may come as a surprise to some—considering the stereotype of the "rocket scientist" as unemotional, analytical thinking machines—that JPL engineers take mission cancellations and mission failures very personally. The public did not hear that actual grief counselors were brought in to help the *Observer* staff get through the sense of loss when, after a *decade* of work, their spacecraft simply disappeared. This was, incidentally, at a time in the aerospace industry when the team members were predominately male. "There were a lot of tears," remembers Project Manager Glenn Cunningham, "when, after weeks of listening in vain for some kind of signal, I had to tell everybody that *Observer* was gone for good. It was very hard." Similar emotional reactions took place over at Lockheed Martin, presenting similar management challenges.

One of John Casani's ways of dealing with both the emotional liability and the nearly obsessive work ethic that seem to go hand in glove was to garner the support of the "other half" of the team members—their families. On the many space missions he has managed, he has gone out of his way to see that the families appreciated the importance of the work that was being done in the labs, when most people in other businesses were at home for dinner. "I tried to have a big get-together for every mission, so that wives, husbands, and kids could see for themselves that we were doing things out here that were worth a little overtime." Casani would lead the delighted family members through Mission Control and out into the assembly area for the spacecraft. There is something about gathering in a circle around an actual deep space probe, most of which have a surprisingly and endearing fragile, "homemade" appearance, soon to be launched into infinity. Casani would post signature sheets in front of the little craft, so that the spouses and children of each team member could sign their names; the sheets were then reduced to microfiche and those signatures went out into deep space, as an interstellar greeting card. That kind of fanciful gesture represents a tremendous outreach to the spouses who must bear with the long work days and missed dinners. When the family itself has an emotional stake in the project, a JPL lab technician, returning late from work, will likely not have to apologize more than once. He or she will also have the understanding of loved ones, should there be a mission failure.

One can imagine that there may be a business manager or two who, while reading this, would rub hands together at the prospect of having a workforce so obsessive that it would burn the midnight oil and yet be afraid to be "caught" at it by claiming overtime. Such a staff is not seen by JPL/Lockheed Martin managers as a resource to exploit but, rather, as a national treasure. The team members, conversely, can sense the sacrifices their managers are making to insulate them from distracting tasks, and the managers are paid back in spades. This protective role of management might be the last thing one would expect during the time crunch of a deadline, but cracking the whip is far less productive than running interference for a team bent on success.

LET THE TEAM DECIDE

Under the accelerated pace of a deadline, the dictator in us all (in our own eyes, the benevolent monarch) asserts itself. There is an urge to expedite every process, even the democratic exchange of ideas within the group entrusted with meeting the deadline. If the team seems unable to make up its collective mind, the "take charge manager" often steps in and makes an arbitrary decision for the sake of the mission. But, by equating the stifling of seemingly inconclusive debate with putting the team back "on course," the manager may have merely satisfied the inner compulsion to get things moving again, and not necessarily in the right direction. George Pace cannot imagine himself in such an authoritative role. "Nobody is that smart," he jokes.

If anybody *were* to be that smart, it would probably be Pace, with the experience of three missions to Mars under his hat. But he steadfastly refuses to intervene personally in team decisions. Even with Time breathing down his neck, he prefers to facilitate a team consensus. "Sometimes I can see that the team is looking at me for the final word. But I want *them* to work it out. And usually two or three individuals will emerge as champions of a particular approach to the problem, while maybe two or three others put up a vigorous defense. One by one, the other members in the middle gravitate to one side or the other. Pretty soon there is a preponderance of people on one side of the issue. Ninety percent of the time, the right path rather quickly becomes evident."

Pace's low-key leadership style is deceptively constructive. By putting the onus on the team members to persuade each other on the merits of their respective arguments, he has created a spawning ground for future JPL leaders. Rather than being relieved of the ultimate responsibility of making a critical decision, the team members are, in effect, forced into a situation in which they must make their case as persuasively as they can before their peers. By laying the merits of their positions before the bar of reason, they expose even their most sacred scientific convictions to objective probing and prodding. Soon a consensus is achieved. And even those who do not prevail must grudgingly acknowledge a moderation of their own views; it is hard to "hold out" in the face of a united front of those who are the best in the world at what they do. Like participants after an exhausting debate, all the team members have a better appreciation of the subtleties of an issue they once thought to be so cut and dry.

Pace does not confirm the team consensus by stating, "Yes, that's what I would have concluded." Nor does he raise an eyebrow at the collective solution. If he is somewhat uncomfortable with the solution, he may ask "Have you considered such and such?" Then, satisfied that the team has indeed considered his concerns, he abides by their decision. After all, the team was empowered to work it out for itself; the last thing he wants to do is pull the rug out from under its authority. It is important to note that, by letting the team decide, Pace does not in any way distance himself from the decision, should there be a failure of the mission. As project manager, he is fully responsible and accountable for the actions of the team he has assembled. Indeed, if he wanted to protect himself from the consequences of a poor decision, he would no doubt be tempted to simply make the decision himself, based on his own considerable experience. By encouraging the team to arrive at the proper course, he probably puts his reputation at greater risk, but that is the managerial style that, in the long run, more effectively serves JPL, as it would any organization.

MAKE YOUR "LAUNCH" VISIBLE

Most of the organizations profiled in this book could have stumbled on the first day of their race against time and, outside a few eyewitnesses, nobody would have known. Had JPL and Lockheed Martin stumbled on *their* public debut, the whole world would have known. A successful space launch would have been news for a day, but a disaster would have had—for the frenetic news industry—a comparatively eternal broadcast life; video clips of the exploding, tipping rocket would have appeared over and over again on every television set in the country. It is no coincidence that many JPL and NASA executives looked positively relieved after the spectacular liftoff of *Odyssey*. American space launches are public and international spectacles. The delivery rockets at Cape Canaveral stand erect on the pad *for months* as the spacecraft is attached, tested, and tuned up; exposed to the national and international media, to the weather, and to the prying eyes of satellites from competitive nations.

But suppose that launch had been done in secret? The American taxpayer would have been treated to the news video of the flamboyant success and, conversely, would have been blissfully unaware of the "state secret" of a failure. The pressure on the teams charged with the success of the mission would have been considerably relieved. It would have been somewhat equivalent to performing "live" on stage in front of an audience of discerning theatergoers or video recording a performance, with all the benefits of editing, which was exactly the Soviet approach. *Their* rockets and spacecraft were assembled in the supine position, beneath the cover of a corrugated warehouse roof, then wheeled out on railroad tracks in the middle of the night and launched immediately. Perhaps the very liability of public exposure, in the event of a launch disaster, is one of the reasons that the NASA space program has been more successful. American rocket scientists must be at least somewhat haunted by the possibility of a fireball at launch. Doubtless, they would be equally dedicated if the projects were done in secret. But the intense public exposure simply has to put an edge on the determination of all involved. Roger Gibbs thinks so. "First of all, we don't want to let the nation down; secondly, knowing the whole world will be watching definitely puts a lot of pressure on us to perform, and I think we perform better."

That kind of "edginess" is needed within any team charged with the responsibility of meeting a deadline. There are certainly business equivalents of a visible "launch" of a deadline; nostalgic newspaper photographs come to mind of CEOs, in top hats and tails, digging the first shovelful of dirt for a major tunnel or skyscraper, wielding silver, ceremonial spades. Modern-day press conferences sometimes attend an opening blue-ribbon ceremony, and of course companies are ever in a hurry to issue press releases of new projects and endeavors. But it is safe to say that many deadlines within the business community are unheralded—some for reasons of security, others because many executives associate fanfare with the *completion* of a deadline, not its beginning. Fully constructed ships are christened with champagne; there is no ceremony for their welding carts on the first day of production.

Yet there is much in favor of treating the beginning of a deadline with the same hoopla accorded its completion. Like any other race against time, a significant deadline merits a good send-off, replete with starter's gun. There is no better way to demonstrate to the team assigned with "bringing it in on time" that success is expected of them—by their peers, by the company at large, by the customer, and by the customer's customers—than a public launch. And, unlike most company activities that begin with a bang and immediately disappear from the consciousness of the rank and file, the deadline should have "legs," perhaps because of an assigned "reporter," who would help keep the excitement alive throughout the organization, and throughout the business community, with timely press releases and updates and progress reports. The company Web site ought to give a running commentary on the project, just as the JPL Web site offered throughout the *Odyssey* mission.

THERE IS MUCH IN FAVOR OF TREATING THE BEGINNING OF A DEADLINE WITH THE SAME HOOPLA ACCORDED ITS COMPLETION.

A highly visible launch is the corporate equivalent of a vast, written affirmation, a public pledge from all within the organization that the deadline will be met. The "pressure," if one wants to characterize public awareness in such a way, is immense; it can either oppress or buoy the team struggling to meet the deadline—*that* depends largely on the corporate culture. If the position of one's associates, from the CEO on down, is, "The world is watching; people are counting on you; don't let them down!" then perhaps the high visibility of the launch would create undue pressure on the team members. But if there is a strong sense of common cause throughout the organization, prompting individuals from every level to offer words of encouragement and confidence, then working in the spotlight is no longer as intimidating. With so much commitment throughout, one feels a sense of momentum, almost of destiny. And, when so much "face" can be lost, employees grow ever more determined to meet that deadline.

DISCOURAGE SUBCULTURES

The managers at Lockheed Martin have noticed over the years—in the aerospace industry at large, and even in their own organization—that subcultures of engineering talent, if allowed to remain insular, can hinder a deadline as much as help it. The larger the organization, the more likely it will have the infrastructure to support subcultures (in smaller aerospace companies, engineers may, by necessity, perform several roles, thereby developing a bigger picture). Seemingly by nature, engineers tend to be very specialized; they also tend to remain within their disciplines. Strong bonds form with fellow engineers, as all contribute to well-deserved departmental reputations for excellence and achievement. Before too long, however, little fiefdoms of very talented people can become indifferent, if not adversarial, to the concerns of other fiefdoms down the hall, all of which compete for budgetary allocations. It is not unusual for an aerospace company to be composed of independently operating teams of specialists who each lunch as a group, socialize as a group after hours, and know very little about the work being accomplished within neighboring departments.

Since most deadlines are assigned to "teams of teams," insularity between the groups can prevent the integration necessary to a seamless, unified effort. All the talent in the world, if compartmentalized, will not make up for a lack of synergy between teams that have little appreciation for the needs and aspirations of each other. "A spacecraft team," says Ben Clark, project scientist and thirty-year Lockheed Martin veteran, "might have little to do with the navigation team, which in turn does not understand the idiosyncrasies of a spacecraft. They are experts all, but out of touch with each other. That can hurt us under normal conditions; under a time crunch it can spell disaster."

Senior management has taken concrete steps to counter the quite natural tendency of departments to harden into little worlds of their own. Continuing with the above example, Lockheed Martin insists that a formal member of the navigation team come from the spacecraft side of the fence and vice versa. Management goes further, by taking a long-term view of the careers of its promising engineers. A significant number of engineers are required to go through a cradle-to-grave rite of passage, in which they participate on all major phases of a mission—from design, to launch, to operations. This "rounding-out" process makes for managers who will, by seeing the Big Picture, become facilitators on a time-critical project, rather than zealous guardians of their own turf. It should be noted that the engineers who have been tapped on the shoulder by management for a cradle-to-grave project feel flattered; the experience, although demanding, is recognized as a good career move.

While keeping a wary eye out for subcultures within its organization, management is also careful that its *dominant* culture—the engineering core that makes up probably 85 percent of the company—does not treat its smaller science cadre as stepchildren. That's because science drives every space mission. While getting a spacecraft to orbit Mars is certainly a great achievement, the mission would be regarded by NASA as a failure if the science instruments aboard were not sending a continuous stream of data back to earth. The contractor's engineers, therefore, are expected to know a lot about the experiments they are making possible for the project scientists, by getting the craft to orbit Mars. Furthermore, says Ben Clark, they are expected to know and appreciate the needs of the "end user": all the university and research scientists who will be analyzing the data for years to come. Without this high level of sensitivity on the part of Lockheed Martin management, their space missions would be in greater jeopardy of being engineering triumphs but scientific failures, nonetheless.

The existence of subcultures is certainly not exclusive to the aerospace industry. Every business organization has its fiefdoms. In fact, many companies unwittingly do more to promote interdepartmental pride and rivalry—through competitions, awards, and increasing managerial specialization—than to prevent it. When forming teams to meet a deadline, businesses would do well to follow the Lockheed Martin example and cross-pollinate these teams with members of other departments and divisions. Efforts should be taken, as well, to put as many managers as possible through an accelerated apprenticeship at a number of departments outside their own. Spending as little as a week at a time in production, quality control, sales, information services, accounting, and customer service, etc., would "round out" one's internal perspective of the organization in ways that could save lost hours or days in bureaucratic delay. And, certainly, a cradle-to-grave project assignment would bestow the Big Picture of the organization's capacity to meet the needs of the most demanding customer. The personal contact, as well, would be invaluable; in the crunch of a deadline, the cradle-to-grave graduate would know "whom to call" for advice and support.

BEGIN WITH A "FAULT TREE" ANALYSIS

One of the problems with determining the cause of a failed mission is that the physical evidence is not in hand. In the case of the two failed Mars missions, "the black boxes" were very likely scattered on the surface of the planet. When there is a sudden cessation of communication with the perfectly functioning spacecraft, there is very little to go on. The scientists, then, have to reconstruct the mission; they do that by a fault tree analysis—a technique that would serve any business enterprise well.

A fault tree analysis seeks out the critical "fault" of a mission; the process, once diagrammed, forms a "tree." For example, the analysts ask: "What has to work in order to get the spacecraft to Mars?" Well, to begin somewhere, the propulsion system has to work; that's a "branch." The propulsion system is broken down into its many subsystems (more "branches" off the main) and the subsystems into their many components (the "leaves"). Once that is done with every system, a "tree" graphically represents the infrastructure of the mission. Eventually, by going down the logical paths, the scientists arrive at some pretty solid deductions.

One of the distinguishing characteristics of the *Odyssey* mission was that the fault tree analysis, instead of being a postmortem, was done at the beginning of the process, before there was, so to speak, a "fault" to trace. "With the two previous failures," recalls Roger Gibbs, "I thought that the only way to keep our credit going was to assure NASA that this mission was going to be OK. The fault tree analysis is always done after the fact, so we *pretended* we had a mission failure even though we were only in the design phase. Then we came in with all the rigor of a Failure Review Board and did the analysis. It was a good thing, too; we found some 'susceptibilities' that we were able to correct easily because we were so early into the project."

Gibbs is referring to the "One/Ten/One Hundred" rule that has come out of the crucible of decades of space launches. Paraphrased, it states that if a problem is identified in the conceptual stage of the project, it takes only "one unit" of the organization's resources to fix it. If the problem appears during the design phase, "ten units" will be required for its resolution. If the scientists become aware of it during the assembly phase, then "one hundred units" of resources will be needed. And, of course, there are mission phases well beyond assembly phase. A design flaw that could have been detected during an early fault tree analysis—if discovered, say, in the cruise phase to Mars—probably could not be resolved without significantly reducing the scope of the mission. Gibbs's *proactive* use of this method may have set the standard for future space projects; JPL has indicated that, from now on, there will be a lot of fault trees diagrammed before the next missions lift off the ground.

Many of JPL's deadline-management techniques, such as the fault tree analysis, make a lot of sense for space missions because of the unique nature of each highly customized project. But, are business deadlines any less unique? Certainly, a deadline for a prominent customer is a "one of a kind" mission: If it is not met, there will never be another deadline for that particular customer. Each major business deadline is also "one of a kind" in that each project is tailored to the customer's needs, and those requirements vary with each and every customer. Just because a company has performed thousands of similar services before is no reason to expect success; more than 300 Delta rockets have been launched, yet JPL treats each one as seriously as if it were the first. This kind of earnest attention to detail would save many a business deadline from unnecessary grief.

Is a fault tree analysis a practical procedure during the crunch of a deadline? George Pace would argue that this kind of proactive scrutiny is even more important on a time-critical project. "You can't afford to *wait* to see if everything is going to work right, because, if it doesn't, you've found out too late." This technique would serve any business team about to enter uncharted waters. Let us imagine a company introducing a new widget into the market. The project team, with representatives from all the branches of the "tree" (design, production, marketing, sales, etc.), would ask: "What can go wrong, and what have we done to protect against that possibility?" By doing its due diligence in the most proactive manner, the team would eliminate to the best of its ability unpleasant surprises down the road, greatly increasing the chances of successfully meeting its milestones. The fault tree analysis, despite its forbidding phraseology, belongs in the world of business and should be applied to every serious deadline—proactively, not after the sad fact of losing the race against time.

> **"YOU CAN'T AFFORD TO *WAIT* TO SEE IF EVERYTHING IS GOING TO WORK RIGHT, BECAUSE, IF IT DOESN'T, YOU'VE FOUND OUT TOO LATE."**

CALL IN A "RED TEAM"

One of the most interesting policies of JPL, as well as one of the most value to the business community, is its emphasis on independent review. At several stages of the *Odyssey* mission, the eager-beaver team members had to submit to a dispassionate critique from a board of aerospace professionals selected by NASA. The experience can be compared to an IRS audit, and, as such, it is not a particularly welcomed interruption of the work in progress. The review board is called a Red Team, dating back to earlier days in aerospace when a Blue Team would be assigned to advocate a certain position or project, while a Red Team would be assigned to look for its inherent flaws. Now, only Red Teams exist; the *Odyssey* team members, obviously biased in favor of their own approach, would constitute a metaphorical Blue Team.

The Red Team review is most definitely *not* a formality begun with a foregone conclusion; it is, rather, a vigorous and intense examination. The chairman of the Red Team reviewing *Odyssey*, Glenn Cunningham, remembers his instructions from NASA: "We were told to turn over every stone, that no question was out of bounds. Our job was to identify any area of risk and report it up line to NASA." Nor is a Red Team an old boys club of familiar cronies; NASA insists that a good portion of the review board be composed of non-JPL, and even non-NASA, specialists. Glenn Cunningham, a good friend and former boss of George Pace on two previous missions, was nevertheless chosen to head the board in the interests of time. NASA, too, is deadline oriented; if it had appointed a complete stranger to the project's concepts, it would have taken far too long to bring that chairperson "up to speed" before he or she could make an intelligent recommendation. Cunningham, then retired from JPL, was the perfect choice. He had been the project manager of a Mars mission that failed (Mars *Observer*) and one that had recently succeeded (Mars *Global Surveyor*). Thoroughly experienced, he was the kind of person whose advice one would covet under any circumstances.

A Red Team, furthermore, cannot be "sold" on the project, and no efforts are made to wine and dine its members or to cajole them into a sympathetic position. Personal contact is kept to a minimum, and every precaution is taken so that Red Team members do not "go native." The colorful phrase refers to the early anthropological studies, in which objective European scientists, too long on the job, began to identify with the very tribes they were supposed to be studying. A suc-

The Broncos Stadium: Turner Construction Company brought in this spectacular $400 million project on time and under budget—an unprecedented achievement in the industry. Sometimes compared to a giant erector set, the stadium required two million pounds of steel, which were fabricated and delivered by Angeles Steel. *Photo courtesy of Turner Construction Company.*

Airborne Express: Every Airborne employee is committed to the deadline. Nobody wants to envision a movie screen that reads, "Ladies and Gentlemen, there will be no movie tonight because Airborne screwed up!" What could be a routine job is never allowed to become routine. *Photo courtesy of Airborne Express.*

The FBI Meets the Ultimate Deadline: Agents Doug Kane (left) and Mark Llewellyn were the lead investigators on the Stephan Phillips kidnapping case. In life-and-death situations, FBI agents have learned how to make fast decisions without second-guessing. *Photo courtesy of Executive Shield.*

FBI SWAT Team: The famous FBI SWAT teams work closely with two other teams—surveillance and technical—on investigation and rescue efforts. Even after a successful conclusion, the case isn't considered "closed" until members of all teams have met to review how they operated and what they could have done better. *Photo courtesy of FBI.*

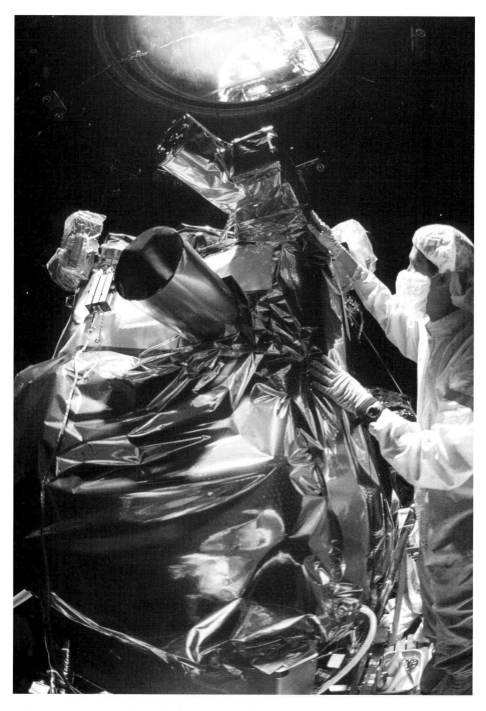

Mission to Mars: Lockheed Martin designed and built the *Odyssey* spacecraft, here undergoing thermal chamber tests. The Lockheed Martin–JPL partnership put an end to a record of failure for Mars missions. *Photo by Pat Corkery, courtesy of Lockheed Martin Space Systems.*

Launch Day for *Odyssey:* The JPL team arrived at the launch site at 4:30 A.M. on April 7, 2001. *Photo courtesy of Roger Gibbs, Jet Propulsion Lab.*

The 2001 Mars *Odyssey*
Photo courtesy of Jet Propulsion Lab.

Boeing's 777: The Boeing wide-body 777 required a team of 10,000 engineers and mechanics to create and assemble more than three million parts. Using a completely new design and building process, the project also required one million hours of training on new systems and technologies. *Photo courtesy of The Boeing Company.*

Into the Air: Five years of effort resulted in a triumphant first flight. "Working Together" with first customer United Airlines, Boeing revolutionized the way planes are built and instilled a new management philosophy that changed the organization. Boeing is now working on its 400th 777 aircraft.
Photo courtesy of The Boeing Company.

Conoco's Weekend of Caring: After tropical storm Allison dumped thirty-six inches of rain on Houston, 1,500 Conoco employees led an extraordinary volunteer relief effort for residents of 333 devastated homes. "We didn't do this just to feel good about ourselves. We had to be effective." *Photos courtesy of Conoco.*

cessive boatload of anthropologists would arrive on the island, only to find that their associates were running about in grass skirts.

The aerospace equivalent of going native has happened when a JPL engineer, sent to "office" in the facility of an industrial contractor—in effect, to look out for the interests of JPL—begins to identify more so with the group of people he or she has been assigned to oversee. The reverse has happened, as well, when an aerospace long-term visitor has gone over to the JPL side. A romantic example of "going native" happened years ago on the Mars/Venus/Mercury project, when a young man from JPL was sent to Boeing to oversee the project and fell head over heels for a Boeing engineer; after the highly successful mission they were married and remain so to this day. As a rule, though, NASA successfully ensures the objectivity of its Red Team members. And, really, so does JPL. "What good would it do," asks Roger Gibbs, "if I were to somehow bias the Red Team into approving a design that turned out to be flawed in some way? The mission could fail. None of us want that."

The initial resistance felt by the *Odyssey* team members toward the intrusion of the Red Team soon dissipated, but not because of a warm and fuzzy evolution of relationships. "In this kind of review by highly technical people," says George Pace, "the facts have to speak for themselves. They asked technical questions; we answered them." Roger Gibbs adds, "After a while we realized that these were pretty smart people and that they could help the success of the mission. They began to feel the same way about us, I think, and about the folks at Lockheed Martin." Asked whether this time-consuming process threatened to jeopardize the deadline, Gibbs shakes his head. "Not really—it goes fast enough if everyone cooperates. At first, I'll admit, I was pretty uptight. I felt like saying: 'You gave us the funding and you gave us the mission, now get out of the way and let us do it.' But then I resigned myself to the process—because it was an honest process. I became pretty philosophical about it. And if it had turned out that we didn't make the launch deadline, at least we tried our best to find the right way to Mars."

The Red Team, no doubt, would not have wanted the *Odyssey* team to miss the deadline, either. After all, they were appointed by NASA to find design flaws that would jeopardize the mission, because NASA could not afford another failure. Surely a missed launch—which would cause a *twenty-six-month* delay—would be nearly as bad as a failed mission, from a public relations standpoint. In its own way, the Red Team was there to help meet the deadline.

Would the independent review process sit well with the fast-paced business community? While many companies require a hierarchical series of "sign-offs," indicating that other eyes have also examined a particular proposal or contract, serious review is usually performed after the fact, once the project has failed. The idea of an indefinite "time-out" for a deliberate review of a *group* of experts, which means possibly even more time to reach a consensus within the group, would be anathema to many a hard-charging manager. But an independent review does not have to be a time-consuming process—if, as in the example of *Odyssey*, the facts are allowed to speak for themselves. It is too often the embellishment of "marketeers," or even the impassioned arguments of the earnestly biased, that takes so much time for an independent observer to unravel. The problems that could truly jeopardize the deadline should be readily apparent to a review group allowed to review the facts without the obfuscation of project cheerleaders. The end result—a stronger plan—should be welcomed by all concerned.

CREATE A TIGER TEAM

The recommendations of a Red Team are always worthwhile, but not necessarily always final. Until NASA itself lowers the boom, there is an opportunity to respond to the verdict of an independent review. On the highly successful Mars *Global Surveyor* project, Lockheed Martin had developed a mechanical arm that would point an antenna earthward, while the spacecraft's science instruments were trained on Mars; this way a continuous stream of data could be simultaneously collected and transmitted. The Red Team voiced concerns that the mechanical arm was too complex and likely to fail. Their suggestion was to do away with the arm, and to program the spacecraft to periodically turn back toward Earth to transmit the data it had collected. But that would mean a temporary cessation of the science experiments. The aerospace engineers, however, again thinking of the "end user," the earthbound scientific community, wanted to keep their antenna arrangement so that nonstop experiments could be conducted. So, management called out a Tiger Team.

True to its aggressive title, a Tiger Team is a task force of experts suddenly called on to clear the obstacles to a successfully met deadline. In an effort to clear *the Tiger Team's* obstacles, as it seizes on the problem, management rolls out the red carpet. A Tiger Team goes to the front of the line (as did the Red Team) whenever it requires company resources, such as lab facilities or the services of the mainframe. The members and the problem they are attempting to solve are given the highest priority. "In a week and a half," Ben Clark remembers, "the team found a solution, and we decided to proceed with the mechanical arm, against the recommendations of the review board." The Tiger Team, of course, had to be interrogated itself, and its solution had to allay the concerns of management sufficiently. But it is interesting that Lockheed Martin does not necessarily follow the recommendations of the very review team it has empowered to identify areas of risk; an equal chance is given to the advocates of the procedure in question.

The system is reminiscent of a city government employing both a district attorney and a public defender to try the same case, doing their best with the identical evidence; in theory, justice should prevail. If Lockheed Martin empowered only the review board to be the final arbiter, it might create a "risk averse" corporate culture. When a Tiger Team is allowed to respond to the concerns of the board, the spirit of adventure still thrives. Together, they form a complementary system of opposing advocates who, in fact, have the same goal—a successful mission—in mind.

It is not difficult to imagine this model applied to a business deadline, because obstacles arise frequently enough during every project. The process need not be time consuming; after all, if aerospace engineers can solve a "rocket science" problem in only a week and a half, less weighty business solutions can surely be found as readily. The results of an independent review do not necessarily have to provoke a response—as the deadline team may gratefully accept their suggestions—but the mechanism for an expert response should be in place. Upper management would have the benefit of two very well considered points of view; both, in their own way, having the interests of the project at heart. The decision may not be an easy one, but, either way, it will be a "wise" one; management is not expected to be omniscient (except perhaps by the shareholder), and it will have done the best it could with the dilemma.

RECOGNIZE THAT SOMETIMES "SLOWER" IS FASTER

The problem with deadlines is that they are so often expressed in such a way as to encourage counterproductive behavior. In an effort to convey the sense of urgency, managers are sometimes all too successful; a crisis condition is created, and crisis behavior is rarely helpful to the successful meeting of a deadline. Whenever the workplace is charged with the electricity of a race against time, clear communication can suffer, sound and practical procedures may be sidestepped, and well-intentioned heroics often unnecessarily duplicate somebody else's work. In an effort to demonstrate that they understand the nature of the emergency, employees frequently mimic the urgency of their bosses and proceed with great vigor—sometimes in the wrong direction. Hurried behavior becomes contagious; even those tasks that only suffer from speed, like taking a message, are done a bit *too* efficiently, as if every second counts, and as if there is no time to bother with the fundamentals, such as courtesy and accuracy. "Hurry," in fact, can become one of the greatest obstacles to making a deadline.

"HURRY" CAN BE-COME ONE OF THE GREATEST OBSTACLES TO MAKING A DEAD-LINE.

At places like JPL, deadlines are approached with premeditated care. As might be expected from those trained in the sciences, the team leaders are methodical, preferring to slow down and do it right the first time, rather than make mistakes and be forced to repeat one's efforts.

Before launching into a project, John Casani scheduled retreats, in which all of his teams came to talk. "I asked every team to tell the other teams what they expected from each other. Once everybody agreed to their obligations, I asked them to put their pledges in the form of a written plan; these plans were then entered into a system and monitored on a weekly basis." Glenn Cunningham is also a firm believer in abolishing ambiguity from the get-go. "It's so important that everybody knows exactly what is expected of them, before they go rushing into the project."

Once into the project, as we have seen, potentially time-consuming practices are put into place, like the independent review of a Red Team, perhaps the considered response of a Tiger Team, and the painstaking exercise of the fault tree analysis. All the while, everyone involved on the project is acutely aware of the ticking of the clock. Yet there is time to "do it right." This patient, methodical stalking of a deadline—as opposed to a metaphorical Charge of the Light Brigade—is responsible for the great successes at JPL. There is a tremendous sense of control, at least of the activities that *can* be controlled by human beings during a space mission. There is also a nearly spiritual acceptance of one's lack of control. Four hundred years ago, Francis Bacon said that "Nature, to be controlled, must be obeyed." The mixture of audacity and servile humility in that statement could characterize the entire NASA space program.

The business community, in dealing with its deadlines, might do well to adopt the slower pace of these "rocket scientists" in their races against time. Speed is often simply a consequence of unobstructed flow. By exercising what many business managers might consider "extreme" care, the folks at JPL and Lockheed Martin manage to eliminate most of the obstacles in the paths of their deadlines; the result is "speed," without the histrionics that so often accompany business projects that are ill planned and that are carried out in an atmosphere of frenetic tension. Although there is often high drama during a space mission, and although these earthbound explorers are, themselves, emotionally liable to the result of the mission, their satisfaction comes from *holding to process* throughout the whole wild ride. Dramatics are not considered evidence of their commitment to the mission.

THE LIGHT AT THE END OF THE TUNNEL

The managers who are attracted to high-risk, high-profile missions—as opposed to organizational management positions at JPL—know full well that their names may become forever associated with failed missions. The high likelihood of failure only seems to add zest to their careers. When George Pace began interviewing candidates for his *Odyssey* leadership team, Roger Gibbs had a comparatively comfortable management opportunity in another department. Nevertheless, he told Pace: "I'll do anything to be a part of this project. I don't have to be a manager, I just want to be a part of this mission." David Spencer distinguished himself during the interview by handing Pace a long letter explaining why, at thirty-one, he was the right choice out of the fifteen more experienced candidates who had applied. Such enthusiasm in the context of a "two-thirds" failure rate of all the missions to Mars made a strong impression on Pace. And Pace, himself, who knew more than anyone the stresses and unknowns associated with a Mars mission, was no less eager to go through it all again.

After long careers at JPL, George Pace and Glenn Cunningham are not ready for the fishing pole yet. Both men are very active consultants to JPL, as well as to national and international clients. John Casani, who was at JPL when it really was a "*jet propulsion* lab," and who mentored both Pace and Cunningham, has returned from retirement to his desk, where he is busier than ever. These three individuals probably have more experience with the trials and tribulations of space missions than anyone on the planet. Yet, they can't get enough of it. From a career advancement standpoint at JPL, perhaps they could have chosen a safer path, one with less personal exposure. But, when they walk down the hall, they are recognized by their associates as the true pioneers, win or lose.

"What I like about projects," says Glenn Cunningham, "is that you can always see the goal. In other areas of management, it's the same old thing, day after day. I remember telling my secretary once, when I was an organizational manager, that I could predict *exactly* what I would be doing a year from then. But on a space mission it's so different. You're doing what's never been done before, and you're doing it under tremendous time pressure. The deadline is the light at the end of the tunnel, and I guess I like to see that light."

For those of us who can also predict exactly what we will be doing a year hence, the finite nature of a deadline is very appealing. Deadlines have an end, and, even on lengthy projects, the end is comparatively near. Every effort must be made, of course, to ensure that it is a *happy* ending, but, in any case, the crisis of a deadline will soon pass. Other challenges will appear, each with distinctive requirements. Had Cunningham remained an "organizational manager," his career no doubt would have been a fulfilling one. But certainly the pace of a series of successively met deadlines contributed to the excitement he still craves as a consultant. The light at the end of the tunnel for these space veterans is simply the shining entrance to yet another passage.

CHECKLIST OF DEADLINE MANAGEMENT
TECHNIQUES FROM THE CRUCIBLE OF THIS PROJECT

- ❏ Be willing to subjugate your personality in the interests of the deadline.

- ❏ Margin can be doled out incrementally or given away up front. Consider creating a marketplace to swap margin.

- ❏ Make use of award-based incentives for your deadline team.

- ❏ Model your team after your counterpart's team structure.

- ❏ Mold your "free spirits" into a functioning team.

- ❏ Prevent burnout proactively on the part of your team members.

- ❏ Cultivate leadership by letting your team decide major issues.

- ❏ Make your deadline highly visible.

- ❏ Discourage subcultures by encouraging the Big Picture.

❏ *Begin* with a "fault tree analysis."

❏ Implement independent review.

❏ Create Tiger Teams.

❏ Remember—"slower" can be faster.

THE ULTIMATE DEADLINE—HOW THE FBI MANAGES A KIDNAPPING

"We have your son. If we do not receive $800,000 by Friday, he will be killed."
—THE KIDNAPPERS OF STEPHAN PHILLIPS

"Kidnappings are the toughest cases; a life hangs in the balance of every decision you make, and there's not much time to make those decisions."
—RON IDEN, SPECIAL AGENT IN CHARGE, LOS ANGELES OFFICE, FBI

"Mark and I tackled him at the phone booth. We both roared in his ears, 'Where's Stephan?'"
—DOUG KANE, FBI SWAT TEAM COMMANDER

◆　◆　◆

While no one would argue that FBI agents are frequently under severe deadlines, there may be a popular misconception of their powers that just slightly diminishes our admiration. For those of us who must brake at every red light in life, frustrated by bureaucratic procedures, stymied by protective executive secretaries who block our calls to customers, and stopped in our tracks by company gatekeepers who, relishing their power, move at the excruciating pace of a Nazi airport official scrutinizing the forged passport of Alan Ladd as he tries to outrun the Gestapo, the FBI agent does not seem subject to mortal delay. After all, he or she need only flash those imposing credentials for all resistance to collapse and all obstacles to fall away. Which of us would not love to wave a similar magic wand in the faces of those who stand between us and our deadlines, transforming the most obstructive gatekeeper into a submissive guide?

But, if the truth were to be known, the FBI agent is hampered and occasionally frustrated by a number of restrictions. Gaining court approval for a phone tap—from a judicial system founded by American colonialists who were infuriated by the arbitrary search and seizure practices of the British—can take weeks. If the judge, persuaded by reams of documentation, does allow a tap, it will be literally for one phone; if there is another phone in the house, that conversation cannot be overheard. If the suspect uses a cell phone, the agents cannot listen. If the suspect drives to a different city, the agents must seek the blessing of yet another judge, who must be convinced that such an extraordinary search warrant (in this case, the search for conversations) is justified. The process can take weeks more. If an individual refuses to talk to an agent, as criminals are wont to do, he or she must be subpoenaed, which is another time-consuming process. Criminals are not unaware of the limits of the law; they often have, in fact, a more practical knowledge of the Bill of Rights than a high school student studying political science. And once the attorneys are brought in, the pace of the investigation can slow to a crawl.

CRIMINALS ARE NOT UNAWARE OF THE LIMITS OF THE LAW; THEY OFTEN HAVE A MORE PRACTICAL KNOWLEDGE OF THE BILL OF RIGHTS THAN A HIGH SCHOOL STUDENT.

Nevertheless, the FBI has a remarkably successful track record from taking a businesslike approach to situations in which "business" is conducted under rather extreme standards of performance. Failure to meet one's commitments in the underworld carries penalties that would make the boldest executive blanch. Yet FBI agents apply many principles in their war against crime and terror that would work equally against the most formidable, but comparatively peaceful, business deadlines. It will be reassuring to those who read on that the deadline management techniques of the world's greatest law enforcement agency can be applied to their own career challenges—without even firing a shot.

THE DEADLINE

Of all the "drop-dead" deadlines profiled in this book, a kidnapping is certainly the most literal. It is a deadline expressed in its most nightmarish terms: "Comply on time or forfeit the life of your child." To have the very existence of a loved one dependent on one's actions creates an unbearable self consciousness; every move could be fatal. It is difficult to think clearly, so difficult, in fact, that not every parent immediately calls the FBI. More often than not, a precious day or two is lost before the professionals are notified. The FBI agents who then respond must often solve the case *before the deadline* or bear the responsibility for the death of an innocent they could not protect.

Not all kidnappings resolved by the FBI fall into the "classic" category, in which an innocent, unaffiliated, victim is taken against his or her will and held for ransom. Many abductions, for example, are committed by an estranged parent; many other kidnappings occur between warring criminal gangs, in attempts to collect bad debts or to enforce drug deals. In the latter example, FBI agents find themselves coming to the aid of the very characters they might be investigating (of course, the victim, usually a child, is innocent). These cases are, in fact, very difficult for the FBI; the family members of the victim are not particularly forthcoming with helpful, and potentially self-incriminating, information. The successful rescue of their abducted child is cause for a happy reunion, to be sure, but not necessarily the spiritual conversion of the mobster mommy and daddy. More often than not, their gratitude toward the agents is restrained and tempered with the fear of new prosecutions for culpability uncovered during the investigation.

Clean-cut divisions between the "good guys" and the "bad guys" are not always readily apparent in a kidnapping case; the agents are understandably open-eyed and open-minded as they proceed with the investigation. In their experience, the "victim" has sometimes been part of the scheme, perhaps even the director of the drama, willing to put his or her parents through an emotional ordeal for the substantial ransom demanded. Sometimes, the grieving parent is the mastermind, hoping to play a convincing part for the insurance company, which will reimburse the "unrecoverable" ransom money. The classic kidnapping case used in this chapter to illustrate deadline-management the FBI way occurred in the 1990s, in an exclusive area of a coastal California community. The names of the victim and his family are fictitious, out of consideration for privacy.

The daily habits of Stephan Phillips, a nineteen-year-old college freshman, had been carefully monitored for months by three young men, who also, very surprisingly, lived in the same fashionable neighborhood. The notes they kept were obsessively accurate, their preparations equally well thought out. Stephan would be taken as he left the house of his fiancée. He would be stuffed for days into what can only be described as a coffin with an air tube, in complete and utter isolation. He would be released (presumably) on receipt of no less than $800,000 in ransom.

At nine o'clock in the morning on a summer day, Mr. Phillips, a highly successful broker, answered the kitchen phone in his usual, chipper tone. The voice in the receiver was startling; it sounded something like a metallic growl, as if an extraterrestrial were speaking. He thought initially there was some kind of technical problem over the lines. Then he heard the garbled words, "We've got your son," and reached for a chair.

STAY IN THE DRIVER'S SEAT

One would think that there could be no more helpless situation, apart from that of the actual victim, than being on the receiving end of a kidnapper's phone call. No matter how businesslike the tone, the voice of the kidnapper comes out of the primal darkness; he is a stranger from an alien world of values, where someone's very life is only the means to an end. If the kidnapper feels any anxiety, it is for the success of his plan, not for the suffering he inflicts upon others. His voice over the phone, even if disguised—maybe *especially* if disguised—fills one's heart with fear. A person of conscience would not even consider making a prank call that threatened the life of someone's child. To actually commit the unspeakable act is to put oneself so far apart from the rest of humanity that true communication is impossible and accomplished only through the exchange of values: money for one, a living being for the other. The kidnapper, through his own voluntary leap into Hell, is in the commanding position of a person with nothing to lose; his potential for harm is universally recognized and feared. He has total control of the captive; his demands, no matter how arbitrary, must be met. At his cruel hints at the consequences of noncompliance, the parents must stifle their outrage and beg for mercy instead. Though evil, this mastermind is surely in a God-like position.

"Not at all," remembers Mark Llewellyn, squad supervisor of the investigation. "The FBI was in control from day one; those guys just didn't know it."

It was, in fact, the kidnappers who were manipulated. Although the father and mother were the only points of contact with the abductors, they were continuously coached by agent Mark Wilson, who lived in their house during the thirteen-day ordeal. "We rehearsed with the parents over and over again. We told them to ask for more time to raise the money and to exaggerate the difficulties of liquidity. We even suggested they be prepared to offer *more* money, in exchange for a little more time. You'd be amazed how easy it is to appeal to the greed of the kidnappers." Both points of contact played on their strengths. The father dealt with the voices on the phone on a businessman to "businessman" level. At Wilson's prompting, he insisted on "proof of life" before any money was to be delivered. The mother was asked to take a more personal approach, and succeeded in keeping the kidnappers on the line well beyond the expectations of the experienced agents. Many ploys were used to keep the kidnappers talking at each conversation, to extend the timeline and to increase the chances of the captors making a blunder. With the expert coaching of the FBI, both parents were playing an agonizing but necessary role in the drama, and, in very subtle ways, they had gained a measure of control.

> "THE FBI WAS IN CONTROL FROM DAY ONE; THOSE GUYS JUST DIDN'T KNOW IT."

The idea of being in the driver's seat of a process that is suddenly thrust upon one is intriguing. Most business deadlines, especially the unanticipated ones, seem to put us in harness, not in command. The customer lays down the challenge; we scramble to keep pace with the customer's expectations. It is a race against time in the literal sense; we race, rather than pace ourselves. We are often unable to clear the way, proactively, for all the nagging fires that must be put out in the present. The end date looms. In near panic, we tell our subordinates, "We've *got* to get this done by 3:00 P.M. on June 15, or else!" rather than expressing with confidence, "This project will be substantially completed by mid-June."

The confidence of Mark Llewellyn and Mark Wilson was based upon a solid foundation of success—close to seventy happily resolved kidnappings between them—but less experienced agents would have exhibited the same assurance, if only out of consideration for the parents. One can imagine the impact on the already distraught family if the agents were to wring their own hands in despair, asking each other with worried expressions, "What do we do now?" Instead, the quiet confidence of the FBI was a major factor in taking control—not only of the bad guys, but of the parents as well. The agents had to become the decision makers almost immediately, which is not always an easy task with strong-willed, competent, professionally successful parents. By demonstrating personal conviction of a successful outcome, the agents were acting out their expectations of the family members, who, to their credit, were able to quell the nearly overwhelming emotions that accompany a kidnapping and play their parts well. Business managers who, likewise, personally exemplify the kind of calm determination they wish to see from their subordinates, will be imitated.

Although customers are most assuredly not to be compared to kidnappers, their demands are frequently expressed in equally nonnegotiable terms, as in "Meet these conditions, or I will find another company that can." Not a lot of time is given for a response—that, in itself, is no accident; the customer is seeking an agreement, not a counteroffer. Although it would be nice to have a "coach" whispering instructions in our ear as the parents do in a kidnapping situation, many of us acquiesce to terms that, in retrospect, could have been amended to our advantage. We tend to focus on our own current position, which may be rather desperate for increased business, without considering the customer's position, which may be equally desperate for a reliable company to make his or her vision a reality.

Being in the driver's seat is an attitude cultivated within the Bureau; agents recognize the potential for violence on the part of the child abductors, but they do not look on them with dreadful awe—unlike the FBI agent portrayed by Jodie Foster in *The Silence of the Lambs*, who gazed on Hannibal Lecter like a mesmerized schoolgirl. In fact, agents have a rather low opinion of the intelligence—not to say of the work ethic—of the "masterminds" they routinely slap cuffs on. They do not tremble at their demands, and their utter lack of fear inspires the parents, who *are* apt to tremble, for understandable reasons. They may encourage the parents to beg, which is music to the ears of any kidnapper, but the pleas are undetectably manipulative. Before he realizes it, the abductor has granted *more time* for the parent to liquidate investments (whether the time is needed or not), has agreed to demonstrate proof of life so that the parents know the money is for an actual exchange, and is negotiating about the exchange process itself, because the parents have been coached to express fear of the proposed drop site.

A "take charge" attitude can be cultivated in any company, no matter how low level the role, and no matter how frantic the need for more business. The customer may "always be right," but his or her deadline, as presented, will surely contain unrevealed margins of time and budget. By appealing and probing in much the same way as the FBI advises the family members, small concessions in the interests of fair play can be gained on many fronts, such as more advantageous payment terms, direct shipments to the customer versus in-house storage, a grudging increase in the amount of the contract because one has demonstrated *why* it cannot be done for the hoped-for amount, or an agreement to substantially meet the end date initially presented, with a few additional weeks to tie up the loose ends. At no time is the customer opposed in an obvious manner. But, in a kind of mental judo—literally translated as "the gentle way"—he or she can be guided to surrender bits and pieces of margin that add to the bottom line of those who serve the customer. In the end, the project will be more comfortably brought in on time, within parameters that are never quite disclosed.

GIVE YOUR PEOPLE THE TOOLS TO MEET THE DEADLINE

The FBI had mobilized within hours of being notified of the Phillips abduction. Technical teams had been set up to trace the incoming telephone calls. Surveillance teams were then positioned throughout the surrounding area to watch for suspicious activity and to close in quickly once the origin of the phone calls had been determined. An FBI SWAT team was ready to recover the victim. A command post had been set up, occupied by the SAC (special agent in charge) of the investigation, Charlie Parsons, as well as his counterparts from local law enforcement. A separate operations center had been established, which served as a briefing area for representatives of all the teams and also as a clearinghouse for all of the puzzle pieces of information gathered by the agents. More than one hundred agents would eventually work on the case, with every resource at their disposal. "Whatever my people needed," recalls Parsons, "they got. And they got it quick."

The incoming calls from the kidnappers were soon traced. Thanks to the prepositioning of the surveillance teams, agents were at the point of the origin of the phone call within minutes. But something was wrong. SWAT team leader Doug Kane found himself peering into the window of a pristine home, occupied by a matronly, silver-haired lady, who was wearing an apron and bustling about the house. "Usually, a kidnap house is a rat's nest, with beer cans and pizza boxes piled on a table and dishes used as ashtrays. This was a house of out of Mayberry, USA. You could smell the cookies baking."

Parsons directed his agents to stay put and watch. As the days passed, more calls came in and were traced to equally unlikely sources—nice homes with absolutely no indications of suspicious activity. Exasperated, Parsons brainstormed the situation with his technical experts. Was it possible that the kidnappers were accessing a central station switchboard? That seemed unlikely, as there had been no reports of break-ins by the phone company. Could they have gained access to one of the junction boxes throughout the city? Parsons directed his surveillance teams to get in touch with the phone company and identify the locations of all the field junction telephone line boxes in the surrounding area. By the end of the day, the results were in. One box, alongside a road and surrounded by bushes, showed signs of being recently pried open; inside, agents found indentations on the phone wires made from alligator clips. The agents put on some clips of their own and traced the calls to the numbers that had already been identified. The kidnappers, who, as it turned out, got the inspiration from a movie, had been placing their calls from this box, using a different wire each time, creating the impression of phone calls originating from all over the neighborhood. Close on the scent, agents now hid behind the bushes surrounding the junction box, day and night.

This was, incidentally, the first time the FBI had ever encountered this telephoning technique. What made the discovery possible was the generous amount of personnel assigned to the case, as well as the availability of all the portable technical equipment required. The Bureau knows full well that, under a critical time crunch, there is no substitute for a massive step-by-step response. With enough agents roaming the area, the chances are good that, perhaps by pure serendipity, something will turn up. If Parsons had been unable to supply and direct the necessary resources and had been forced, instead, to depend on a handful of agents with little equipment, the same conclusion may very well have been reached but never in time to have saved Stephan Phillips.

Often business deadlines appear unannounced. In an earlier chapter, we saw how Angeles Steel found itself in the not unpleasant, but nonetheless electrifying position of receiving an overnight order, representing a 25 percent increase to their annual business: two million pounds of steel to be fabricated and delivered within a few short months. Their unanticipated challenge was not unique; businesses every day are hit with the unexpected demands of customers. The problem is, "lean and mean" organizations, having downsized to please investors, often find themselves unable to respond immediately to increased orders; they must ramp up quickly and cannot be too particular about whom they hire. Stocking actual inventory is considered a sign of mismanagement in the modern business world, so emergency orders must be placed to suppliers who, in turn, may have cut their own inventories. Just as a human physique can be *too* fit, not having enough body fat, for example, to withstand a bout of flu, many companies find that they haven't the reserves to withstand the business equivalent of a few missed meals. Daily cash flow can be so critical that even a short period of reduced activity can bode disaster. Even prominent mega-corporations like the major airlines were openly concerned about bankruptcy after only two days of drastically reduced air travel, following the September 11 attacks on the World Trade Center and the Pentagon.

Imagine the FBI functioning under the severe, self-imposed asceticism of many companies: a kidnapping call would trigger a purchase order for surveillance equipment; Human Resources would be pressed to cast about within the organization for kidnap experts, having laid off most of the experienced agents during a "kidnap lull"; and black boxes must be requisitioned to trace telephone calls. This sounds absurd, because we expect the FBI to be ready for such contingencies; yet many businesses, which are expected by *their customers* to be similarly prepared, function in precisely the manner just described. While the customers may inventory as little as possible themselves, they expect the companies that serve them to have bulging warehouses and a standing army of technicians ready to commence work the following day. There is always a slight loss of face when the vendor or contractor must tell an impatient customer that the items are not in stock and must be ordered, and that the personnel are not immediately available. And, admittedly, it does seem strange that the "expert" in the field is not fully prepared and, more disturbingly, must rely on a supplier's ability to have forecasted the needs of the market accurately enough to have the necessary items in stock himself.

NOT TO HAVE THE BASICS, IF ONLY IN A SYMBOLIC AMOUNT, IS TO CREATE AN IMPRESSION OF BEING UNPREPARED.

While no one could run a business with items on the shelf gathering dust "just in case" a variety of deadlines should appear, there is a basic "stopgap" inventory in every industry that, if stocked, will give an *impression* of readiness, while buying time for the ramp-up operation to meet the customer's needs. Not to have the basics, if only in a symbolic amount, is to create an impression of being unprepared—and worse, the vendor or contractor actually will be unable to take swift action in response to the unexpected deadline. And sometimes the ability to respond immediately, even if followed by a period of inaction, has an effect on the customer's appraisal that is out of all proportion to the actual work accomplished.

Customers are not the only ones who must have sufficient confidence in a company's ability to get the job done; the person or persons charged with the responsibility of meeting the deadline must know that all the necessary resources will be forthcoming. Business deadlines are often presented in very specific terms of the desired end state, while the *means* to that end may not be discussed in detail at all—as if how one gets there is up to the intrepid soul who accepts the challenge. There is no doubt that there *is* a challenge ("That's why we picked you, my boy!"), but asking for more specifics regarding the company's capacity to meet such a challenge might be interpreted as evidence of indecision or a lack of self confidence. Just as we might refrain from asking the CEO during a hiring interview for specifics on the company's vacation policy, we may save questions regarding the tools that will be available for meeting the deadline for a more appropriate time and for a more appropriate person. As we accept the challenge, we assume that the resources we will need come part and parcel with the challenge itself. It may be weeks after the congratulatory handshakes and shoulder pats from relieved executives when we realize that our hands are tied metaphorically, or empty, in the battle against time we have voluntarily entered.

Being entrusted with a deadline but not with the means to meet it would seem a contradiction so blatant that the situation should never occur. Yet many a businessperson has found him or herself in precisely such a position: denied access to needed information during a time-critical project, unable to make a tactical decision when the supervisor is nowhere to be found, and without the field manpower or administrative support to meet the urgent, immediate needs of the customer. It may very well be that an authority figure, when finally contacted, will release the company resources and will make the command decisions, but precious time lost is rarely recoverable. Later, during the postmortem to determine the cause of failing to meet the deadline, the "lack of organizational support" is considered an unseemly excuse; the executives are disappointed, having had higher expectations of the deadline manager.

As important as the provision of the needed tools is the *removal* of internal, organizational obstacles that, in some cases, might be the managers and executives themselves. Getting out of the way of one's team requires a certain humility, as well as confidence in those selected to bring the project in on time. The highest compliment an FBI agent can pay to management is that "he/she stayed out of our way and let us do our job." Since the majority of its managers (SACs) come from a tactical background, they have both the willingness to subjugate their own roles in times of crisis and the confidence in those who report to them to transfer authority comfortably down to the agents closest to the task. Decisions that must be made within seconds, on the spot, cannot be forwarded up line for approval. "My job," says Pat Patterson, assistant special agent in charge of the Los Angeles office, "is to provide all the tools for the agents to do their job; *their* job is to get it done."

There is one caveat to this concept having to do with a too literal interpretation of "providing all the necessary tools." In an age of downsized organizations, *too many* tools are sometimes provided to the lone individual, who is then expected to fulfill multiple roles once played by secretaries, administrative assistants, order clerks, and assorted support personnel who no longer have a place in the "lean and mean" reorganization. In these cases, the tools are provided in an effort to cost cut, by off-loading onto one person tasks traditionally done by many. The end result can be a burden of time-consuming peripheral chores that prevent the individual from pursuing his or her primary responsibility—be it sales, customer service, or just about any level of management, which are all activities requiring face-to-face contact with the customer. Hours spent *away* from the desk can be the greatest deadline management tools of all.

DECISION MAKING WITHOUT SECOND-GUESSING

Even trivial decisions made in the pressure cooker of a deadline can be difficult to make; throw in the life-and-death factor present in every kidnapping or hostage situation, and it's a wonder decisions can be made at all. There are moments when an agent must choose among several viable alternatives, knowing full well that the wrong choice could mean the death of an innocent captive. Should they risk blowing the case, for example, by arresting the person picking up "the drop," when he may be an unwitting tool? Should this car or that car be followed? Do they apprehend the man making the call at the pay phone, when he could be under the gaze of the mastermind? Dozens of literal life-and-death decisions confront the agent during the course of a kidnap investigation, under conditions during which there is no time for reflection.

When *is* there time for reflection? Months, even years later, these decisions can return in dreams or in quiet moments, to haunt an introspective conscience. Even the popular "shoot 'em up" action films all seem to have the obligatory "dramatic" scene in which a law enforcement veteran, drinking alone in the wee hours of a sleepless night, questions for the millionth time a fatal decision once made under crisis conditions. When asked whether *he* ever had doubts over past decisions made during numerous kidnap and hostage rescue operations over a twenty-seven-year span with the Bureau, Doug Kane answers with untroubled eyes, "I've never second-guessed myself."

"THE SECRET TO DECISION MAKING DURING AN EMERGENCY IS TO ALWAYS DO WHAT IS BEST FOR THE VICTIM."

"Neither have I," agrees Mark Llewellyn, whose long FBI career includes an equal number of life-and-death situations. Noticing my incredulity, he adds, "Not once."

"The secret to decision making during an emergency," explains Kane, "is to always do what is best for the victim. You don't think about catching the bad guys, or retrieving the money, or what this case might mean for your career. You simply pretend that victim is your own son or daughter and you do what's best for their well-being. If you follow that guideline, how can you second-guess yourself?"

Knowing that the agents are thinking primarily of the well-being of their child is what makes most parents surrender control of the case to the experts. But while the FBI and the victimized parents share the initial goal—the recovery of the child—it could be argued that both entities have somewhat conflicting secondary priorities. Once the child is safe, the family would no doubt prefer to have the ransom recovered, while the agents have a duty to society to capture the bad guys so that they do not kidnap again. Llewellyn and Kane's secret to guilt-free nights is to always share the primary goal with the "end user," always preventing the secondary goals from ascending to the top. This advice seems most appropriate to the business deadline.

There can, after all, be a great deal of second-guessing during a time-critical business project and even long after its completion. Even a successfully met deadline does not guarantee the customer's satisfaction, if he or she has been a stepping-stone on the race to the finish line. From the beginning, the customer and his or her vendor and/or contractor have somewhat conflicting fiduciary duties, in that both want to profit at the other's expense. Certainly, vendors must do what is best for them, but what is best for them is continued business with that customer. If decisions are based on the *secondary* priorities—one-sided profitability, sales commissions, less-than-necessary change orders, inflated service contracts, etc.—there will be a loss of trust. While a *competitor* helps the customer with the next deadline, the original vendor will be left to second-guess his or her fatal decisions.

KEEP A DEADLINE LOG

Although it would come as no surprise that FBI agents have occasional bouts of paperwork, we may be inclined to think of those mundane tasks as occurring *between* the action-packed cases that surely must sweep an agent along in their momentum. Certainly, Hollywood portrays an FBI agent, in the midst of a suspenseful investigation, as having no time to shave or sleep, much less attend to distracting paperwork. Once the plot is foiled, with much shooting and rushing about, the exhausted, haggard "agents" drive off into the sunrise, presumably to finally go to bed. If there is any reference to paperwork, it is left to the supporting actors—desk sergeants and long-suffering secretaries—to sort out the details and to take care of the bureaucratic chores unbecoming to men and women of action.

A more accurate portrayal would have FBI agents spending hours at the keyboard, updating their case documentation, even as, metaphorically, the bullets fly. Agents are expected to stay on top of their cases in every way; each step leads ultimately to the courthouse. All the long hours put into an investigation will have been in vain if the agent cannot produce, within ten days of the apprehension of the accused, a clear, unambiguous, specific report to the federal or state prosecutor. Without that documentation, the prosecutor may not be able to make a case beyond reasonable doubt, resulting in reduced sentencing or even freedom for criminals caught red-handed. Anyone who reads the newspapers knows this *does* happen in America's courtrooms, although very infrequently when the FBI has done the investigative work. "We don't want these people to walk," says Charlie Parsons, "the paperwork has got to be complete. And we don't want a last-minute reconstruction of the investigation, because it's hard to recall the specifics." The agents, though action oriented, do not have to be persuaded to keep an accurate case diary; the very real possibility of their "catch" being freed, to prey upon society once again, is motivation enough.

But there is another reason why paperwork is so important to the FBI. "It helps us solve our case," continues Parsons. "By reading your own notes, patterns emerge; things begin to suddenly make sense. That's how we figured out Stephan's kidnappers were tying into the junction boxes." Structure the agents may not have been conscious of in the heat of an investigation is often revealed during the quiet time of paperwork. And brainstorming sessions, with the butcher paper sheets familiar to Hollywood taped to the walls, all marked with specific times, dates, and events, are productive to the degree to which the information is accurate. One can imagine the erroneous conclusions that would be possible with wrongly "remembered" data.

Paperwork in the business community is a fact of life accepted by some and avoided, to the best of their ability, by others. Salespeople, for example, who are often on the front lines of a deadline, are not fond of paperwork, or of any chore that takes them away from pursuing their next commission. Employers are aware of this trait and actually seek out those who have it. It has been reported that Navy "top-gun" pilots are chosen, in part, for their *affirmative* answers to questions such as, "Have you ever gotten a speeding ticket?" or, "Did you ever take your Dad's car out for a joyride when you weren't supposed to?" In similar ways, sales managers search for personalities who are apt to push the envelope, as opposed to applicants who prefer, for example, a steady salary versus commission. The only paperwork these hotrods enjoy is the order-entry process. But there are other members of a deadline team who dislike paperwork—and that often includes the managers themselves.

The deadline manager, like the FBI agent in charge of an investigation, must insist on a daily log from the key team members. While there is no legal case to prosecute (although a deadline team could find itself in litigation, in which case an accurate diary would be most impressive), a clear, concise history of the team's achievement can be invaluable to the prosecution of future deadlines. Important contacts have been recorded, and quoted prices and commitments are there on paper. A deadline log is evidence of one's style. Customers, vendors, and bosses, alike, are impressed and perhaps somewhat taken aback by the professional statement a project history makes. In addition, a deadline log offers the quiet time that gives one a sense of control over even the most frenetic pace of events. Just the act of entering the day's critical moments into a volume thickened with similar comments from previous days can have a calming effect; one has passed through the whitewater before and survived. Finally, a clear, concise diary, in retrospect, can tell one *why* the deadline was successfully met. Without a written history, the experience may well remain a blur of active images that will only become even more incomprehensible over time.

One should not underestimate the protective role of a concise deadline log. If a project, for whatever reason, fails to meet the end date, management may come gunning for someone to hold responsible. Often the "guilty" party is the one with the least documentation. A concise history of one's actions during a project is an indication of more than just a conscientious personality; it is a polite warning to all that one is prepared to defend one's actions. Just as an IRS auditor may throw up his hands in surrender when offered a massive ledger of tiny handwritten entries documenting the issue in question, so will a manager when confronted with a fearless subordinate who has built up a solid "defense." It may be unfair, but the manager bent on finding the cause of a failure may fasten on the team member who saw no need to account for his or her actions.

CONDUCT AFTER-ACTION REVIEWS

On the thirteenth day of the Phillips kidnapping, the abductors used a gas station pay phone, rather than the junction box used previously (and now guarded by hidden agents). As Mrs. Phillips did her usual, wonderful job of keeping the kidnapper on line, the call was traced. Agents Mark Llewellyn and Doug Kane, already in the field for another sleepless vigil, were directed to the gas station. They radioed visual contact of the suspect to Charlie Parsons. Parsons asked: "Do you need help?" Kane replied in the negative. A moment of silence followed, as Parsons considered the possible consequences. By now, he knew they were dealing with a kidnap *team*, having had distinguished at least three disguised voices over the phone. Arresting one member of the team, without first rescuing the victim, could blow the operation. For all he knew, the drama at the gas station could have been monitored by a second kidnapper with binoculars, from a remote location. "Busting" one could cause the others to go into a murderous panic. On the other hand, attempting to follow the "bird in the hand" was also risky; contact had been lost in the past, because of traffic or because the suspect had hopped on a motorcycle and zipped down a couple of alleys, or turned off the road. But Parsons's voice was decisive: "OK. Take him."

Later, in court testimony, the kidnapper would remember two guys, about seven feet tall and three hundred pounds apiece, bursting out of a car, yelling and screaming, and throwing him on his face into the pavement. Llewellyn and Kane smile at the recollection; they *are* big guys, but not quite seven feet tall. "Whenever you take someone down," explains Kane, "there's always a few seconds when he'll respond to orders. I don't care how tough a guy he is, there will be that one brief window when he'll respond. Once he gets his wits about him, of course, he won't talk without an attorney." Llewellyn adds: "We were hoping to find out where Stephan was in those first few seconds of confusion, not hours later in the downtown office. By that time, Stephan could have been killed or taken out of California. So we simply asked him, 'Where's Stephan?'" The question roared into both ears simultaneously, as all three went to the pavement, was answered readily enough; the kidnapper, who had sounded so menacing over the phone to the parents, suddenly did not seem so menacing at all. Within the hour, an FBI SWAT team, commanded by Kane, burst into the house, then into the bedroom, where Stephan Phillips lay, disoriented but alive.

The weekend following Stephan's return and the arrest of the kidnappers, the grateful parents insisted on throwing a big backyard California barbecue for the agents who had rescued their son. Unsure as to the propriety of accepting such a gesture, Llewellyn ran it up the chain of command. The agents were given permission to attend, as long as the celebration was kept modest; it was, in fact, suggested to Mr. Phillips that he provide

"WE WILL ALWAYS FIND SOMETHING WE COULD HAVE DONE BETTER IN EVEN THE MOST SUCCESSFUL CASES."

"hot dogs." Phillips agreed to provide them. "When we got there," Doug Kane recalls with a grin, "there was an enormous buffet set up by the pool: ribs, steaks, chicken, all kinds of salads, beer." Off to the side, untouched, lay a plate of the obligatory hot dogs.

This happily resolved, classic kidnapping case was not formally "closed," however, until there had been an earnest review of how the investigation had been handled—by the very people who handled it. Most significant FBI cases are promptly reviewed by representatives of the various teams involved (surveillance, technical, SWAT) and the kidnap squad, itself. Even apparently flawless investigations are put under team scrutiny. "We don't get together just to slap each other on the back," says Ron Iden. "We will always find something we could have done better in even the most successful cases." The purpose of these meetings is to discover ways in which the next similar investigation may be managed more effectively. In that spirit, the team members examine their own behavior with the objectivity of third parties. Techniques that worked well are mentally reinforced, while actions that may have actually hindered the investigation are frankly acknowledged by agents who are eager to find better ways. Since most of them will remain, by choice, street agents, they are not thinking in terms of increased knowledge for career advancement. The lessons learned in these debriefings will help them—and the generations of agents who follow—in the practical fight against crime.

The successfully met business deadline is very often celebrated but not carefully reviewed, the postmortem being reserved for the deadline that was missed. If there were mistakes made in the happily resolved case, benevolent managers wave them away; results are what count, so why be a killjoy? The FBI would argue that the successful endeavors should be put under the same scrutiny as the failures, perhaps even greater scrutiny, because whatever *worked* should be identified and codified, so that it can be implemented the next time. If, as is often the case, luck seems to have been a deciding factor, the celebration should be tempered with the sober realization of just how fortunate the team was. Since luck cannot be counted on again, it is important to "replay" the events, in an attempt to discover what practical decisions *could* have led to the same joyful conclusion. By a kind of reverse engineering, deadline management techniques can be "identified," even though they are not actually implemented during the project.

Not only are the successful actions sometimes forgotten in the flush of victory, but the mistakes made in the unhappy case are *also* forgotten—but not the individual who had the misfortune of committing the fatal error. The business equivalent of an "after-action review" is more often than not a faultfinding session for failed missions, frequently attended by silent executives who took no part in the struggle themselves. They are there not to find out *why* but *who;* they are searching not for the fault, but for the faulty. The sad result is that the organization itself does not learn from the mistake, because the mistake is not studied. Uncomfortable team members are not open with their thoughts; few in the room are thinking long term, because management is making it perfectly clear to them that a twenty-year career may not be likely. Most of one's mental energy is spent frantically thinking of a clever, self-protecting answer to the interrogations of a solemn inquisitor who wants to "get to the bottom" of the story.

The idea of the team endeavoring to find new ways to deal with the next deadline—for themselves and for the generations of employees to follow—would seem laughable. Yet this is precisely what the visionary manager must encourage; he or she, after all, has a fiduciary duty to prepare the organization for the next time-critical challenge. If a self-corrective spirit can be created within a team of tested deadline "veterans"—and sustained even in moments of defeat—they will be positively eager to find fault in their own actions and committed not to make the same mistake twice. New approaches that had not been previously considered will also reveal themselves. The debriefing sessions for projects won or lost will not be dreaded. And no project, including the "flawless" ones, will be considered complete until the after-action review.

INSTITUTIONALIZE THE "LESSONS LEARNED"

From a managerial standpoint, the FBI produces agents like a shark produces teeth; when one falls out, another fills in the gap. Young faces, fresh from the academy, make up a goodly portion of every branch office. Although beneficiaries of the best training in the world, these agents lack practical experience. Many of their fellow agents, however, have decades of experience under their hats—experiences that serve the veteran agent well throughout his or her career but, unshared, do little for the organization as a whole. If *all* are to serve the nation competently, the lessons learned by the experienced must be passed on, throughout the entire, global Bureau; otherwise, an agent off on an investigation may waste precious time searching for a way to get around a problem that has already been discovered, perhaps years ago, on a similar case.

The FBI shares its experiences in a number of ways, all easily incorporated into a business environment. Student agents are taught at the academy by mature, experienced FBI veterans. After graduation, the fledgling agent is paired with a mentor—paired, but not abandoned by management, which recognizes the spell an experienced agent can unwittingly cast over a newcomer. The special agent in charge of the field office is not necessarily looking for a clone of the veteran; the beginner must be allowed to bring his or her uniqueness into the organization, so an active interest is taken by management as well. "The reason I left the 'fun stuff' to become a SAC," says Ron Iden, "was to help pass on what I've learned over the years and what was taught to me by some great agents."

After the resolution of the Phillips case—a classic kidnapping—a couple of team members were sent back to Quantico to re-create the experience before classrooms of student agents, who will have listened to many more "war stories" from the real world before they graduate. A best practices Web site has been created to house the practical tips from agents all over the world. The hope is that an agent, confronted with an apparently unprecedented enigma, will find, with only a little research, that his or her problem is not unique, after all. Many of the lessons learned "the hard way" are also institutionalized into FBI methodology. As head of the elite Los Angeles–based FBI SWAT team, Doug Kane did not want his people reinventing the wheel. "If we found in the debriefings something that really worked, we'd work it into our response plans from then on."

FBI tactical agents and managing agents are, of course, thinking long term, in the best interests of the organization they love. In corporate America, it is safe to say that not all managers are planning for the generation of leadership to take their place, and some may not be thinking very far beyond the next paycheck. Not only are valuable personal experiences not shared, they are intentionally kept secret, to increase the value of the upwardly mobile employee. *Teams* are not promoted to assistant vice president, individuals are, and tricks of the trade learned over the years are very often kept close to the vest. To the degree to which there is any sharing, it is often in as ostentatious a manner as possible, such as at a corporate awards banquet, in front of the CEO, where an ambitious associate may finally share his or her knowledge—as a kind of spotlight mentor. The odds of a one-on-one, unseen transfer of valuable experience may be slim.

The problem is that deadline management is an acquired skill; it is a disservice to the organization to allow these skills to remain in the heads of those who have conquered significant time-critical challenges. That "head" may leave for another company, retire, or await his or her next chance to single-handedly grab the glory, while others in the company, who will eventually be entrusted with a deadline, are in sore need of that experience, whether they know it or not.

Some businesses are better than others at broadcasting the success stories of their own, via company newsletters and intranet announcements. Sometimes, however, these communications are no more than internal press releases, puff pieces that cheer the victory without examining the near-fatal mistakes, which, if unexamined, will certainly be made again by uninformed associates. Team debriefings may take place within many organizations but within a context so sensitive to the self-esteem of the team members that the mere hint of constructive criticism would have employees running to HR in righteous indignation.

No businessperson would argue that something new is learned on every project, but how many have actually witnessed the mechanism by which this newfound knowledge is incorporated into company policy? Worse yet, corporate policy is often held in contempt by a company's own employees, who want to be recognized as "thinking out of the box" and who prefer "street-smart" solutions to the excessively protective ways of the patriarchs and the matriarchs of the company, whose portraits hang in gilded frames on the wall, like ancestors from an irrelevant age.

Without a conscious effort on the part of management to perpetuate the experiences of the few into helpful, perhaps project-saving, suggestions for the many, the organization will suffer unnecessary hits to the bottom line. With just a little proactivity—in the form of debriefing sessions, presentations by triumphant (or even defeated but wiser) deadline managers, in-depth employee newsletter articles with checklists of useful tips, and managerial recognition of *all* who contribute to the successful conclusion of a deadline—the organization will survive a brain drain of experienced retirees or a loss of key players stolen by the competition. The deadlines that subsequently appear will not be looked on with dread by inexperienced employees, for they will have had the benefit of shared experience so real that it has become part of their own consciousness.

PREPARE A DEADLINE TEMPLATE

FBI cases not only appear without warning, they sometimes seem to appear without precedent. Every kidnapping and hostage crisis is as different as the individuals perpetrating them. Like snowflakes, or, more appropriately, like fingerprints, each case is unique. The FBI could not function, however, by facing each challenge as if it presented something heretofore unknown to the Bureau, forcing it to develop a plan from scratch. Accordingly, a template has been created to deal with not only kidnappings but also bank robberies, attempted assassinations, hijackings, etc. "We don't know when the crisis will occur," admits Doug Kane, "or how it will occur, but we do know for sure that certain things will be required. So we prepare in the area of the known. Then, when you face the unknown, at least you're not preoccupied with getting the preliminaries done."

"The first thing we do," says Mark Llewellyn, "is make sure it's a real kidnapping. The last thing you want to do is mobilize law enforcement all over the state for a hoax. Once it is determined to be the real thing, we want to know the motive. Is this a business transaction or a punitive act? If it's all about money, we can play with the greed of the abductors; if it's revenge for something, that's harder to manipulate. While we're determining that, the kidnap squad, *which is always ready to go*, is sent in. The command post is established, and the Ops Center becomes a very busy place."

Charlie Parsons compares the activity at the Operations Center to something like the apparent chaos of a movie set. "Once I did a little consulting for the first *X-Files* movie. When I walked into the studio, dozens of people were talking all at once. At first I thought it was a Tower of Babel, but, as I listened, I realized there were a number of groups going into action: camera teams, lighting and sound experts, and the actors themselves, each knowing or finding out exactly what to do. It seemed like chaos, but it wasn't; it was a very organized bunch of professionals communicating with each other." Parsons grins, "That's what a stranger might think of an FBI Operations Center; there's so much activity going on that it looks confusing. But we know what we're doing, and, really, we're going pretty much by the book."

The various action plans that fill the FBI manual are not looked on as a sacred text; plans are frequently updated, modified, and perhaps replaced. But the templates are helpful, consulted frequently by neophyte agents, and carried in the heads of the more experienced men and women of the Bureau. But even the very experienced, like SAC Ron Iden, frequently test their own knowledge of recommended responses. "While I'm driving, I'll put myself in various imaginary situations. What would I do if the guy I'm tailing suddenly turns and rushes me? What if I found myself in the middle of a bank robbery? Suppose I'm on a plane and a hijacking situation erupts?" He then goes over in his mind the best course of action. "I have the advantage," he laughs, "of being both the director and the actor, so I finally get it right." These daydreams, however, have a deadly serious purpose, and that is to reinforce in his own mind the proper action to be taken in spontaneous tactical situations. The "what if?" game can be, depending on one's personality, either a constructive or destructive mental activity. In Iden's case, the imagined scenarios are not meant to create anxiety but to provoke thoughts (i.e., mental action plans) that will reduce anxiety.

Whatever the intricacies of a kidnapping case, the broad "kidnapping plan" applies. Business deadlines, while as varied as the industries in which they appear, share enough characteristics to be dealt with immediately in similar fashion, using a deadline template. The day the deadline appears should not be the first day one gives serious thought to how to cope with deadlines. Preparations should be made to create a business counterpart for at least some of the components in the FBI template. The corporate equivalent of the command post is easiest to visualize: upper management summoned into a conference room. The operations center, likewise, is not difficult to imagine: another room, necessarily separate from the command post because of its incessant activity, with a sufficient number of outlets to link the team members to all required databases, as well as plenty of telephones, a dedicated printer and fax machine, and even a coffee pot.

Many companies do have action plans, but they are tucked away in manuals, which gather dust on the shelves because the employees have never been persuaded of their usefulness. Often, deadlines are met with emergency planning sessions that need not be emergencies at all; a simple enactment of previously identified procedures would have been enough. Management really has to go out of its way to demonstrate the applicability of tried-and-true action plans, often to associates who have serious doubts that the corporate soldiers of the past could have possibly anticipated the "out-of-the-box" challenges of today. Every new generation tends to think of itself as unique; the challenges it confronts, therefore, must also be unique. It is a somewhat humbling realization—but a comforting one—to discover that one's problems have already been anticipated, perhaps decades before, by a company strategist who still lives as a virtual coach in the company manuals. Every effort should be made to acquaint employees with the resources—and the relevance and value of those resources—at their disposal.

> IT IS A SOMEWHAT HUMBLING REALIZATION—BUT A COMFORTING ONE—TO DISCOVER THAT ONE'S PROBLEMS HAVE ALREADY BEEN ANTICIPATED.

CREATE A SENSE OF DEADLINE READINESS

An FBI kidnap squad does not sit around a cracker barrel waiting for an abduction to take place—in fact, it may not be a "squad" at all until the kidnap call comes in. Each member may also be engaged in a variety of investigations that may require (as with organized crime investigations) years of plodding research. The "kidnap squad" is actually a potential assembly of specialists, who drop whatever they're doing and come together to deal with the intense short-term deadline of a kidnapping. There is very little they have to be told in the way of instructions; after years of formal and on-the-job training, each team member knows his or her role. After the briefest of mobilizations, the squad is in high gear. The parents of a kidnapped child are both astonished and relieved at the speed with which these professionals take control of the situation and at the synergy of their individual efforts. "It's like a symphony," says Pat Patterson, "when all the elements—surveillance, technical, SWAT, and the squad—come together to rescue that victim."

The coordination comes not only from working together on previous cases, but also from intense practice during frequent exercises. As busy as FBI agents are (and they are *very* busy) the Bureau insists on putting its managers and rank and file through realistic drills, which may include a kidnapping, hostage situation, bank robbery, or terrorist attack. In every case, the familiar elements of a command post and operations center are formed, while the various SWAT, technical, and surveillance teams come together. Not only do agents and managers get to know their respective roles, but they also get to know each other. When the real thing comes along, they already have a working relationship. It is interesting that no one, despite the years of accumulated experience, is exempt from the drills. During the critiques that follow, even senior agents are open to suggestions that might improve their performance the next time; managers themselves evaluate and are evaluated. Not all drills are as dramatic as the one mentioned above; moot court is sometimes held, so that agents can practice being in the hot seat under questioning from a hostile defense attorney. Individual qualifications are also held quarterly, in which every field agent and manager in the Bureau must demonstrate skill with firearms, under stressful simulations.

At least some degree of the FBI's readiness for "drop-dead" deadlines can be achieved in private enterprise, if enough thought is given to a structured response *before* the deadline appears. No one, for example, should have to stare at a demanding, time-critical purchase order in a state of even momentary, incredulous paralysis. Many things can be done proactively, so that one's personnel can be ready. Deadline workshops could be held, in which the members brainstorm possible action plans in response to hypothetical challenges. Roundtable discussions and guest speakers from consulting firms could create an awareness of what has to be done in a major deadline and of what can go wrong. Potluck lunches, in which senior managers and the CEO pass down war stories of their own, may prevent the repetition of mistakes made on past deadlines. Deadline "drills" can be enacted, in which all explore their roles in bringing simulated challenges under control. When the real thing comes—be it an unexpected order, a government mandate, or a unique request from a customer who is under the gun— there will be no initial panic, because panic is simply not knowing what to do. Employees properly prepared will have a pretty good idea of what, in a conceptual if not specific sense, must be done immediately. They will certainly have a leg up on those who have not given a lot of thought to the crisis of a deadline.

An "A-Team" of deadline busters can be formed out of the likeliest and even the unlikeliest employees. Even office veterans who have settled into a predictable, comfortable routine, and who resent intrusions, would no doubt be flattered to be selected as part of a deadline management team, especially if upper management adds an extra helping of prestige with every appointment. The recognition of one's peers often puts spring in the step of the most cynical employee. The deadline management team might include representatives from Accounting, Production, Quality Control, Sales, Information Services, and Engineering—all of whom would probably welcome a chance to drop what they're doing in order to live on the edge of a major deadline. Those who wish to belong to the team should rightly (and only slightly) tremble at the prospect. Membership in the most exciting unit in the organization carries certain obligations: the willingness to work overtime occasionally and the voluntary acceptance of stress that other employees will not have to bear. The "perks" may be nothing more than an enjoyment of an *esprit de corps* that does not exist to such a degree anywhere else in the company.

Prestige as a motivational tool should not be underestimated, as it should not be cynically used. Even FBI agents, who already have worldwide respect, are not immune from the lure of belonging to an elite squad within the organization. There are many such units, each with their own specialty, such as espionage, organized crime, and bank robbery, but there is something about membership in the C-1 squad that both attracts and gives one pause. This is the group that deals with kidnappings and hostage situations—cases that literally involve "drop-dead" deadlines. The investigations are intense, time compressed, and often end with SWAT teams breaking down the door; the hours, accordingly, are long and charged with emotion. Only mature agents are considered for membership, reminiscent of the Army Rangers, an elite unit that accepts only those with the rank of sergeant or above. Like the Rangers, members of the C-1 squad are looked on by their fellow agents as being biased toward sudden, violent, quick turnover cases; whereas those in another unit might prefer equally daunting but longer-term, more complex investigations, such as the ones that result in the collapse of a criminal dynasty, or the exposure of a terrorist cell.

Management can help create a deadline mentality and, at the same time, reduce the anxiety deadlines provoke, by the frequent establishment of minideadlines during the business year. When a staff, department, or assembly line must meet periodic end dates, they become accustomed to working calmly and accurately under the gun; success becomes a habit, and deadlines lose the aura of impossibility. FBI agents live under so many BUDEDs (Bureau deadlines) that they come as no surprise. Business management, of course, would not want to bury its people under arbitrary deadlines, stacked one after the other, but their judicious implementation will certainly develop the necessary calluses for the major deadline to come.

These minideadlines also offer management opportunities to keep the enthusiasm going on a long-term project. Charlie Parsons had a reputation, during his tenure as head of the Los Angeles Division, of being aware of what he called the "narrow victories" of his agents.

Perhaps the organized crime kingpin still walked the streets freely, but one of his people had been "turned" into helping the FBI—that would be a narrow victory. It might be years before the agent would eventually get the main target, but, as a manager, Parsons did not want to wait years before he praised his people. He made a point of monitoring the small successes and of walking by the agent's desk when a number of associates and staff "happened" to be near, congratulating the agent on his or her piece of good work. More often than not, the agent would be pleasantly taken aback—surprised that the boss even knew his or her name, much less about his or her small contribution to a complex, long-term case. As Charlie walked away, the head would bend earnestly over the desk with newfound energy.

If a manager has any doubt as to the usefulness of drills, all he or she has to do is ask subordinates questions such as: (1) What would you do if a customer calls in a panic? (2) Whom would you call if you needed help? Do you have their cell and home phone numbers? (3) What is the quickest way to identify who can deal best with this customer's issue? (4) Where would you look in the system if a critical shipment hasn't been received? (5) What is the password to get online? (6) What are the names of our corporate officers? Employees who have been "prepped" to handle the initial phase of a deadline will be much more relaxed during the typical business day, and under the pressure of a time-critical challenge. Customers can sense this; anxious themselves, they will be comforted by the apparent readiness of an organization that has prepared itself for contingencies such as the one they are facing.

MAKE YOUR DEADLINE TEAM LIKABLE (IT'S MORE IMPORTANT THAN YOU THINK)

FBI agents are the first to admit that not all cases go like clockwork, and that very often investigations are resolved because somebody living "on the other side of the fence" voluntarily provided the agents with strategic information. Nationwide gangs have been broken up, and prominent, heretofore invulnerable, Mafia bosses successfully prosecuted, simply because a petty criminal did an agent a favor. Most informants, in Pat Patterson's experience, "help us because they want to, not because they're being paid. In fact, the intelligence we get from paid informants is highly suspect. But when a guy you've known for years calls in some information *as a favor*, it's usually accurate." In his twenty years with the Bureau, Patterson has cultivated informants that, to this day, continue to be . . . well, friends.

"You wouldn't take them home to dinner, but that doesn't mean you don't treat them as human beings." Many of Patterson's sources of information were cultivated outside the office or police station. "I've converted most of them in a bar," he grins. But there have also been some who, when arrested, remember being treated fairly by him and who then ask for him by name. The same holds true for many of the agents in the Los Angeles Federal Building, some of whom receive seasons greetings cards from the people they have personally put in jail! "A lot of times, there are no hard feelings," he explains. "They know we've got a job to do and don't hold it against us. A lot of them say, when it's all over, 'You treated me square.' Some of these folks, when they get out, occasionally tip us off."

While there are some violent criminals who would like nothing better than killing the agent who brought them to justice—and who, in fact, have put out "contracts" from behind bars—it is interesting that productive relationships can be developed with *any* of society's renegades. "I think what makes the FBI different from a lot of law enforcement," continues Patterson, "is that we're good with people— law-abiding people, and not so law abiding. Sometimes, we'll take a chance and step out of a surveillance situation, take a guy aside on a hunch that he might cooperate, tell him who we are, and just say 'Let's talk.' Every now and then, they talk when they don't have to; we haven't really got anything on them." Patterson describes the transaction as gentle; the Hollywood version of agents slamming uncooperative denizens of the underworld up against the alley wall would not, he points out, be a particularly effective way of creating a relationship. And a relationship, of sorts, with a "wise guy" whose heart has not completely hardened, is precisely what an agent may need during his or her career. Why would a borderline criminal cooperate? "I know it sounds funny, but most informants tip the FBI off because they *like* the agent."

There really *is* something to the "good guys" versus "bad guys" representation of the conflict taking place on America's back alleys and streets. The face of an FBI agent does not look like the sinister faces on the wanted poster beside his or her desk. The fundamental differences in character are recognizable, even by petty criminals who, themselves, may be fearful of the ruthless predators invading their neighborhood. Although FBI agents are perfectly capable of meeting a violent criminal on his own terms, if necessary, it is refreshingly apparent that they are not, themselves, cut of the same cloth. They have an aura of decency and sanity about them, as well as a vigilant, sheepdog mentality, that people tend to like and trust.

> **"I KNOW IT SOUNDS FUNNY, BUT MOST IN-FORMANTS TIP THE FBI OFF BECAUSE THEY *LIKE* THE AGENT."**

The successful meeting of a business deadline often requires favors from strangers—not to mention strong relationships with vendors, distributors, and manufacturers. Managers must remember that efficiency and focus on the part of the team members entrusted with the deadline are not necessarily endearing traits; being "likable" is equally important. Someone in a position to help—a shipping clerk, credit approval manager, gatekeeper, or assembly line supervisor—usually does not do so simply because of one's efficiency, or even because of one's *need* for a favor. Sadly, the reverse is often true: The individual appealed to may have been saying "Yes" all day to his or her supervisors and customers and is finally in a position of fleeting authority, able, perhaps for the first time in months, to say "No!"

It is crucial that the manager charged with a deadline cultivate the character of his or her team members. Even in an age of electronic communication and video conferencing, personal attributes, or the lack thereof, are still obvious to the discerning customer. Managers must also remember that a deadline can transform the gentlest soul into a clock-watching monster; suddenly, there doesn't seem time for small talk or for courtesy. Often, our sense of urgency puts others off, at a time when we most need them onboard. Help may not be forthcoming, purely because people do not like to be pressured into going out of their way; it's so much easier to decline. But, when it is clear that the one asking for a favor is a nice enough person who happens to be in a bind, a fellow human being is inclined to lend a helping hand. That kind of personal projection cannot be faked; those in a position to help will spot a feigned conviviality a mile away. Like the FBI agent on the street, those selected for a deadline must be the "good guys"—likable and decent—rather than company agents driven to desperation, trying to force or beg a favor.

THE LURE OF DEADLINES

One might expect veteran FBI agents, who have lived a good part of their lives on the periphery of corruption—within the worlds of child abductors, hostage takers, serial killers, violent gangs, organized crime, and terrorists—to be a grim and disillusioned fraternity. But I was struck by the good cheer of all those interviewed and slightly taken aback when I heard the first of many describe his and her career as a "fun job." The FBI agents in the movies (which is all most of us have to go on) are certainly not portrayed as chipper team players who love their jobs; rather, they are moody, troubled figures who have seen too much and who are always on the verge of tossing their badges on the supervisor's desk and walking away from the Bureau and from a bitter life on the streets.

But, of course, a career, even a dangerous one, must be some fun, in order to be sustainable. Normal people could not enthusiastically spend thirty years doing something they hate. It *is* fun, no doubt, to put violent criminals away, thwart terrorist attacks, and generally witness good prevailing over evil. "Can you imagine," asks Charlie Parsons, "anything more satisfying than knocking on the door of a distraught couple, in the wee hours of the morning, to return their two-year-old baby? There is nothing like it. Moments like this happen throughout our careers. If you interviewed a thousand agents, nine hundred would tell you there is no greater job in the world."

Retirement for many agents does not come as a relief, nor as a longed-for event. The Bureau mandates a comparatively young retirement age—fifty-seven—which is, in the view of many who must leave, still the prime of life. Retirement parties often have a false gaiety; the spectacle of agents being forced by regulations to leave the Bureau when they are, in their own strong opinions, perfectly capable of continuing at a level of excellence, can bring tears to the eyes of a staff. Given the opportunity, most agents would remain on duty, despite the long hours, the personal danger, and the endless deadlines. Ron Iden, in charge of the Los Angeles Division, is nearing that time himself. Looking about his office wistfully, he grins. "On my retirement day, they're going to have a barricade situation on their hands."

The time-management challenges faced by most agents closely parallel those of the comparatively peaceful business world: middle- and long-range projects suddenly interrupted by extreme deadlines. Kidnapping cases, because of their compressed nature, require eighteen-hour days, thoroughly uncomfortable duties, and physical danger; yet the agents I spoke with recalled them as almost fond memories. When asked to recall the most dramatic, exciting moments in a long career, their minds leapt instantly to such cases, as opposed to even highly successful but longer-term campaigns against organized crime. These "drop-dead" deadlines, enforced by an arbitrary set of nightmarish rules concocted by the perpetrator, seemed to be the spice of life. Nearly every agent I spoke with had somehow contrived to stay "in the field" for their entire careers, side-stepping, or downright rejecting, promotions that led to more managerial challenges but perhaps less action. Contrary to the urgings of concerned spouses, and their own financial needs, they voluntarily remained in pretty much the same pay grade, in order to live the life of a tactical agent.

Many of these agents enter the business world still in their prime. Accustomed to working with others who shared that "deadline mentality," some are dismayed to find the sense of urgency somewhat lacking in private enterprise. Mark Llewellyn and Doug Kane, after twenty-seven eventful years with the Bureau (careers that included no less than seventy-five kidnappings!), are now in business together in Los

Angeles, as partners of Executive Shield. "Probably one of the most frustrating things we deal with," says Llewellyn, "is other people who don't have deadlines, who don't understand how to get things done, who don't return phone calls, and who don't follow up on their commitments."

Mark Llewellyn's frustrations will be familiar to all of us who must contend with counterparts who do not seem to share our sense of urgency. But Llewellyn and Kane have found that, rather than adapting to this new environment by abandoning the habits of a career, they have been able to effect a change on those they deal with, by personally exemplifying their high expectations. Scrupulously punctual themselves, they implicitly put pressure on their customers to also honor the exact time of every appointment. Target dates established by the customer are met early; the final reports are clear and satisfying, followed by a detailed, understandable invoice for services rendered. Before long, the partners found that their reputation for efficiency preceded them; the word was out: "These guys are former FBI agents—don't keep them waiting." To the degree to which we can all build a reputation for meeting our commitments on time, our customers will feel an obligation to respond in kind.

CHECKLIST OF DEADLINE MANAGEMENT TECHNIQUES FROM THE CRUCIBLE OF THIS DEADLINE

❏ Remain in the driver's seat throughout the deadline.

❏ Provide your team with the tools needed to meet the deadline.

❏ Put the customer first to eliminate subsequent second-guessing.

❏ Maintain a deadline log.

❏ Conduct debriefings after each deadline.

❏ Incorporate "lessons learned" into company policy.

❏ Create a deadline template to deal with a sudden deadline.

❏ Maintain a state of readiness—departmentally and personally.

❏ Make sure your deadline team remains "likable."

CHAPTER FIVE

BOEING'S RACE TO DELIVER THE 777 WIDE-BODY

"Our first inclination, of course, was to modify a 767—to travel farther with more passengers. Then we realized the airlines were asking for a totally new design, a brand new family of planes for the twenty-first century."
—JOHN MONROE, BOEING

"Boeing doesn't come out with a new design every day. I've been here since the early seventies, and this is only the third wholly new plane that's come down the pike. It's such a major undertaking."
—ED CALLAHAN, BOEING

"Because of our Working Together philosophy, I sat in on some serious meetings. They let me in their war room, with schedule charts all over the wall. It had been so secret, for so many years, I felt like I should be taking a blood oath."
—GORDON MCKINZIE, UNITED AIRLINES

◆ ◆ ◆

The Boeing 777 is one of those rare creations that occasionally emerge from a process as equally revolutionary as the finished product. That Boeing would have had the capacity to design and deliver a technically advanced aircraft for its customers will come as no surprise; Boeing has built many planes before. What makes the 777 more intrinsically beautiful than any of its predecessors is the manner in which it was created. Just as the significance of Henry Ford's Model T lay not only in its affordability, but in the revolutionary "assembly line" technology that made its mass production possible, the new jet embodies a profound change in the philosophy of management that can apply to any deadline and in any industry.

This fundamental change is known throughout the organization (and throughout the companies that either buy from or supply Boeing) by a phrase that may have seemed initially prosaic; it is called, simply, "Working Together." But Working Together is much more than a corporate motto that is paid lip service to in committee meetings; it is a sweeping, radical philosophy that pushed down barriers as rigid as the steel infrastructures that comprise a Boeing manufacturing plant. Working Together liberated some employees and filled others with trepidation. It nudged prestigious customers, such as United Airlines, British Airways, and All Nippon Airways, off their pedestals and into the problem-solving arena, while it gave Boeing's suppliers the courage to deal on a peer-to-peer level. It was a working ethos that permeated every activity at every level, eradicating the concepts of departmental "turf" and even individual ambition. Communications between employees who had formerly been strangers would become, comparatively, telepathic. The few engineers, designers, and mechanics occasionally brought in from outside companies would feel, for better or worse, as if they had stumbled into a Utopia, where everything was shared—the credit for a job well done and the responsibility for another's failure.

It is not hyperbole to suggest that Working Together created not only a new airplane, but a new organization. Which achievement is greater may depend on its respective life span. Airplanes can fly, with proper care, for decades; corporate philosophies sometimes do not outlive their champions. The original sponsors of Working Together, Phil Condit, Alan Mulally, and others, still lead the Boeing organization. But the new ethic has no doubt taken on a life of its own; future CEOs will inherit a working spirit, along with the massive infrastructure, that, like freedom itself, is perpetuated by successive generations of employees.

WORKING TOGETHER CREATED NOT ONLY A NEW AIRPLANE, BUT A NEW ORGANIZATION.

A new working philosophy may not have been necessary, had Boeing simply modified a 767 to meet the demands of its customers—primarily United Airlines, which wanted a plane smaller than a 747 that could economically transport more passengers more miles than the next step down, the 767. And, in fact, many changes were suggested for the tried-and-true 767. Design concepts were submitted with a stretched fuselage, modified wings, and bigger engines. When the Boeing execs realized the airlines were asking for an entire new family of planes within five years, they also discovered that, in order to build it, things would have to change across the board, both internally and externally. The "fences" that had traditionally separated one venerable Boeing department from another would have to come down; so too would the barriers between Boeing and its customers, suppliers, and the FAA. In no other way would a new family of airplane, incorporating more than three-and-a-half million parts and space age technology, emerge from the design phase to delivered product in five short years.

THE DEADLINE

In the early 1990s, three manufacturers were scrambling to meet the requirements of a major "launch customer," United Airlines. UA was prepared to commit to a significant order of aircraft, once it had identified the plane of its dreams. McDonnell Douglas offered its wide-body, the MD-11, Airbus the A 330, already in test flights in Europe, and Boeing the *design* of the 777, at the time a paper airplane—or, more properly, an airplane on paper. All three manufacturers cooled their heels in three separate waiting rooms at UA's corporate headquarters during the final negotiations, which included two grueling all-night sessions. "It was a horse race," recalls United exec Gordon McKinzie. "We rated all three planes in various categories, and the overall scores were close. What swung us to Boeing? We loved the design of the 777, and Boeing, if the need arose, had the resources to help us with the financing."

Boeing's contract came in the form of an order for thirty-four of the jetliners, when not one—not even the prototype—had been built. The leap of faith on the part of United Airlines was both gratifying and sobering: Boeing now had only five years to design, build, test, and deliver the most technically advanced airliner on the planet. The project would require a team of no fewer than 10,000 engineers and mechanics to create and assemble more than three million parts, big and small. The first 777 would cost Boeing billions of dollars to create.

The Boeing execs knew that five years was pushing it. The 767 had taken nearly that long from the design phase to delivery, utilizing the reliable, familiar procedures that had also created the 757 and 737. The method to build this new aircraft would not be anything like that which created its predecessors. In fact, the process had to be built simultaneously, as it were, with the plane. The projections indicated that one *million* hours would be needed for training alone on the new systems and technologies that were to be implemented. Because of Boeing's reputation in the industry of meeting every deadline, UA had begun to develop its own schedules and to prepare its own infrastructure, for the on-time arrival of a fully certified 777. Delays in delivery were, from a business standpoint, unthinkable. United Airlines had made its commitments to its customers and to Wall Street; its execs had marked their calendars, expecting the jetliner of the future to be delivered, ready for transoceanic service, on the very day it had been promised.

LISTEN TO THE CUSTOMER

The concept of Working Together began, ironically, with a lesson learned about what happens when organizations do not work together. Boeing had tried once before to interest the airline companies in a new plane for the twenty-first century. Called the 7J7, it was an engineer's dream. The company had gone to considerable expense, packing into the 767 derivative every bell and whistle its designers could imagine. The 7J7 then went on a road show—to a less than enthusiastic response from the airline companies. "They weren't interested," recalls John Monroe, a forty-year Boeing veteran. "We had put a major investment into the 7J7, but we had forgotten to ask the airline companies what they wanted in a plane. We thought we knew what they wanted. Boy, were we wrong. We forgot that they had to make money with it. The 7J7 ended up being priced such that it could never close the cost-price-market loop."

"After the 7J7 flopped," says United Airlines exec Gordon McKinzie, "Boeing called in the Gang of Eight—the eight major airline companies—and asked us, 'OK, what *do* you want to see in a new airplane?' Their willingness to listen impressed us. We decided that, when the time came to order a new wide-body, we would keep the communication going, with whoever won the contract. And, in fact, part of our eventual agreement with Boeing included a handwritten MOU (memo of understanding) in which we all pledged to work together on this new product, on an unprecedented level of cooperation." Having agreed to a new working relationship with the customer, the Boeing leadership turned inward, deciding to emulate this new concept within its own organization.

"Listening to the customer" may not sound like a radical suggestion; many business leaders no doubt consider themselves good listeners. Heads will always nod in agreement while the customer speaks, but if he or she is asking for fundamental change, it may not be forthcoming. Management knows full well that, while the customer may have a wish list, there are only so many options available throughout the industry and that, ultimately, pricing will bring the customer back to earth. "Listening to the customer" often amounts to lip service in the early stages of negotiation. Then, things get practical, and both organizations end up pretty much where they began. The seller would much rather tell the buyer about the available options than listen to his or her unique needs. The moment the seller starts to really listen, a measure of control is lost. The specter of the customer being in the driver's seat of a project fills one with dread; customers often have only a vague idea of the fiscal impact of their suggestions. And worse, those suggestions are not always consistent. Last-minute changes evoke the image of a long-suffering interior decorator trying to keep pace with the whimsical, often contradictory, impulses of the homeowner.

"Listening to the customer" can be just as disastrous as paying no heed, at all. True communication requires a sensitivity to the requirements of both parties; in order to be "heard," the customer must be acutely aware of the supplier's practical considerations. The agreement to "work together" simultaneously affected the respective positions of both organizations: Boeing would open the doors to heretofore confidential operations, while United would voluntarily shed some of the mystique of being the *customer*, roll up its sleeves, and join in on the problem solving. Both adjustments are slightly painful; there will be customers and suppliers who do not wish to make the sacrifices required and who will prefer the traditional master-servant relationship—both, ironically, considering themselves to be the master.

Today, Boeing continues with its own memo of understanding for each new customer. It is not a legally binding agreement but a mutual pledge to work together. Prospective buyers of airplanes are asked to read and to consider carefully the words that describe the working relationship desired by Boeing. But in this age of litigation, the memo, not being a legal document, is sometimes given a cursory glance. Recently, John Monroe sat before a new customer and watched his eyes sweep down the text of the MOU. Shrugging his shoulders, the customer said, "Sure, where do I sign?" Monroe was not impressed. "He was sitting there, pen in hand, ready to close the deal, but I told him to sleep on it. I asked him to read the memo carefully and to even make a change here and there, to reflect his own situation. Then I'd know he understood what we were trying to say. It has to be our pledge to each other."

It is important to note that this was a competitive situation: Airbus was waiting in the wings, perhaps with no such informal understanding required. One wonders how many companies would tolerate its representatives taking such high ground on a sale exceeding $100 million—in a tight economy, with competitors beating on the same door. If a sales manager were to ask how it went with a prospective customer and was informed, "Oh, it went great. He was just about to sign on the dotted line, but I told him to sleep on it," the office doors might close for a private, heart-to-heart discussion. Although a veteran Boeing exec, surely John Monroe reports to somebody in the organization. Yet, he was perfectly comfortable in the stance he had taken. He had learned on the 777 project the practical virtues of Working Together; it was in the interest of Boeing, and that of the customer, to secure such an understanding.

"YOU CAN'T MANAGE A SECRET"

Implementing a new working philosophy within a venerable institution such as Boeing was not a matter of simply coming up with a new, snappy corporate slogan and pasting happy faces throughout the facilities. It required radical change, and change generally meets with some resistance. There were those within the organization who questioned the necessity of a conspicuous new work ethic, noting that "if it ain't broke, don't fix it." And Boeing wasn't "broke"; the corporate giant was perceived by the business community to be at the top of its game, cranking out 747s, 767s, 757s, and new-generation 737s in record numbers to meet global demands. Just why the new wide-body project should differ fundamentally from these other highly successful ventures was not entirely clear to a number of old-line Boeing folks. In order to introduce Working Together, the Boeing execs had to deal with obstacles inherent in the very nature of the organization, and of the human heart. Not only would departments have to cooperate on an unprecedented level, but individuals would have to be persuaded to bare their professional souls.

"You can't manage a secret," Alan Mulally would preach, in his appeal for a more open working environment. "The secret manages you. You spend your whole day, or week, or year, trying to keep that secret to yourself, and trying to resolve it yourself." The problem with trying to work it out alone, he reasoned, was the inordinate amount of time required and the high probability of failure. "Let the secret out, so that everyone knows about it, and the best and the brightest can help you." The kind of openness Mulally envisioned would be much more likely to occur when the fences between departments—as well as the barriers between Boeing and its customers, its suppliers, and even the FAA—had been removed. The grand plan could certainly begin where Boeing had the most control: in the departments, where time-honored divisions of responsibility were now looked on by the leaders of the new plane project as simply time consuming.

"In the old days," says John Monroe, a Boeing exec who looks much too young to have already spent thirty-six years with the organization, "our departments were insulated from each other. The folks in Structures would make their design, then toss it over the fence to Systems, who would shake their heads and say, 'No, this won't work,' make their corrections, and toss it back over the fence. Eventually, they would work it out, and the design would then go down the line to Manufacturing, who would make *their* corrections and return it to Engineering. The revised design would go to Tooling, who in turn would make changes . . . and on and on." All that had to change, says Monroe, if the 777 were to be delivered on time. But there was a tremendous amount of rethinking and retraining involved, because "nobody really knew *how* to 'work together.' When you went to college," he asks with a grin, "did you ever take a course in Working Together"?

Putting everybody in a room together, both metaphorically and literally, was certainly a step in the right direction, but encouraging these "strangers" to communicate openly and frankly was another matter. Engineers can be introspective, quiet types at best, proprietary and self-protective at worst. Management had to cultivate a level of trust between teams and between itself and everybody else, so that the open admission of problems was forthcoming. Boeing associates may be dedicated professionals, but they are also human; "sharing a secret" in front of one's peers and one's boss or bosses is not an easy thing to do. Management had to create the conditions in which even the most recalcitrant team members would feel comfortable "confessing," in effect, to having a problem that was too much for them alone.

"WHEN YOU WENT TO COLLEGE, DID YOU EVER TAKE A COURSE IN WORKING TOGETHER"?

The managers themselves, led by Alan Mulally, set the example by openly soliciting help with their own issues from those in the room. Perhaps nothing symbolized Mulally's own freedom from the fear of "exposure" more than a PR photograph of himself, posing in the newly designed restrooms for the 777. Flanked by Boeing executives at either side of the open lavatory door, Mulally smiled obliviously at the camera, in a natural position, atop the pneumatic toilet seat. Surely a project leader with such a self-effacing sense of humor could create an atmosphere of open exchange, in a room filled with the most recalcitrant engineers.

Eventually, Boeing's suppliers caught the spirit. "We had an issue with the floor beams," recalls Kevin Fowler, who oversaw the development of the interior flooring of the plane. "In the 777, we went away from metal floor beams, because composites were lighter and stronger. Early in the program, the supplier of the beams came to us with a problem: the sections, which were beautifully straight when they came out of the tool, would eventually warp a good three inches. Years ago, no supplier would have had the guts to come to us like this; they would have tried to figure it out themselves, and, if they couldn't, we wouldn't find out until much later in the game, when it costs a hell of a lot more to fix." True to Mulally's promise, the "best and the brightest" experimented with the problem. "Somebody suggested we bend the tool itself, so that the beams would intentionally come out slightly warped but would then cure into a straight line. We thought he was joking at first and got down to some serious brainstorming. But, do you know what? That's exactly what we ended up doing. And I think the idea came from some guy on a totally different team."

That the supplier was comfortable in bringing up his problem before it turned into a crisis, and that a team member from another department felt comfortable in offering an out-of-the-box solution, is an indication of the sense of freedom created by Boeing management. Certainly, many of us would not be comfortable airing our own problems out in front of our peers or bosses. And, having done it once, we might not open ourselves up again, as the Boeing members felt free to do, during this complex, five-year project. It is ironic that, in so many organizations, it is management itself—prone to ask, "Why didn't you come to me with this issue before?"—that is the cause for reticence. If only the manager could see the cold, judgmental image that he or she presents, the answer would be self-evident: The subordinate was afraid to come forward. In a competitive working environment, in which employees are measured against each other's performance and many covet the identical promotion, it is very difficult to express what may be interpreted as an inability to handle one's assigned goals. There is the fear that management may toss that assignment to someone who *can*, or, in an effort to create "self-reliance," simply push it back and demand more effort, when lack of effort is definitely not an issue.

Some problems are not expressed, it is true, because one may feel the solution is just around the corner. Many of us who seem to be chronically on the verge of the resolution may not see the need to share, when victory is imminent. We also may keep our problem to ourselves because there is "no time" to subject it to the democratic cross talk of a brainstorming session, which could unravel the very progress we have been able to make. Sometimes, we are simply being courteous; the problem is *our* responsibility, and we do not want to burden associates who have problems of their own. But it would not be an overstatement to suggest that, in general, we keep our secrets to ourselves as a matter of self-preservation. After all, if one is considered the "expert" in an area, one has to act like one, and experts either have the answers, or express confidence in acquiring them soon. To voluntarily expose one's lack of ability to come up single-handedly with a solution requires courage and, above all, trust.

Creating the level of trust necessary to emulate Boeing's Working Together environment is definitely a leadership issue. Management must demonstrate an unconditional acceptance, so that its team members need not fear to raise their hands and ask for help. Not only must management accept, but it must *forget*, so that there is no fear of overt or subtle retribution once the project is completed. Team meetings should be robust enough to encourage innovative thinking but never be intimidating to the shy. The wise manager might demonstrate through role play, beforehand, what would be considered unacceptable behavior, such as a timid question being met by derisive laughter. And a group discussion of what is about to happen might be in order, so that all enter into the spirit of the brainstorming session with open hearts and minds. A debriefing afterward, especially if there have been moments of clashing personalities, would also be worthwhile.

Brainstorming sessions, though often very serious, due to the nature of the emergency responsible for the session, should be as much fun as possible, with the manager always poised to come to the rescue, if the humor gets a little too personal. But one can imagine the relief that would flood the soul of a reticent problem sharer once he saw the lively, productive, even entertaining discussion his "problem" had provoked. The manager who can oversee this kind of exchange of ideas and solutions will save himself or herself much grief down the line— when the "secret" would have otherwise been discovered—and will have created a bonding mechanism that will serve the organization well through deadlines to come.

It should be noted that Working Together, once established, did not require committee meetings or the benevolent presence of management; if it *had*, it wouldn't have been Working Together. During the day-to-day operations, a committee meeting could not be called at the slightest disagreement, nor could a manager be summoned to referee. "Working Together meant relationships," explains Ed Callahan. It meant that we would work things out at our own level, because we had gotten into the spirit of the thing, and because we had become more than team members; we had become friends."

SHARE EARLY, SHARE OFTEN

Not all sharing has to be about problems, just as not all team meetings must be brainstorming sessions. During the five-year project, frequent meetings were scheduled simply to share the progress of the respective teams. But these sessions, too, were uncomfortable for some. "We engineers tend to be perfectionists," admits Kevin Fowler. "There is a reluctance to take the wraps off of one's creation until it's just right." Part of Working Together, however, meant laying out one's "work in progress" for all eyes to see—*early* in the project, so that unpleasant surprises down the line could be avoided, and *often*, so that there were no shared illusions about the status of the overall project. John Monroe recalls another purpose of the frequent updates. "You'd want to know what the engineers were doing, because sometimes you would have to say, 'Enough, already, it's beautiful. You can stop now.'" There was a point where obsessive tinkering with a design, purportedly to improve on it, was no longer in the interests of the project or the customer.

Since these meetings frequently involved Boeing's suppliers and the launch customer itself, United Airlines, a number of potentially troublesome issues were spotted well before it was too late or too expensive to do anything about them. UA exec Gordon McKinzie and representatives from the seven other airlines actually had offices at Boeing during the five-year project and sat in on numerous design meetings. It was discovered, during one of these early sessions, that the fuel port was so high up on the wing that none of UA's fuel trucks would be able to reach it. "In the old days," posits Boeing veteran Ed Callahan, "that probably wouldn't have been discovered until delivery day. United might not even have noticed it until they tried to gas up the plane. They would have come to us, unhappy as hell, and we would have had to say, 'The design has been released; you'll have to buy taller trucks.' Not a very nice surprise on delivery day."

As it was, the work-in-progress reviews saved all parties many headaches down the line. It saved real-time headaches, as well, not because this incredibly complicated project did not have problems, but because Alan Mulally and his leadership team became aware of the problems well before the migraine stage. "Weekly progress review meetings," says Lars Andersen, who worked closely with the European equivalents of the FAA, "were Alan's way of making sure that everybody was paying attention to the right things. Working hard was a given; there was no question of the effort being expended, but you can work hard and still go down a blind alley. These weekly meetings would have caught that."

There are a number of reasons why sharing early and often may meet with resistance in one's own workplace. On the perilous climb up the ladder of success, we are told that "timing is everything," and that, if we are to make the most of an announcement, the time, place, and persons present must be considered. Why, for example, squander an opportunity for recognition from the CEO by prematurely revealing the status of the project to a room full of peers? "Timing," however, is important only for those who desire full credit for their labors. The sharing of progress in front of our associates makes us uncomfortable because it opens up the possibility of friendly advice; suddenly, our "ownership" of the project is jeopardized; we must now acknowledge the contributions of others. Team players, of course, couldn't care less about taking credit for the project; they are committed to the mission, not their ambition. "Alan was incredible about getting us to focus on the mission, rather than personal accomplishment," recalls Kevin Fowler.

Another reason one might dread "share early, share often" meetings is the lack of anything of substance to report. These are, after all, progress-sharing meetings—suppose one has no progress to report? Here again, management must take the lead by recognizing that, on a long-term project, there may be periods of less-than-spectacular results. In fact, these meetings would have to be handled with the same deft touch of the secret-sharing sessions, so that all team members would feel comfortable in delivering their status reports. What made the Boeing managers so successful in creating a productive meeting environment was their sensitivity to the personalities involved; attention was focused not so much on the individual reporting, but on the mission itself. Those who might have otherwise felt "on the spot" lost their self-consciousness in the collective enterprise taking place.

The frequency of progress-sharing sessions would vary with the nature of the project, but frequency is certainly a factor that could be abused by a "hands-on" manager, overeager for good news. If the team members, for example, begin to resent the meetings as intrusions into their already hectic schedules—and, further, view them as evidence of a lack of confidence on the part of management in the team's ability to get the job done without compulsive supervision—the lack of enthusiasm will be apparent. If they're anything, progress-sharing sessions must be uplifting. If the news is good, with all groups on schedule, a buoyant team will leave the room in anticipation of victory. But even the "bad" news of a department falling behind schedule will also be motivating, as the team assesses the situation and regroups to implement the solution. The meetings, therefore, must be productive, not formulaic, and must be seen as none-too-soon opportunities to reaffirm, once again, that everyone is on schedule and of the same mind.

PEER PRESSURE AS A DEADLINE MANAGEMENT TOOL

Anyone who has ever tried to read the blueprint of a house will appreciate the imaginative effort required to "raise" the flat lines on the paper into a mental construction of what the house will eventually look like. Traditionally, jetliners have been assembled from detailed images, rolled up in blueprints that also demanded the conceptual ability of the reader, in effect, to bring the drawing to life. Not only were there a lot of drawings of the planes designed in the past—each with millions of parts to assemble—but there were contradictions that were not apparent until the actual parts, manufactured to specifications, didn't fit. These discoveries, made toward the end of the development of an aircraft, were always disproportionately expensive to fix, since parts and assemblies had to go back to the "drawing board."

To avoid these unpleasant surprises, Boeing made use of extensive physical mock-ups as it developed the 767 and 757. Planes that would never fly were put together to simulate the real thing, so that the engineers would know, for a fact, that the designed parts would fit together after manufacture. And even with these time-consuming and costly safeguards, it was not unusual for drawings to go through four or five revisions, each one representing much work that had to be redone, before the final product rolled out of the plant.

Those mock-ups were an attempt, using the technology of the time, to construct a virtual airplane to serve as a model for actual manufacture; employing the technology of the future, Boeing engineers had developed a software program for the 777 that could "assemble" the new aircraft before the parts were even built. CATIA would revolutionize the science and art of building airplanes. For the first time, engineers could see on the screen a 3-D "solid" of what had previously been a flat representation on paper. It was the difference between an X-ray and a CAT scan. The complete 777 could now be *seen*, not visualized, and manipulated on-screen from any angle, years before it would emerge from the plant. That this technology would speed up the development process of the airplane would come as no surprise, but that it would also serve as a deadline management tool in a motivational sense was an unexpected bonus.

"What CATIA allowed us to do," recalls Kevin Fowler, "was project the work in progress, in a 3-D solid, recognizable to everybody present. If somebody's piece was not there in the puzzle, it was immediately obvious. Heads in the room would turn to the individual or group that had committed to have their piece completed." The lack of contribution—as evidenced by a cable running smack into a beam, instead through a hole in the beam—was now witnessed by all of the team members. Rather than trying to interpret verbal progress updates, the engineers could see for themselves who was, and who was not, on schedule. Those meetings, held on a regular basis, proved to be enormously motivational, because no one wanted to be singled out as the person responsible for jeopardizing the deadline, and there was no way to obfuscate one's current status—not when wherever one happened to be on the schedule was as graphically represented in the form of an actual assembly. "None of us," remembers Fowler, "wanted to be singled out as an obstacle to the deadline, or as somebody who couldn't Work Together."

The very term "peer pressure" evokes, for the HR Department at least, negative images of unwarranted vigilante management by the rank and file, which would (and rightly should) be grounds for an employee complaint. But the other side of peer pressure, which is the desire to be an accepted and respected part of the team, is a very powerful deadline management tool. A team committed to a collective goal manages itself, through the expressed expectations each member has of the other. If senior management has done a proper job of creating a sense of mission, the team will take care of itself—on and off the job. When one's associates are living and breathing the project, it is clearly no time to offer one's irreverent impression of the team leader (unless, of course, it really is funny). The Boeing Working Together meetings were not a matter of lip service in front of management, followed by "treasonous" behavior in private. Those working on the new plane felt as if it were the most important project of their careers, and a temper tantrum on the part of an individual or a carefree attitude that allowed slippage on the schedule were considered metaphorical, though unwitting, acts of sabotage.

PEER PRESSURE IS A VERY POWERFUL DEADLINE MANAGEMENT TOOL.

Leading the mission themselves, managers have to remember that all eyes are on them. To the degree to which they, too, live and breathe

the project, the rank and file will follow. *All* managers must show the way, because each represents factions of the workforce involved in the endeavor. There was a time, during the very early stages of Working Together, when there was some initial resistance on the part of some in various departments, who were accustomed to their own procedures and their own authority that were now jeopardized by the new work ethic. Alan Mulally at that time represented Engineering, while Dale Hougardly led Manufacturing—two departments traditionally insulated from each other and, at times, even slightly adversarial. "There were a few people," recalls Ed Callahan, "who were looking for signs of discord between Alan and Dale, so that they, too, could then break ranks. But it never happened. What we all saw was a united front of management, committed to this new way of doing things. Before long it was accepted even by the hard-liners."

PANIC EARLY

One of the great challenges of any long-term deadline is instilling a sense of urgency on day one, when the end date may be years away. Of course, Boeing management had the great advantage of dealing with professional engineers who understood the nature of sophisticated deadlines—and the need to stay on schedule—but nothing would be taken for granted. "I never realized," recalls United Airlines' Gordon McKinzie, "how schedule-driven Boeing was, until this project. On the development of the 767, I had been 'the customer' and, as such, kept at something of a distance. On the 777, because of our Working Together philosophy, I sat in on some serious meetings. They let me in their war room, with schedule charts all over the wall. It had been so secret, for so many years, I felt like I should be taking a blood oath. It gave me some real insights to how committed these people are to the schedule."

Boeing's schedule was so refined that the teams involved in the early phases of design could know, to the day, the impact of falling behind. Kevin Fowler, in fact, tasked with the development of the 777's flooring, realized to his dismay that, according to schedule, his team was approaching a "day-for-day slide." "That means, for every day we are late, the plane will be delivered to the customer a day late; if we're three weeks behind, the delivery will be three weeks late, which means twenty-one more days of paying interest on a $100 million airplane that won't be paid for until delivered. Not just that, but United would have lost revenue because they planned to put their first Boeing 777 into service immediately."

Fowler called his team of sixty-five engineers together and explained the problem; they knew full well the implications of a day-for-day slide. As a team, they worked overtime for thirty-five days, nonstop, to recover pace on the schedule. Fowler remembers one engineer logging eighty-five hours on his computer for a one-week period! All this activity was for a delivery date *years* down the line. It is significant that not one engineer questioned the accuracy of the projection. Boeing's scheduling ability is legendary; they knew the forecast was accurate—and that when the schedule showed recovery, it had indeed recovered.

"Panic early" is a phrase one might not expect from the cool, unflappable types we imagine to be engineers, but it is Boeing's somewhat tongue-in-cheek way of impressing on all the importance of not taking time for granted, even if—especially if—the end date happens to be years away. Many managers, confronted with long-term deadlines, may not have Boeing's advantage of seasoned team members, who sense the impending doom of even distant end dates, but there are ways to impart that sense of urgency. Breaking up a long-term deadline into a series of urgent milestones, each right around the corner, will help prevent one's team members from taking refuge in the long days before the end date.

Holding each team member to his or her commitment for these milestones is also critical. Boeing's Ed Callahan, on the manufacturing side, remembers how Engineering at first balked at the idea of "going public" with a schedule slippage. "If our people slip in Manufacturing," he explains, "we ask them to put a series of dots on the schedule, connecting their committed date with the revised date the work was now expected to be completed. Those dots showed everybody who had slipped. But Engineering would simply tear up the old schedule and produce a new one with the new dates. Looking at it on the wall, one would never have suspected any slippage had occurred. We asked them," Ed recalls with a smile, "to kindly put in the dots."

The opposite of panicking early is, of course, panicking late—a situation familiar to us all—when time is truly in short supply. Any margin built into the project for safety's sake is usually depleted by that time, so that the later stages of any project seem unfairly compressed to those tasked with the remaining work. With the lack of time, options are reduced. Fundamental changes, such as in the design itself, are either out of the question or disproportionately costly. The best way to deal with these situations is to monitor the slightest slippage of the schedule proactively and to treat each case with the greatest concern. Nothing will kill the momentum of a team with the fear of God in it as much as an "understanding" manager who accepts delay philosophically. This is the time when it is proper to overreact. A manager who is unfazed by delay will serve as a poor role model for a team equally untroubled by its own inability to keep to the schedule.

PR AS A DEADLINE MANAGEMENT TOOL

One tends to think of a public relations "event" as a contrived, tightly controlled, and choreographed opportunity to debut one's program and to update the public periodically—in this case the flying public. Boeing, like any other company, makes extensive use of PR, but, unlike many companies, it is willing to take the risk of incurring a PR disaster, by broadcasting events over which it had little control.

From the beginning, the 777 project opened itself up to unprecedented public scrutiny. The entire five-year endeavor was chronicled, for example, in an incisive, five-hour PBS documentary. Like most PBS productions, this was definitely not a press release. Boeing had given its producer, Karl Sabbagh, *carte blanche*, surrendering, in effect, editorial control. And there are moments in the production Boeing might have preferred not to have been included, such as very frank discussions during emergency brainstorming sessions. This film series may be the most honest portrayal yet of the trials and tribulations of a major business venture. The lasting effect of the production is tremendous admiration for Boeing, in great part because the organization opened the doors on what most of us would have expected to have been a confidential R&D project.

Boeing also took some chances by inviting the world's media to witness, alongside their engineers, two events that could have had unanticipated results: the airplane "Static Test" and "First Flight." In the first test, the long wings are incrementally stressed upward until they literally snap off the fuselage. The engineers had designed the wings to withstand anything the plane would encounter in the air, but this was the first actual physical demonstration. The goal, in terms of pounds per square inch, had been announced before the test began. If the wings had broken too soon, the image on the news broadcasts would have been a public relations catastrophe. Who would book a flight on a plane with "weak" wings? Ironically, if the wings had broken "late," way beyond the design point, the flying public might have been gratified, but the airlines would have balked at carrying the excess weight of overly designed wings during millions of passenger miles. "I think we would have been in more trouble had the wings broken too late," recalls John Monroe. Fortunately, the test was a total success; the flying public was comforted to know that the wings of a 777 can "flap" twenty-two feet, through any sort of turbulence. But the test certainly could have been done behind closed doors, had Boeing played it safe.

IF ANYTHING HAD HAPPENED, THE WORLD WOULD HAVE KNOWN ABOUT IT THAT EVENING.

The first flight of the 777 was equally successful and equally risky—risky enough to provide the test pilots with parachutes and to rig the passenger door with explosive bolts, should an emergency exit be necessary. If anything had happened, the world would have known about it that evening. The Boeing execs shrug their shoulders; if there *had* been a problem, they say, word would have gotten out anyway. That may be true, but a picture of an engine on fire, for example—

played again and again by the media whenever the topic of the plane arose—is infinitely more expressive than a verbal description.

The more likely motivation behind inviting the media to even chancy events is that their involvement is the logical consequence of Working Together. The project environment by this time was so open that it would have been seen as absurdly conspiratorial *not* to include the media at significant events. Surely the presence of so many cameras and recorders had an impact on the Boeing team members, who already must have had a sense of history taking place. The inclusion of public relations in all aspects of the 777 program was a natural extension of Alan Mulally's caveat, "You can't manage a secret." It also proved to be a great deadline management tool.

Not every company can afford or will attract the attention of the news media. But to the degree that it is possible, the media should be brought in to chronicle one's race against time. There are some very cost effective ways to get the word out, such as press releases, articles written for newspapers and trade magazines, and radio talk show interviews (local radio hosts are generally eager, if not desperate, for interviews). If affordable, a "countdown" series of ads, announcing the days remaining before the grand opening (or the beginning of a new service, for example) would not only help create public anticipation, it would also put a great deal of pressure on the deadline team to meet these publicized goals.

Internally, similar announcements could be broadcast throughout the company intranet. Colorful posters on the walls and kinetic representations (such as a movable boat on its journey to its destination) of the company's progress would serve to remind all employees of their race against time. A company photographer might be enlisted to chronicle the endeavor and to display weekly collages of employees strenuously working toward the goal. Frequent company-wide deadline updates and in-progress awards ceremonies, replete with team jackets, coffee mugs, and caps, would help to sustain the sense of common cause. Colorful "campaign buttons" that symbolized the shared deadline would also, if worn by all, create the impression of collective effort and responsibility.

Boeing's willingness to make potentially damaging events a public affair requires a great deal of courage and confidence but certainly ought to be considered by any organization facing a deadline. When the risk is great, employees tend to close ranks in support of their supervisors, managers, and CEOs, who have also put their reputations on the line. It should be impressed upon the media that the company is taking a real chance by opening the event to the scrutiny of the public; in fact, *that* should be part of the story—so that, in the event of a mishap, there will be at least a lingering admiration for the company's courage. The public tends to forgive and forget the transgressions of open, aggressive corporate ramrods, who are not afraid to take a chance.

The Public Relations department, when it has a bold "do or die" attitude, associates itself with the mission of the rank and file, much like the combat photographers who accompanied the Marines landing at Iwo Jima. And like those photographers, PR can spur performance just by being an active, appreciative participant. But when the PR department is seen as a fussy choreographer, trying to get everything "just right," its lack of confidence in the uninhibited abilities of the men and women on the job is palpable and destructive.

HAVE ONE PLAN, NOT MANY AGENDAS

Boeing management recognized from the beginning that, with a team of more than 10,000 members from multiple departments, it would be imperative that all associated with the project have the identical "Big Picture" in mind. The development of the 777 could not be allowed to become simply a series of successfully met departmental milestones. Working Together not only had to break down the barriers separating these subcultures, it had to redefine "success" in terms that would discourage any goal setting other than the on-time delivery of the world's greatest passenger aircraft. It even had to be established, in fact, that achieving one's assigned goals, though commendable, may not always be in the best interests of the overall mission. In theory, if all the smaller goals are met, the larger goal would be realized. But there could be times when a department might willingly sacrifice its own record of success, so that another department could be more profitable. Ed Callahan, in Manufacturing, remembers an instance when he went to an engineering team and asked it, in effect, to fail.

"An engineering department really doesn't have recurring costs," he explains, "they design their piece of the project, and they're done. I, on the other hand, have to build the plane, so I'm never done. We're approaching the four-hundredth 777 now. Suppose an engineering department has a budget of one hundred hours to do their design, and they meet that budget and throw a celebration party. But I spot something on the design that, if tweaked, could save me a hundred hours on every plane we build. In the old days, I probably would have been stuck with that design—and the recurring costs. But under Working Together, I could go to Engineering and ask them to tweak the design—which means I would be asking them to voluntarily fail to meet their budget goal, so that I can better meet mine. Maybe I'd have to take them to lunch," he grins, "but they would do it. And, somewhere down the line, that department would be rewarded for 'going over' their budget, by a savvy manager who understood what Working Together really meant."

Whether the deadline team is composed of ten, or ten thousand, the very division of labor will tend to create myopic goal setting. Departments evaluated for their contribution to the overall project will understandably focus on their scope of work and not on the responsibilities of others. Moreover, on an undertaking of any duration, it is very possible that there will be individuals or departments that will complete their portion of the work, while others attend to the later phases of the project. They may feel "done," while those on the later phase may have felt uninvolved during the initial kickoff. Management must do its level best to keep everybody focused on the Big Picture from day one, until the deadline is successfully and collectively met. Those who have "finished" their portion should be incorporated back into the venture

THE VIRTUE OF LARGE MEETINGS IS IN THEIR INCLUSIVENESS; THE SENSE OF COMMON CAUSE AND COLLECTIVE RESPONSIBILITY BECOME PALPABLE.

and assigned to new teams, while those who have not "begun" should attend every planning session of the actively involved.

Large, comprehensive meetings of the entire team are dynamic opportunities to create—or update—the Big Picture. It may be true that the larger the meeting, the less specifically accomplished, but the virtue of large meetings is in their inclusiveness; the sense of common cause and collective responsibility become palpable. With time allocated for socializing, for open discussion, and for "team player" recognition awards, these get-togethers are a tonic for all involved. More than just a pep rally, these meetings can be instructive; when the Big Picture is properly presented, one begins to understand better one's own contributions. It is amazing how many individuals involved in a large endeavor do not really appreciate the significance of their own efforts. Eisenhower, on the eve of D day, did not successively address the paratroopers, the artillery men, the fighter pilots, the infantry, and all the other specialized units, on their particular vital roles; he prepared an inspirational speech that took the entire Allied armada into account. Alan Mulally would blush at the comparison, but he frequently assembled his "forces" for project updates. Microphone in hand, he would address the thousands before him, all seated in one of the vast Boeing hangars, to share the Big Picture, and to solicit comments and concerns from anyone who raised his or her hand.

When the deadline team has one clear, shared, image of the collective enterprise in mind, its individual members will think beyond their immediate responsibilities and, if given the forum, may have suggestions on how to integrate their efforts better. At the very least, they may ask, when finished with their own assignments, "How can I help?" If management has conveyed the Big Picture properly, no one will rest until the moment comes when all may rest. The apparent contradiction of sacrificing one's personal achievement goals for those of the team—when the team's success is dependent on the personal achievement of its members—is resolved: The complete, finished product *is* the goal of all involved, as each member scrambles to match the contributions of the other. When a major deadline is presented as a "shared destiny," the person who has a hidden agenda will stick out of the crowd. "You could spot the empire builder a mile away," recalls Ed Callahan, "but somebody trying to take advantage of the mission to further his personal plan didn't, and couldn't, last long. Working Together had really taken hold."

The Big Picture must include the customer's recurring costs, as well. Making our own deadline by burdening the customer with our own protective margins may be an unspoken temptation. To use a possibly oversimplified illustration, perhaps Boeing could have met its own schedule sooner by overdesigning some of the characteristics of the plane, rather than going through so many time-consuming procedures to optimize the design. UA might very well have received its first plane ahead of time but would also have been saddled with the additional margin (in terms of unnecessary weight or lack of interior space) that had made life easier for Boeing.

In our own deadlines, there may be temptations to provide a product or service that meets the contractual obligation but that, if "tweaked" (perhaps at our own expense) will save the customer a lot of money over the years in recurring costs. When our Big Picture factors in those considerations, we will have become true advocates for the customer.

IN THE MIDST OF A DEADLINE, CELEBRATE SIGNIFICANT MILESTONES

One of the ways the Boeing execs could keep the drumbeat going on a five-year project was to celebrate the successfully met milestones of the various engineering and manufacturing teams. Pizza parties were thrown at work, while the local pubs benefited from occasional invasions of triumphant engineers. But by far the biggest celebration of them all occurred when the first Boeing 777, its major components joined, rolled off the blocks and onto the hangar floor, a recognizable jetliner. What made this party unique was its size, its emotionalism, and the thousands of children gazing up at just about the biggest thing they had ever seen.

With an overall team of 10,000, one would expect a large number of attendees. But Boeing invited all employees, and their families; more than 100,000 people would be guided around the gleaming airplane by excited team members who would proudly explain or point out their handiwork. There were several showings on this weekend event. Choreographed by Dick Clark Productions, the presentations were memorable. United exec Gordon McKinzie remembers being shown to his seat via penlight. "It was so dark, I had no idea where the plane was. Then, when the spotlights came on, along with the swelling music, I saw that the wing was actually over my head." The huge plane, painted pure white, glowed in the darkened hangar and loomed over the audience—one great, hollow shape—even stopped, it seemed to move. The music swelled into a kind of instrumental choir. The effect brought tears to the eyes. There were executives, engineers, and mechanics who did not, for many moments, trust themselves to speak and who instead nodded solemnly at the creation shining before them. Those tasked with the introductory words had to clear their throats, as if they had colds.

One has to wonder whether Boeing's accountants were among those who cried; the tab for this celebration was substantial. And it could have been argued that the event was totally unnecessary. There were, after all, two years of work remaining on the schedule—did the Boeing execs plan to throw yet *another* expensive bash on completion of the project? Hundreds of employees had already seen the plane in their daily work at the hangar. Would they come on a Sunday, when they could be watching football? And, why invite the families? Surely a celebration for the 10,000 employees would be deemed sufficiently extravagant. Furthermore, the airline industry, cyclical at best, was in a downturn; the country was in a recession. Perhaps this was not the time, nor even the occasion, for such an expansive gesture.

A PARTY AFTER THE PROJECT IS A REWARD; A PARTY SLIGHTLY MORE THAN HALFWAY THROUGH THE PROJECT IS A MOTIVATIONAL STRATEGY.

While Boeing's leadership no doubt had warm feelings for its 777 team members, the big celebration was a practical business decision. A party after the project is a reward; a party slightly more than halfway through the project is a motivational strategy. The timing was, in fact, perfect—now that the deadline had taken physical form. The 777 project was no longer an abstraction. Though much remained to be done, the swept-back wings and rounded nose of the assembled jet seemed to express an impatience. This plane clearly did not belong in the shelter of a hangar. The effect on the team was such that it almost felt responsible for holding the plane back from its release into service and had to move quickly to get that craft into its natural element.

Boeing's "open house" celebration theme was very significant. From strictly a public relations viewpoint, 100,000 people were not at all necessary. The PR for world consumption could have consisted of sound bites from a few Boeing and United executives and dramatic camera shots of the plane itself. Boeing did not require the presence of thousands of giggling children, stamping through the hangar, tugging on the hands of their parents, and begging to go for a ride on the big airplane or at least to sit at the controls. This million-dollar bash was, above all, a celebration for the rank and file. By inviting their families, Boeing had provided an opportunity for its employees to shine in front of the people who mattered most. And from that moment on, support for the new plane deepened; an informal layer of "management" had been created; team members would not only be asked at work about their progress, but at the dinner table as well. New meaning had been given to the corporation's "family" of employees.

If a company has the resources for but one celebration, Boeing's example of throwing the party in the midst of the deadline, rather than after its completion, should be considered. A properly designed celebration can be inspirational—why hold it after the fact? The time to pump people up is in the course of their work. Nine out of ten employees will be positively affected by a sincere and emotional commemoration of a successfully met milestone. It should be noted that management itself, although having arranged the ceremony, is not immune from its motivating effects. The evidence: the Boeing execs reaching for their handkerchiefs during the celebration that they orchestrated. Extravagance is unnecessary; a "potluck" gathering of the deadline team at significant milestones can have lasting effects out of all proportion to the investment. The inclusion of the families is truly the icing on the cake—management will have created the conditions under which friendships are made, and commitments to complete the work at hand are reaffirmed.

OFFER 'EM A CHALLENGE THEY CAN'T REFUSE

Twin-engine passenger jetliners are desirable because of their inherent fuel efficiency and because two engines are less maintenance intensive than four. But there is one certification hurdle that a "twin" must pass that planes like the three-engine MD-11 and the 747 can skip. The certification required is called ETOPS, for extended-range twin-engine Operation. The FAA wants to be assured that the two engines and the plane itself are reliable enough for "extended" flights over the ocean, where there are no airports nearby for emergency landings. ETOPS requirements are considered by many experts to be anachronistic, dating back to the days of propellers, when four engines really were desirable for transoceanic flight. It is an indication of the conservative nature of the FAA that ETOPS is still a requirement, after the airlines have for decades demonstrated the incredible reliability of jet engines. But it is very definitely a requirement, and United Airlines, which was also considering the three-engine MD-11, which did not require the certification, was assured by the Boeing execs that the 777 would be ETOPS certified out of the blocks, on delivery day.

Golfer Lee Trevino once scoffed at a sports writer's characterization of a "pressure putt" and described *real* pressure as trying to sink the eight ball, as a young man in a rough border town bar, on a hundred-dollar bet, when he didn't have the hundred dollars. The Boeing execs would probably have sympathized with that description of stress along about that time, having promised United ETOPS certification without the pledged cooperation of the FAA. Ever since transoceanic flights had been considered by twin-engine planes, ETOPS certification had been granted only after planes had proven themselves over the years in actual "revenue service," carrying passengers on commercial flights. To make matters worse, extended service approvals had traditionally been awarded incrementally. Initially, a twin-engine plane is allowed to fly sixty minutes away from the nearest alternate airport, then ninety minutes, and later, two hours—at which point the plane is certified to fly the Atlantic. Boeing had guaranteed ETOPS certification out of the box, before its new jet had carried one paying passenger. It would have to find a way to get the FAA, a notoriously conservative—some would say "stodgy"—bureaucratic agency that was beholden to no one, to agree to a radical, unprecedented certification process.

"We offered," explains Lars Andersen, "to compress years of revenue service into a torture test of the 777 that would exceed the FAA's requirements. We would dedicate a plane exclusively to a nonstop one thousand cycle (take off, flight, landing) test, while we also ran two engines on the ground through a three thousand cycle test." The FAA considered the proposal, while the Boeing teams continued to build the airplane. From the agency's standpoint, there was no hurry; Boeing was the one under a deadline, not the FAA. "I think they finally agreed," Andersen grins, "just to see if the plane could do what we said it would do." Actually, the FAA had everything to gain from the experiment and nothing to lose. If the new Boeing jet could not perform as promised, it wouldn't be certified; if it could, it would deserve certification. Either way, the grueling test might yield valuable information that would ultimately further the cause of aviation safety. (Boeing had also garnered enthusiastic support for the proposed endurance test from the Pilots Union, which was equally curious to see how the 777 would perform.) In the end, the new plane would pass the test easily. By offering the FAA a challenge it couldn't refuse, the Boeing team had met its bold commitment to its customer: The 777 would roll out of the factory certified to fly across the world's oceans. What would have taken two to three years, traditionally, had been accomplished in five short months.

The Boeing example of offering a challenge so attractive that it had to be accepted should be remembered by all who must deal with agencies that do not necessarily share one's sense of urgency. Drug companies are no doubt occasionally frustrated by the snail's pace of the approval processes they must contend with, as are automobile manufacturers who must prove the efficiency of a car to an environmental board. It must be doubly frustrating when one's technology is actually ahead of the regulatory agencies involved or when one's testing procedures are superior. Those of us who must get the blessing of internal corporate guardians, recalcitrant customers, or bosses—in order to accomplish the same end, but in a compressed time-efficient manner— might suggest, in so many words, "If I can do *this*, would it demonstrate to you the soundness of my proposal? If not, what would?" As long as it is clear that *time* is the only factor that one wants to accelerate and that the actual requirements can be met or exceeded, one should receive a sympathetic hearing. And if the challenge is phrased in terms that spark the interest of the person whose approval is required, it may be accepted out of pure curiosity.

It should be pointed out that Boeing did not leave the FAA out in the cold when it came to Working Together. Overtures were made to keep the agency "in the loop" throughout the development of the new jetliner, and its members were invited to many design and operations meetings. And, of course, it wasn't as if Boeing were a stranger to the FAA; relationships have surely developed over the decades. But Boeing had been turned down by the FAA before, and it could have happened again with ETOPS. Certainly, if Boeing had made no contact with the agency officials up until the point it "needed" them, things could have been different. So the challenge alone may not have been sufficient incentive for the FAA to deviate from time-honored, and time-consuming, procedures; the credibility of the organization or individual offering the alternate method must be taken into account. There are times, certainly, when one is a "stranger" to those who have the power to expedite a process. That's when personal attributes, such as candid honesty and courage, may well be as important as the provocative alternative one is proposing.

THINK BEYOND THE DEADLINE

Not everybody at Boeing agreed with the sweeping changes brought about by the institution of Working Together and CATIA. Interestingly, the most frequently heard objections were that these implementations actually jeopardized the deadline. There just wasn't enough time, it was argued, to build a brand new airplane and, simultaneously, spend the hundreds of thousands of hours necessary to train people on complicated new programs—and to make them adjust to revolutionary working concepts that were never implemented on the 747, 767, 757, or 737. *Those* deadlines had been challenging enough; why introduce so many time-consuming innovations now, when there wasn't a moment to spare?

Had Boeing not met the delivery date, those objections may have found a sympathetic ear. The judgment of United Airlines and Wall Street could very well have been that Boeing had tried some noble experiments on the wrong fast-track project. As it was, the 777, though delivered on time, did take three or four months longer to build than the 767. But so much more was created! In building the 777, new systems and processes had been developed for *all* the planes to follow; new management principles had been created to tame *all* the deadlines to come. In the end, it was in the best interests of the launch customer, United Airlines, as well as every future customer, for Boeing to think beyond the delivery date of plane number one.

It may be difficult for some companies to encourage long-term thinking on the part of its managers—especially, if at the same time, they are asking, "What have you done for me lately?" Boeing has many, many senior executives who have never worked for another organization; they are "company men" and "company women" who joined Boeing right out of college and have remained there for decades. A management core that does not consider itself a body of free agents, who may jump to the competition at any provocation or at the next offer, is apt to think in the best long-term interests of the organization. How does a "dot-com" company, with a legacy of all of fourteen months, engender far thinking on the part of its managers when the business community is told by every career-consulting guru that "gold watch employees" are afraid to leave their comfort zones, and that one should periodically interview with other companies in order to assess one's current market value?

Senior management can engender loyalty and long-term thinking, if it is loyal and far thinking itself. To the degree to which it presses for immediate results, it unwittingly encourages a shortsightedness on the part of middle management and the rank and file. Of course, the senior execs themselves are in the hot seat, expected to deliver positive news at each quarterly meeting, and if the board of directors is not far-seeing, no one in the company will look beyond the next paycheck, much less the next deadline. So it really is a leadership issue. The manager who can buffer his or her own people from the "What have you done for me lately?" line of questioning—whether from impatient superiors, board of directors, or institutional investors— will help create the fertile ground for business yet to come. One who establishes criterion by which to measure long-term strategic thinking—and who praises one's people for thinking beyond the immediate challenge—will foster a creativity within the workplace that can pay disproportionate dividends for the future.

> **IF THE BOARD OF DIRECTORS IS NOT FAR-SEEING, NO ONE IN THE COMPANY WILL LOOK BEYOND THE NEXT PAYCHECK, MUCH LESS THE NEXT DEADLINE.**

Deadlines must be met, it is true, but the end date should never become the end of the synergy developed along the way. If no consideration is given to *what happens after the deadline is met*, the end date becomes the edge of a cliff, where one teeters on the brink of an immediate success, with no plans for the future use of all the wonderful principles and practices that made the victory possible. But when deadlines are looked on as opportunities to explore solutions for future time-critical challenges, a head start is gained on the ones to follow.

DON'T LET THE CUSTOMERS MISS THEIR DEADLINES

After the delivery of United's brand new, ETOPS certified 777—the first Boeing plane ever to be accepted by a major airline without a "re-flight"—Boeing's part of the bargain was, in a literal sense, completed. The company had met its deadline by delivering the plane on time; the fact that United Airlines had associated deadlines of its own was not, strictly speaking, Boeing's concern. But United was not out of the woods yet. There are some elements of a jetliner that are "buyer pro-vided," usually having to do with the custom interiors that distinguish a United plane from a Delta or an American Airlines jet. The features and colors of the seat are highly distinctive, so the seats are often pro-vided by specialty contractors. United had hoped to capture market share also because of its unique passenger entertainment system, which was also buyer provided. And because the galleys (kitchens) in a plane are set up to accommodate the in-flight procedures of each airline, they are very often purchased separately. United was having problems with all three systems.

The FAA had mandated that the seats in the newly developed pas-senger jetliner must be able to withstand a force of 16 Gs. This repre-sented a quantum leap from the existing 9 G crashworthiness standard. As evidence of the independence of the FAA (and further evidence of Boeing's risk of promising ETOPS out of the factory without initial FAA agreement), the agency held firm while the seat manufacturers and the airlines argued that the human body, itself, could not withstand an impact of 16 Gs; such a standard, though having the best of inten-tions, was clearly excessive. The entertainment system, as well, was giving United fits; the music stations and video screens would work for a few seats, but, when expanded to the hundreds of seats in the 777, the system mysteriously failed. The manufacturer in Portsmouth, En-gland, though frantically working on the problem, could not find the cause. And, finally, the galley module presented problems. In the 777, the flight attendants sat in their familiar places, facing the passengers during take off and landing; those seats, as well, had to withstand a force of 16 Gs, and they were attached to the wall of the little kitchen. The galley manufacturer was desperately trying to figure out a way to beef up the module wall to meet the new criterion, so that United could keep its promised schedule of flights.

Though having met its own deadline, Boeing jumped into the breech. A team of engineers was immediately sent to the seat manufacturer. "We helped," recalls John Monroe, "with interpreting the requirements, the actual design and integration, the test plan development, the actual testing, documenting the test results, and probably most importantly, we provided program management assistance." To resolve the entertainment system issues, no less than sixty Boeing engineers spent thousands of hours with the manufacturer. Another group was dispatched to the galley manufacturer, to help with the issues involved in fortifying the module wall and with testing the solution. In all, tens of thousands of hours were spent—all of the work at no charge to United Airlines. John Monroe shrugs his shoulders. "We had to do it. We couldn't let United down, and we couldn't let passengers sit down in a Boeing plane with music systems and video screens that didn't work; they wouldn't relate that to a struggling manufacturer in London—they would only think 'Boeing.'"

While it is true that the passenger might associate Boeing with these difficulties, United Airlines would not, and could not, have held Boeing responsible. "It was our problem, alright," admits Gordon McKinzie. "And we've had last-minute issues before with buyer provided equipment." He adds significantly, "Other airplane manufacturers in the past have told us it wasn't their problem, which was technically true. But Boeing would go to our trouble-prone suppliers and barge into their factories and *fix it* for us. We don't forget that; we have long memories here at UA." A cynic might argue that Boeing was compelled to go the extra mile, in order to evade misplaced blame, but if that were the case, all airplane manufacturers would feel similarly responsible and take corresponding action. United Airlines has not always experienced that kind of commitment from its manufacturers. "Boeing takes its sense of obligation to the customer to the final degree; *they will not let you fail*. And, don't tell anyone," he jokes, "but I haven't seen the bill yet."

Boeing's real deadline, then, was United's deadline. The fact that Boeing had the means to carry its obligation further is not the only explanation; so did other airplane manufacturers, who, in the past, did not feel a similar compulsion. The commitment to meet the *customer's* deadline should be emulated by any company hoping to win the loyalty of a long-term customer or eager to build a reputation within the industry as stand-up ally, willing to go the extra mile.

> **"BOEING TAKES ITS SENSE OF OBLIGATION TO THE CUSTOMER TO THE FINAL DEGREE; *THEY WILL NOT LET YOU FAIL.*"**

The reasons we may not think in precisely those terms are understandable. Sometimes, our very focus on our own deadline blinds us to the customer's obligations to the end user. Fear of possible litigation can be a factor; we are loathe to "barge in," as Boeing might, on the territory of another's responsibility, where even the best of intentions could embroil us in a legal endgame. And, to be fair, we are reluctant to do anything without being paid for it. The "bottom line" is what we are most frequently evaluated on, and heroics above and beyond the letter of the contract will have a negative effect on the immediate project. Since we may be forced to think in terms of the immediate by the expectations of management, we may not particularly care if one last, selfless effort would guarantee future projects for somebody sitting at our desk in the years to come. This is where enlightened management will find a way to award, or at the very least recognize, last-minute heroics on behalf of the customer.

Of course, helping a customer meet its obligations need not be costly. Sometimes a word to the wise is all that is required. A customer forewarned is more than grateful; he or she is aware that his or her best interests are being considered. The logical consequence to friendly advice is an offer to include project management on the next endeavor, to spare the customer from similar headaches. The customer will come to rely on us to not only perform our part of the bargain, but to oversee the remaining effort. Another possible result of our going the extra mile would be that we are awarded that "buyer furnished" business our customer has been withholding the next time around—having proven to him or her that it really isn't worth the hassle to rely on third parties. Failure on the part of our customer reflects poorly on us, despite our own on-time contribution. So, in the broadest sense, helping the customer meet his or her deadline is good for us and for the industry. Going the extra mile will not be forgotten. Not only will we reap the rewards of repeat business, we may have created a sense of reciprocity: The customer may, one day, go the extra mile for us.

CHECKLIST OF DEADLINE MANAGEMENT TECHNIQUES FROM THE CRUCIBLE OF THIS PROJECT

- ❏ Be sure you are *listening* to the customer.
- ❏ Create conditions in which your people are forthcoming about their problems.
- ❏ Share early and share often.
- ❏ Constructive use of peer pressure is a management tool.
- ❏ Panic early.
- ❏ Public relations, when it shares the risk, can be a great partner in meeting the deadline.
- ❏ Have *one* plan, not many agendas.
- ❏ Celebrate the significant milestones, rather than wait until the end date.
- ❏ Offer your customers a challenge they cannot refuse.
- ❏ Think beyond the immediate requirements of the deadline.
- ❏ Don't let your customers miss *their* deadlines.

CONOCO'S WEEKEND OF CARING

"I've got a huge opportunity. I'm going into battle tomorrow, and I need you by my side."
—KIRK HEINRITZ, GENERAL MANAGER, HUMAN RELATIONS RESOURCES, CONOCO

"When I got there, it was no longer a business plan. The devastation was unbelievable. But then, because it was so unbelievable, I realized it had to be a business plan."
—MARY JANE MUDD, DIRECTOR, CORPORATE COMMUNITY AFFAIRS, CONOCO

"This was the highlight of my career. I've been at Conoco for twenty-six years and have met a lot of wild deadlines. But, looking back over the years . . . this was us at our best."
—TOMMY DUNCAN, DIRECTOR, HUMAN RESOURCES, CONOCO

◆ ◆ ◆

Not all deadlines are assigned mandates from the customer; some are thrust upon the general public as an open challenge, awaiting a taker. In June 2001, tropical storm Allison presented such a challenge to the citizens of Houston. Thirty-six inches of rain fell within a twenty-four-hour period, completely overwhelming the intricate system of bayous designed to contain predictable overflow. Twenty-two lives were lost, as downtown streets turned into rushing rivers. The news stations, displaying images of missing persons, were flooded while on the air. The damage was so overwhelming that it took an experienced eye to see if effective assistance could even be rendered. For the residents of 333 devastated homes, Conoco will be remembered as the leader of an unforgettable relief effort, willingly assumed and efficiently executed. The intense short-term deadline recounted here can serve as a model for any business that must take control of an urgent deadline, inside or outside the workplace.

Ironically, *outside* the workplace may provide the greater opportunity to train and cultivate a business team that will sweep through any deadline. The organization that overlooks volunteerism as a way of cultivating a workforce that will be accustomed to impossible challenges, biased toward victory, and willing to sacrifice, is missing out on a great opportunity. No deadline will seem insurmountable to a workforce that has emerged from the crucible of a major community outreach, exhausted but radiant, filled with admiration for one another's heroics, and powerfully aware of the mountains that can be moved through passionate, collective effort.

THE DEADLINE

It was difficult, even for many Houston residents who lived through tropical storm Allison, to truly comprehend the devastation caused by a deluge of thirty-six inches. Even the news footage of submerged houses with people and pets stranded on the roofs could not convey the extent of the damage that would linger *inside* those homes, once the waters had subsided. The storm eventually passed, and in many areas of Houston, the world sparkled again in the bright sunshine. But for those living in the neighborhoods built on the low-lying areas near the bayous, the ordeal was far from over. Although many welcomed checks were written to many relief agencies and churches, comparatively few of the citizens who did not actually live in the affected areas would know of the human suffering that continued in the aftermath of a "perfect storm."

As so often happens, the people most affected were the ones least able to afford the damage and least able to respond physically. The neighborhood hit the hardest was made up of the elderly, many of whom lived alone, all of whom existed on low, fixed incomes. The conditions under which they now lived were appalling. The flood waters had left behind carpets covered with mud and sewage. Walls were stained—some as high as the ceiling—and still saturated behind the gypsum board; the houses reeked of mildew. Cars were still flooded. Refrigerators and air conditioners were ruined. Many houses had lost electricity, gas, and water. In the dangerously hot and humid weather, men and women in their seventies and eighties lay exhausted on wet, moldy mattresses, some with mold actually growing on their own bodies. Despair, helplessness, and hopelessness characterized the emotional state of hundreds within the twelve-block radius of the greatest flood damage.

The weather reports and the rate of flood water recession made it clear that Friday, June 15, would be the first opportunity for any practical assistance for those hit hardest by Allison. The houses, like drained aquariums, steamed in the humid air, but the streets were no longer flooded, power had been restored, and help could be sent. That gave the leadership at Conoco, headquartered in Houston, less than three days to plan a response that would require fifty-five dedicated buses, thirty tons of cleaning and safety supplies (at a time when the city's building supply stores had been depleted because of the storm), 4,000 prepared boxed meals, and the energy of 1,500 volunteer employees— and another two days, in effect, to use it all up, in the intensive relief effort they named "Weekend of Caring."

RECOGNIZE THE IMPORTANCE OF FRONT-END LOADING

It was clear to many at Conoco that some kind of corporate assistance would be forthcoming, well before the announcement from Conoco CEO Archie Dunham. As the rain fell Sunday, phone calls were being made between managers, who anticipated a demand the following day from Conoco employees *to do something*. Dunham had already signed a $100,000 check for the Red Cross and had established a corporate matching program for employee contributions. But he soon came to the realization that "money wasn't enough." He directed a steering committee to see what might be done with "feet on the street"—lots of feet.

Fortunately for the citizens of Houston, Conoco was not exactly a stranger to bad weather. "All the easy oil has been found," explains Executive Vice President Rob McKee, "so that puts us in places like the polar ice cap or the North Sea, which can have thirty-foot swells on a 'good' day. We make our living in bad weather." Nor was Conoco a stranger to house renovation; the Houston corporate office had long ago adopted a small number of older homes in the city, where volunteers spent weekends refurbishing, painting, and landscaping. Perhaps more important, Conoco, with its global presence, was no stranger to crises. In 1998, during the overthrow of the Suharto government in Indonesia, violence had broken out in Jakarta. With people being killed outside the windows of the Conoco facility, complete and utter anarchy was a distinct possibility. Three hundred employees and their children, scattered throughout the city, had to be gathered up and spirited out of the country. After long hours of evading mobs, they were met at a Singapore airport by the Conoco team that had helped make their escape possible. "It was like being welcomed by Green Berets in business suits," Steve Brouillard recalls. "I saw the buses and the Conoco name everywhere, and I knew we were safe at last."

In spite of its experience, or, more appropriately, *because* of its long experience, Conoco management approached this short-term deadline as it would have any other, that is, with extremely careful planning. The lack of time to prepare only made the planning more necessary. "We've learned that the more thought and energy we put in front of any project," says McKee, "the fewer problems we'll encounter on the job." The concept of "front-end loading" being ingrained in the relief effort project leaders, the first thing they did was sit down at the conference table and talk. Accountabilities were accepted; phone calls were made; the planning staff grew in size; site visits were scheduled. The very real possibility of well-intentioned chaos, involving an army of employees and tons of supplies, loomed large in the minds of those who were attempting, at this point, just to get an appreciation of the scope of the work needed. A day or so later, as ideas solidified into action plans, the front-end loading approach would be applied downstream—on a block level, a house level, and, in cases of extreme damage, on a room-by-room level.

THE LACK OF TIME TO PREPARE ONLY MADE THE PLANNING MORE NECESSARY.

Front-end loading was possible even in the realm of the hypothetical. The legal folks at Conoco knew that the company was about to take on a very risky endeavor, from the perspective of liability. First, there were the homeowners to consider. In today's litigious society, in which even good Samaritans are sued by the very persons they have helped, it was not at all out of the question that some homeowners, out of more than three hundred targeted for assistance, might file a claim against the company. They were, after all, distraught; most of what they owned had been destroyed in front of their eyes. There could be some confusion after the clean-up operation as to what items of value had survived the flooding and what were now "missing." And there might be legitimate cases of inadvertent loss; after all, an army of Conoco employees would be dumping tons of water-soaked trash; certainly mistakes could happen. Furthermore, it was not beyond imagination that some homeowners, strangers all, might sense an opportunity to sue for compensation, claiming a swarm of "do-gooders" had swept through and further damaged their homes.

Then there were the Conoco employees themselves to consider. Site-visit reports had confirmed that they were about to enter houses in which electricity sparked in pools of water, and in which the sewage systems had backed up and overflowed onto the floors. The issue of infection was taken very seriously, especially considering that the hospitals in Houston were critically short of the tetanus vaccine. There was a concern about venomous snakes in the houses, another byproduct of bayou flooding. Back injuries were a real possibility, with all the furniture and refrigerators that would have to be muscled about. An employee (or homeowner) could have an allergic reaction to the cleaning fluids being used. The devastation aside, this was also a somewhat dangerous, low-income neighborhood, and not all the residents were elderly or sick. Thought was given to the personal safety of the Conoco volunteers, as well as their family members, many of whom would want to come and help.

Those in Legal were torn between a desire to render aid and their fiduciary duty to protect the company from exposure. The liability concerns raised questions that went around the conference table. "Would the homeowner's Permission Form offer any protection for the company in a court of law?" ("Probably not.") "Should the Conoco employees themselves sign a waiver holding the company harmless in the event of injury?" ("No way!") The conversation went in circles that always returned to the same point of departure: *There was great need; this was the right thing to do.* If there were going to be aftereffects, then so be it.

But the conscientious front-end loading would not be wasted, even in a courtroom. "I think we could have demonstrated," recalls corporate attorney Ralph Burch, "that we had put a great deal of forethought into this project and had taken every possible precaution." The organizational approach to the relief effort would be self-evident. There was a command structure, manifested by the street/house/safety captains, each with a clear idea of what to do, and what *not* to do (such as removing drywall or addressing structural problems). Conoco's own emergency assistance mental health counselors, trained in crisis intervention, were on-site, comforting the anxious. First-aid tents had been set up, with medics prepared to call the emergency rooms about town if necessary. Great care was also taken to prepare the homeowners gently for the massive effort. Should the corporation ever be taken to court, it would have been apparent that this humanitarian endeavor had been studiously planned by an experienced organization, which had felt compelled to render assistance, despite the exposure to liability. But that exposure doubtless dissuaded many companies from a similar, aggressive volunteer effort. It was so much easier—and safer—to write a check.

That Conoco plans its projects will come as no surprise; all successful companies do the same. What is noteworthy here is the disproportionate amount of planning for what was only a two-day operation—a very large operation, to be sure, but still short term. The planning took longer than the implementation! Can one imagine a screenplay of this highly dramatic undertaking, with high-energy, charismatic actors spending two-thirds of the plot *planning*? In today's culture, where "actions speak louder than words"—and where an athletic shoe slogan "Just Do It" seems to have been adopted as a philosophy of life—slow, deliberate consideration in the face of urgent need might be seen as an unnecessary exercise of caution or even as timidity.

It could have been argued that, in view of the extreme nature of

"WE DIDN'T DO THIS JUST TO FEEL GOOD ABOUT OURSELVES."

the situation, there simply wasn't *time* to sit around and put pencil to paper. But the degree of "front-end loading," at all activity levels, is precisely why this relief effort was so effective. The unbridled enthusiasm of a small army of good Samaritans is a wonderful thing to behold, unless it is an invasion of goodwill stumbling all over itself. Without the discipline of a structured approach, this relief effort could have been a fiasco. "We didn't do this just to feel good about ourselves," recalls volunteer coordinator Juanita Garner. "We had be *effective*. We had to change things."

RECRUIT BY PERSONALITY

During the initial stages of the front-end-loading, the steering committee of five selected its field generals. "We needed help, initially, just to get our arms around this thing," recalls HR General Manager Kirk Heinritz, "so we called in some very capable people. It would have been difficult to pick 'experts,' though, because at this point we didn't know exactly what we were going to do. All we really knew was that it was going to be *big*. So, we wanted people who start to salivate at the prospect of a major challenge." The qualifications Heinritz sought had nothing to do with house renovation per se; he wanted "attitude." He continued, "I called Tommy Duncan late at night and told him I was going into the battle the next morning, and that I needed him by my side."

Heinritz, by his own admission, does not make such dramatic phone calls often. He knew Duncan well enough to use these provocative words; further explanation would have been unnecessary. "Tommy is one of those individuals who responds to challenge. In fact," Heinritz smiles, "the best way to get him going is to say, 'It can't be done.' I knew when he heard that we were going to take on the worst hit part of Houston, he'd be fired up." As expected, Duncan appeared in the planning room the next morning, curious, eager, and hoping for a tough assignment, whatever this undeclared project may be.

"Personality" would also be required at the commencement of the relief operation. Not all of the homeowners were comfortable allowing four or five complete strangers, covered with dirt from cleaning the previous house, into their homes, despite the great need. A deft touch was often required, as was sensitivity to the modesty of the elderly. Sensitivity to what might be of *value* to each homeowner was also paramount, especially when the scope of the work was essentially a whole neighborhood, tempting a team of volunteers to think of "moving on" to the next house as quickly as possible. Rather than allowing the relief effort to turn into a juggernaut, steam rolling through the twelve-block radius with the best of intentions, the house captains took pains to consult with each owner. That's why in the middle of a flurry of activity, involving carpet removal and the relocation of couches, tables, and other large items, one might find a volunteer off in the corner, layering paper towels between the pages of an ancient, water-soaked scrapbook, the letters and photos inside being priceless to the homeowner.

These personality traits—love of challenge and sensitivity to the needs of "the customer"—are precisely what every team tasked with a business deadline requires. It would serve little purpose to meet the literal terms of the deadline while trampling one's relationship with the customer. When recruiting for a deadline team or for a new addition to the workforce, "personality" can be as important as the more obviously highlighted entries on a resume. Rather than screen out all but the highly accredited, Conoco managers are alert for the right balance of personal traits. Candace Stephens, now an indispensable member of Conoco's finance department, recalls her initial employment interview with the company. "I'd been working part-time in a noncorporate environment since the birth of my son, so my experience in the corporate arena was a little dated. I told them the truth: that I had just gone through a difficult divorce, and that I was reentering the workplace, and that I probably wasn't at my best right now." Her future manager didn't bat an eye; he had seen "credentials" such as honesty, perseverance, and leadership that would serve the company well. Additionally, he had noticed references to pro bono activities on her résumé. To a Conoco manager, a personal history of volunteerism is an indication of abundant energy, concern for others, and an ability to juggle the demands of a vigorous life—all attributes needed on the job.

CULTIVATE LEADERSHIP THROUGHOUT THE RANK AND FILE

A personality who is attracted to challenge is not only a product of life experience—it can be cultivated at the workplace. At Conoco, a major, corporatewide effort has been in force for decades to prod employees at all levels of responsibility toward increasing their capacity. Nearly everyone at Conoco goes through Targeted Development, although it is a voluntary program—a course of action plans designed to improve the professional capacity of each associate. Nearly all employees (again, it's voluntary, but strongly encouraged by supervisors and peers alike) have attended some version of Covey's Principle-Centered Leadership course; hundreds of Conoco managers have spent a week at a time at these and similar leadership and team-building workshops, at significant expense to the corporation. Refresher courses are offered and taken throughout one's career. There is also a major emphasis, encouraged from the top on down, on putting one's subordinates into situations just slightly "larger" than their image of themselves—while keeping, from a ready distance, a protective eye on them. It is perhaps, more than coincidence that a number of current and former CEOs (among them Keith Bailey of The Williams Companies, and Jim Barnes of MAPCO) are all "products" of Conoco leadership development.

But what makes this investment worth highlighting is its across-the-board application. One would expect a corporation to make an effort at developing its managers, but Conoco goes after its rank and file as well. "Almost everyone I've *ever* known here," reflects steering committee member Julia Ericsson, "has taken leadership workshops and is going through Targeted Development. That's why it didn't matter to me who was going to be a house captain or a street captain, or who took on *any* responsibility role. I was confident that whoever volunteered—whether I knew them or not—could do it."

A major investment in leadership cultivation of the rank and file is a lot to ask of companies in today's leaner and meaner business environment. But the benefits are most dramatically obvious when challenges arise with only days in which to respond. As important as inspirational managers can be, there is simply no time to prepare a large force of employees for the responsibilities that must be assumed; they have to be "there" already. For a company to move with speed toward a business opportunity, tremendous assumptions have to be made. Every level of management must be confident that its workforce will rush into "battle stations" without needing hands-on supervision. For better or worse, there is a point at which even very powerful organizations must trust to the discretion and the competence of its employee base. Certainly, many companies would shudder at the prospect of releasing 1,500 personnel—unsupervised by traditional management—into more than three hundred homes belonging to strangers, in a potentially unsafe part of town, in a communal effort fraught with legal liabilities. The fact that senior management at Conoco could do so readily is a testament to the confidence it has in *all* of its people.

Of course, volunteerism in itself is a crucible of leadership for employees who have been thrust into a situation calling for personal leadership, organizational talent, team building, and interpersonal skills. Leaders and managers are often born on volunteer weekends. Obviously, the donation of one's personal time cannot be mandated, but it can be encouraged and supported. Companies that wish to emulate the Conoco example may find, however, that its support of volunteerism creates a few unsuspected internal challenges having to do with the blossoming leaders returning from a community project. A popular song during World War I expressed a significant cultural shift in America. Entitled "How 'Ya Gonna Keep 'em Down on the Farm (After They've Seen Paree?)" the lighthearted ditty actually described an awakening of American youth, who, on returning from the war in Europe, had no interest in resuming their lives on the family farm. It would be sad, indeed, if one's volunteers—after having "taken charge" for a weekend—looked at the following Monday as a *step down* from their temporary ascendancy. The company must always be sensitive to the character it is helping build through volunteerism and be prepared to provide continuing opportunities for growth at the workplace for its budding new managers.

ENSURE TOTAL EXECUTIVE SUPPORT

The decision to *do something*, in addition to writing out a substantial check to the Red Cross, came from the top. In a gesture both symbolic and practical, Conoco CEO Archie Dunham turned his executive boardroom over to the steering committee for the relief effort. After the committee had assessed the magnitude of the challenge, it somewhat breathlessly reported up line, outlining a shopping list that would exceed $150,000, not to mention the countless dollars of "sweat equity" subsidized by the corporation. "For a moment," recalls Julia Ericsson, "we just sat there, looking at Archie, stunned at our own estimate. What I remember him saying was: 'OK, go do it.'"

Implicit in this terse approval were unspoken paragraphs of mutually understood assumptions, all based on a sobering amount of trust. "Go do it" meant that seeking additional approvals from senior management would not be necessary, but it also put an enormous sense of responsibility on those entrusted with the task. It meant that those who would be authorized to purchase the thirty tons of cleaning and safety supplies were expected to be good stewards of the stockholder's money. "If somebody had to go to the local store and buy every electric fan and mop in the place," recalls Archie Dunham, "I expected them to bargain for one heck of a discount. They did." Above all, it meant that Dunham had complete confidence in the abilities of his project leaders and the feet on the street to do the company proud without executive oversight.

It is significant that all of senior and middle management expressed a similar confidence, in a unified show of executive support. Dunham's decision to begin on a Friday, with a paid day "off" for the cleanup operation, and finish up on Saturday—as opposed to declaring a weekend volunteer effort—meant that there would be business to do, as well. A small workforce was selected to hold down the fort on Friday, while the vast majority took to the streets. But there would be no undue distractions from the office; the cell phones on the belts of the volunteers did not ring with inquiries of pending contracts or work in progress. The managers and personnel who stayed behind worked just as hard to protect the cleaning crews from being pulled in other directions. Sometimes the total support of upper management is manifested by a silent cell phone.

It is extremely doubtful that this major operation could have succeeded in any other way. There was simply no time for seeking the approval of top management. Decisions had to be made by those closest to the task, without fear of being second-guessed by someone who was not at the scene of devastation. The more intense the deadline, the more the expressed support of upper management is required. A workforce that can sense the commitment from on high will go the extra mile, confident that the resources of the organization will be there for them, and confident that they won't run out of "ammunition."

DECISIONS HAD TO BE MADE BY THOSE CLOSEST TO THE TASK, WITHOUT FEAR OF BEING SECOND-GUESSED.

For its part, upper management, when it expresses unbounded confidence in the rank and file, must do so within a strictly defined scope of work, not only for the sake of the corporate pocketbook, but for the protection of those engaged in the deadline. If the execs at Conoco had encouraged their volunteers to, in effect, "go save the city," they would have set them up for a tragic fall. There is only so much even 1,500 enthusiastic warriors can accomplish in two short days. By defining the neighborhood that would be targeted, a realistic, though daunting, goal had been established. The teams could eventually walk away with a sense of accomplishment, instead of a haunting feeling of despair for all that had yet to be done. As it turned out, the scope *did* grow—but only because it became clear that it was possible to do even more effectively.

Out in the devastated neighborhoods, an advance team had spread the word to the residents, nearly all of them elderly and hopeless, and all of them too exhausted to continue on their own. But their cooperation would be necessary, at the very least, for access. *They* had to be ready, too. Thursday, signs were posted on every block: *Conoco is coming tomorrow.*

RELEASE THE PASSION

It is significant that Conoco's decision to take action did not come after it had become clear that the local authorities were overwhelmed by tropical storm Allison; in fact, it came well before. Manager of Corporate Community Affairs Sue Reed arrived at the office after the weekend deluge fully expecting her voice mail and E-mailbox to be full of messages from Conoco employees asking variations of the same question: "What are we going to do about this?" She was not disappointed. By this time, the television news images had made it clear that the residents near Houston's bayous were really in desperate straits. Reports from the steering committee's site visit had already gotten around; it was known, now, that fellow human beings were living under appalling conditions only fifty miles away. Julia Ericsson remembers, "The nervous tension here was tremendous. Giving money was great, but we wanted to use our hands, too. I think everybody was expecting Archie to commit the resources of the company. When he did, you could see the smiles everywhere. We were ready to help, and we would have Conoco behind us."

From a managerial perspective, one of the great prerequisites for the success of any project—sufficient motivation—was a nonissue. These employees were already primed; all that remained was the substantial challenge of organizing the effort. Tommy Duncan's scheme of street, house, and safety captains had been quickly adopted, as was the use of colored vests for role identification. As Friday approached, project leaders scrambled to assemble the supplies, buses, and boxed meals. The weather reports were not encouraging; another front of threatening skies had moved in. On the morning of the relief effort, the volunteer employees, plus hundreds of family members—all wearing red Conoco T-shirts—were packed into the buses about to depart the company parking lot.

Then it began to pour.

Because the ground had already been saturated for days, the rain began to pool almost immediately, raising the very real possibility that the houses in the targeted neighborhood could soon be in standing water, once again. As the Conoco parking lot itself began to flood, the project leaders were now confronted with another problem: How do you tell an army of pumped up volunteers that, to be effective, the relief effort may have to be postponed for another week? It was clear from the faces in the bus windows that the rain would not dampen spirits. The energy of so many people simply had to be used.

Phone calls were quickly made around town, to see if at least some busloads could be immediately diverted to good use, while a "reconnaissance" bus of street and house captains was dispatched to the bayou neighborhood. The city's main Goodwill facility was delighted at the prospect of more assistance in sorting the huge donations of clothing, food, and bedding recently received from the citizens of Houston. Hundreds of Conoco employees, perhaps fearful of the operation being postponed, headed off to the Goodwill shelter, making its over-burdened staff's day. The remainder of the volunteers waited for the report that the reconnaissance bus had arrived. "We asked them by cell phone," recalls Kirk Heinritz, "if it was too wet to work in the neighborhood. Their answer was, 'Don't make us leave. Send more people!'" Within minutes, all the buses rumbled toward the bayous, cheered on by their passengers. Even the weather began to cooperate, although the steaming humidity that followed the appearance of the sun was not much of an improvement, in terms of comfort.

The next two days did nothing to diminish the spirits of the volunteer force. The suffering witnessed firsthand seemed only to strengthen the resolve. The ensuing gratitude of the stricken rendered the volunteers speechless, as they doggedly pushed on to the next home. While "organization" had to be supplied, inspiration did not. There is a question as to what made the strongest impressions on the Conoco employees: the plight of the people they were helping or the selfless actions of their own associates and supervisors, working in houses without air flow, in the ninety-five-degree heat. There was no question of having to "manage" the effort, in order to spur performance. The only time management had to assert itself, during the entire operation, was to *stop* its people from working at the end of each day.

Certainly, passion is one of the greatest attributes any team tasked with a deadline can have. But is it possible to get one's people to feel equally passionate about a business deadline, in which there are no flood victims and no way to appeal directly to the heart? Absolutely! When the workforce feels passionate *about the company* it serves, it will go the extra mile. After events like the Weekend of Caring (or its annual 10K Rodeo Run or its ongoing Keep 5 Alive house renovation project), Conoco headquarters is fortunate enough to have many employees eager to, in some way, repay it for making such experiences possible. This culture of volunteerism exists at virtually every major Conoco facility. And there is a sense worldwide among Conoco's employees that the company *deserves* success in the marketplace, not as recompense for its community outreach programs, but because, in the big scheme of things, there just aren't that many organizations out there willing to put their "feet in the street."

A workforce that feels good about itself from such an effort has energy to draw on that the competition may not. One only has to imagine a deadline being laid down by a manager who is not respected, to a workforce that does not feel good about itself or the organization, to see the competitive advantage of company pride. An employee base pleased with the corporate culture wants to preserve it; the only means to do it is through winning more business. Passion for the company, however, is not a resource to manipulate cynically or to take for granted; nor is this admirable end state the reason behind volunteerism. Passion for the company cannot be harnessed; it can only be released. And when an organization supports opportunities to make a difference in the world and to gladden the soul, it will be humbled by the reciprocity of its rank and file.

CLOSURE AS A DEADLINE MANAGEMENT TOOL

There comes a point at which every completed deadline must be left behind for another. Those who performed so well before must be able to confront new challenges with clear minds and renewed vigor. Closure, therefore, can be a significant deadline management tool—for the subsequent deadline.

Conoco EAP counselor Evelyn Malone remembers a number of people having a difficult time "letting go" after the Weekend of Caring. Some would express feelings of guilt for living in an undamaged home, in a better part of town not prone to flooding. Aching muscles attested to the fact that much was done, but, for many, there still seemed so much more to accomplish. Hundreds of other homes had also been damaged—who would help those families? The 333 homes that had been cleaned were better for it, certainly, but what about the damaged drywall that remained or the need for new furniture? For many who had not seen poverty on an intimate level, the realization that Allison was not the only factor behind the sad condition of the neighborhood was beginning to dawn. Not having ever visited the homes of the very poor, they hadn't known the conditions under which they habitually live. So the flush of victory—totally deserved—was somewhat tempered by a deepening sense of civic responsibility.

Perhaps the most poignant and dramatic example of the need for closure was unwittingly expressed by Conoco attorney Ralph Burch. He had been called in the middle of the volunteer effort, because PR needed his immediate verbal approval of a press release. Burch had, moments before, been hugging one end of a large, ancient freezer, ruined by the flood and filled with putrefied meat. A bloody liquid spilled out of the seals and onto his clothes and shoes, as he manhandled the freezer to the curb. In that distance of twenty feet, he had paused three times to rip off his dust mask and vomit. Now, exhausted and shaken, he listened dutifully to the press release being read to him over the cell phone.

The volunteer effort had been described accurately enough; he nodded his head in affirmation as he listened to the remainder of the text. The final blurb, however, caught him by surprise. In a symbolic gesture of outreach, and as a remembrance of the Weekend of Caring, Conoco Care Bears were to be distributed to all of the homeowners who had been helped. This perfectly legitimate, sweet gesture suddenly struck Burch, in the heat of the day, as an attempt to tie a ribbon around a social ill of enormous proportions. He began to sputter with emotion. "This isn't about Care Bears!" he shouted into the phone. "These people are desperately poor. Even if we had restored their houses to their original state—which we couldn't—they would still be desperately poor. We can't pass out Care Bears and dust off our hands, as if the job is over!" And then, Conoco's corporate attorney burst into tears.

Strong emotions are still evident, nearly a year after the Weekend of Caring. Of the twenty men and women interviewed for this chapter, all had to make an effort, at some point, to control quavering voices; all had to blink back tears when summoning up images of the suffering of those in the neighborhood and of the endurance of their fellow employees. Oddly enough, they also had closure. They were proud of what they had accomplished as a company, as a team, and as a person. Tommy Duncan, who had helped organize the massive effort, considers this to have been the highlight of his twenty-six-year career with Conoco. At 270 pounds—a "macho"-looking guy if there ever was one—he has to look away, clear his throat, shift positions in his chair, shuffle papers, frown at a hangnail, before he can begin to speak of the pride he feels in his company and in his associates.

Conoco senior management did many wise things to bring about closure within its rank and file after that emotional weekend. Sensing that an overview of the accomplishments of the volunteers might be therapeutic, the CMC (Conoco Management Committee) invited the project leaders to give a presentation in the executive boardroom. As fifteen of the organizers walked into the boardroom, the CEO and execs all rose to their feet and applauded. Offering their own chairs at the conference table, the executives *remained standing* throughout the forty-five-minute presentation and discussion. It was a gesture and a simple tribute none of the project leaders would ever forget. And, sure enough, the act of discussing the experience from the perspective of a concluded job did have a beneficial effect for all concerned.

A big lunch was held in honor of the company volunteers. All received citations, signed by Archie Dunham. Senior executives took to the podium and expressed their heartfelt appreciation. By this time, nobody was shocked to see a corporate leader well up with emotion. It was a happy event, with great food and ample opportunity to reaffirm newly found friendships, one of the great by-products of a corporate volunteer effort. Employee comments on the memorable weekend had been solicited via E-mail and were now "published" in a journal for all who cared to read them; so they, too, had a chance to express and to release their emotions. This major undertaking had come to an end, and rightly so; there would be new challenges to face, in the office, and out in the community. The employees of Conoco had closure. But, to be fair, they had had a head start. In the final moments of the relief effort, as the volunteers dragged their feet toward their assigned buses, makeshift signs had been put up by grateful homeowners—some as simple as lipstick written on a broken mirror or painted words on a warped, dried out piece of cardboard—all reading, "Thank you Conoco!"

Business deadlines, too, undeniably take a personal toll. The lack of sleep, fewer homecooked meals, less time with the family, the final string of fifteen-hour days—not to mention all of the frustrations that seem to occur only when one is in a tremendous hurry—can all contribute to a brittle emotional state at the project's end. Following Conoco's lead at the conclusion of a significant deadline makes perfect sense. Debriefings, a celebratory lunch, a forum for team comments, certificates of appreciation, and above all, a meaningful, eye-to-eye "thank you," are all cost-effective ways to clear the mind and free the spirit for the deadlines to come. Not all major deadlines will be as emotional as Conoco's, but "closure" is essential, and very definitely a managerial responsibility.

VOLUNTEERISM, THE ULTIMATE DEADLINE MANAGEMENT TOOL

There were other organizations at work that weekend—businesses, charitable groups, local agencies, churches (most notably the indefatigable Second Baptist Church of Houston, under the leadership of Dr. Ed Young). But none had been able to summon the resources or the "people power" of a major corporation. Looking back, it is clear to Conoco's employees that if their company had not reached out to the homeowners of that devastated area, assistance would not have been forthcoming—perhaps for weeks or perhaps not at all.

The Monday morning following the Weekend of Caring, Conoco employees did not, as might be expected, drag themselves into the office, complaining of sore muscles. "Street captain" Debbie Hill remembers quite the contrary. "Everyone was so pumped! It was as if we had learned together what we could do as a team, the mountains we could move." The unassuming, quiet personalities who had turned into "tigers" over the weekend were amazed, and rather pleased, at their own unsuspected leadership potential. Previous strangers, who had worked side by side and who had cried together and triumphed together, were now comrades. Executives and managers who had spent the brutally hot and humid weekend in rooms without air flow, cleaning carpets strewn with sewage, would forevermore be looked on in a different light by their staff members. Is it even conceivable that this workforce, after having accomplished so much in so little time, would be intimidated by the announcement of a business deadline?

It should be stressed that volunteer efforts do not have to be as dramatic as the one profiled here in order to build such confidence and such pride in the organization. A 10K Run, a community car wash, a highway cleanup, or a hundred other projects can make similar demands on the employees, who will return to work with an increased capacity to respond to business challenges. There is no dichotomy between "business" and "volunteer" projects; every successfully completed charitable deadline owes its success to the discipline of the business plan imposed on it. In fact, having a business plan for the implementation of an awarded grant is one of Conoco's main criteria for donating. "We have requests from charitable organizations from all over the world," explains Sue Reed, "any one of which will break your heart. But, we can only honor a few, and those with the best business plans usually win. We want to make sure our donation is effectively put to use."

It must be remembered that well-planned, corporate-sponsored volunteerism is a partnership with the passion of the workforce. Sharing the burden by supplying the resources for the project and for the well-being of its volunteers is critical. If Conoco had supported its people with lip service, rather than with thirty *tons* of supplies, meals, and transportation—over a volunteer weekend rather than a paid Friday and a volunteer Saturday—the effort and resulting pride in the company would have been significantly diminished. As it was, the synergy created between the organization and its employees was evident the following Monday morning, as the army of volunteers returned to take on more traditional Conoco deadlines. Any company that wishes to develop this kind of dynamic relationship with its workforce can do so. Oddly enough, it all begins outside the walls of the office, in the community. Effective corporate-sponsored volunteerism really raises the question of who benefits the most—the community or the corporation?

IF YOU HAD HAD MORE TIME . . .

Tommy Duncan remembers being asked, during the debriefing that followed the Weekend of Caring, "What would you have done differently if you had had more time?" His considered response surprised even himself. He realized that he wouldn't have done anything differently. The very lack of time, which had been his enemy, had also spurred compensatory performance in both himself and his associates. The deadline, being impossible, had created possibilities that may not have been realized if there had been more time to respond. One only has to candidly appraise his or her own company's chances at mobilizing and implementing such a massive and effective operation in less than five days to appreciate Conoco's achievement and to realize that a shortage of days does not doom an organization to failure, as long as the time-consuming tasks, such as leadership cultivation and partnering with the passion of the workforce, have already been accomplished.

CHECKLIST OF DEADLINE MANAGEMENT
TECHNIQUES FROM THE CRUCIBLE OF THIS PROJECT

❏ Even short-term deadlines require front-end loading.

❏ Recruit by personality as much as by expertise.

❏ Invest in across-the-board leadership cultivation.

❏ Present a unified front of executive support.

❏ Partner with the passion of the workforce.

❏ Closure is a managerial responsibility.

❏ Volunteerism may be the ultimate deadline management tool.

RECURRING THEMES OF DEADLINE MANAGEMENT

◆ ◆ ◆

In a determined effort to avoid the repetition of deadline management principles from chapter to chapter, techniques that had been previously examined were not reexamined, even if they were crucial to the success of the particular deadline in question. It seems incumbent on me, therefore, to highlight a number of themes that became apparent—no matter whom I interviewed, no matter what the deadlines.

SCHEDULE IS SACROSANCT

The deadlines profiled in this book were approached from different angles by the respective task teams, but all concerned expressed a reverence for "the schedule" as the single most important deadline management tool. Ironically, scheduling is often the least credited success factor when company newsletters, magazine articles, or talk show hosts examine a business triumph, probably because the writers are in search of more colorful, personality-driven keys to victory. But it is precisely that implacability that makes a schedule so stable, incorruptible, and enforceable.

While all of the project timelines had mechanisms by which the dates could be altered, the number of "sign-offs" required ensured that amendments could not be made capriciously. Changes were rare and agonizing; since the end date could not be moved, each adjustment threatened to compress the final stages. The schedules, consequently, became great enforcement tools, because they could be referred to impersonally, as an authority that would not respond to appeal. The manager could say, in so many words, "It's not *me* that's chewing you out, it's the schedule that's pushing us all, and we've got to keep pace."

It must be noted that these schedules were not in any sense arbitrary or dreamed up by uninvolved executives who then handed them down to the task teams, along with the end date. All of the long-term projects were guided by realistic, *believable*, timelines that had the benefit of insight from those who would be doing the work. The short-term deadlines, such as the FBI kidnapping case or the Conoco relief effort, were prefaced by intensive scheduling sessions, without which the various teams would have been crashing into each other. In both the long and short of it, a schedule codifies the ambition of the organization; without one there could be no synergy. Imagine, for example, Boeing's team of 10,000, like a Lilliputian army assembling a giant craft of more than three million parts, trying to bring the project in on time without the strictest control of the efforts of each individual.

Within each timeline, significant milestones were established— and celebrated as they were met. These minideadlines made the overall program more manageable, attainable, and more comprehensible to the individual focused on his or her piece of the puzzle. When milestones were in jeopardy of not being met, alarm bells went off in the minds of every manager and team leader on the project, because all would have been affected by slippage along the critical path. A milestone would not be "bumped" unless, and until, the team knew *why* it was in jeopardy, because simply allowing more time would not necessarily correct the process. Margins of time and budget were also factored into each schedule and either doled out parsimoniously, or surrendered immediately for the teams to manage themselves.

In each and every case, those involved in the deadline felt driven by the schedule, which is not, incidentally, as emotionally overwhelming as it may appear. In fact, enforced schedules can offer a tremendous sense of relief: One knows exactly what must be attended to on a daily basis in order to be victorious, and even when "off schedule," one knows what must be done to get back on track.

There is a famous and funny workplace cartoon, in which a circle of kneeling office clerks raise their hands in worship of the Coffee God—a giant coffeemaker, elevated in the center of the adoring throng; it captures, for many of us, the importance of the ubiquitous brew in our workday. An equally apt characterization could be made of the successful teams of deadline-busters profiled in this book, as they willingly bow to the Schedule God, recognizing and obeying the truest guide to victory in the race against time.

PARTNERING

The deadlines profiled in this book that involved major, long-term projects were met jointly; the traditional distance between customer and "those who serve" bridged in the interests of expediency. Turner partnered with a heretofore adversary, the esteemed architectural firm HNTB; they were partners not only in process, but also in risk assumption. The venture embarked on by Airborne Express and Technicolor was so fraught with unknowns that the two companies found their way hand in hand. Under NASA's "faster, better, cheaper" mandate, which cut project timelines by two-thirds, JPL and Lockheed Martin came to the conclusion that the venerable customer-contractor relationship would prove too cumbersome. Boeing's radical Working Together philosophy took the concept of partnering with the customer to its logical conclusion—applying it internally, within its own traditionally insulated departments, and externally, in its relationships with suppliers and governmental agencies. And Conoco partnered as well—with the passion of its employees—in a relief effort that would not have been possible without the support of the corporation. It was abundantly clear to all of the above organizations that their respective races against time would have to be run in unison.

While these companies may have discovered many rewards in the closer relationships and found, perhaps, that the doors of communication, once opened, are difficult to close, their original motivation was to save time. "Business as usual" would not suffice under the highly unusual conditions of a significant deadline. These companies *needed* each other in order to win. Deadlines are very often joint ventures for the simple reason that few organizations can go it alone. Even global industrial leaders, such as Turner Construction and Boeing, were dependent on the unstinting cooperation of customers and suppliers if they were to bring their projects in on time. Conversely, much was expected of them. Reciprocation was possible by modifying billing and payment practices, or by waiving long-standing bureaucratic requirements, or by rerouting time-consuming communication paths, or by modeling one's teams to reflect those of the partner. It was clear, during every interview, that customer and contractor alike felt part of the delivery process.

WILLINGNESS TO ACCEPT RISK

Each of the deadlines described in this book involved risk. Turner Construction had begun work on its new stadium even before the citizens of Denver had voted on the controversial proposal to replace cherished Mile High Stadium. Airborne Express had taken on a challenge so full of uncertainty that UPS and FedEx had declined to join the initiative. The *Odyssey* 2001 team members had begged to be on the project, even though two-thirds (and two out of the previous three) of the Mars missions had failed. The members of the FBI "reactive" squad count themselves fortunate to be tasked with very high risk assignments, such as hostage rescue and kidnap recoveries. The executives of Boeing took great risks, not the least of which was promising United Airlines that its first 777 would roll out of the hangar certified for transoceanic flight, even though the FAA had not agreed to deviate from its certification practices. And Conoco willingly exposed itself to great liability from both those whom they would help and from its own employees.

Yet, one could not find more conservative organizations! The inherent risks in these projects were not accepted by corporate swashbucklers who revel in danger. These challenges were accepted by serious professionals who immediately went about finding ways to *reduce* the risk, by preparing backup plans, by brainstorming creative solutions, and even by taking out literal insurance policies. The risk was accepted, then cut down as much as possible, in order to succeed, to make a profit, or, in the case of the FBI, to reduce the possibility of casualties. The willingness to take a chance defines an organization in ways a thousand Madison Avenue advertisements could not. Airborne Express, which doesn't advertise, is nonetheless known throughout the industry as the carrier to go to with unusual requests. The owners of the NFL teams were not unaware of the courage shown by Turner as it encountered unprecedented obstacles in building the new stadium. Word simply gets around. And companies and individuals who take on risk, and then prevail, develop reputations as giant killers.

There is also something in the nature of "risky" operations that binds teammates together. The "sink or swim" mentality of the teams interviewed surely was responsible for some of the innovations that brought their respective projects in on time. Participating in these deadlines was not simply another day at the office for those involved; these were adventures, the stuff of reunions. Those who had passed through the whitewater of a serious deadline could look on the "nervous time" with a kind of nostalgic pride. "Risk" creates common cause even more than "reward." The most lackadaisical group of soldiers will suddenly become "squared away"—focused and very serious—once the element of risk is introduced.

COMPANY MEN AND WOMEN

Without exception, the challenging deadlines profiled here were successfully met by "company men" and "company women." Their most obvious credential was tenure; the many team members interviewed averaged twenty-five years of service to their respective organizations. No one looked forward to retirement (in fact, they seemed to dread the day), and all seemed to thrive on the formidable tasks assigned to them. While those people were no doubt ambitious, success seemed to be measured less by personal recognition and more by participation on a job well done. None of them were coy about their futures with the company. "I love it here" was heard so frequently, I began to take it for granted, until I realized how unusual it had been, in my own career and in my own circles, to hear so many expressions of unabashed affection and loyalty to the company.

Being considered a "company person" may not be particularly flattering in today's age of the entrepreneurial pioneer. A "company man" is thought to be an unimaginative figure, a corporate soldier who plods obediently to the orders of management. If someone says of another, "Ah, he's a company man," it is to suggest that he cannot be trusted, either with corporate gossip or to come up with the creative strategies required to meet critical projects. In fact, company men and women are usually portrayed as *obstacles* to the bold, forward-thinking newcomer, who is desperately trying to make the changes necessary for the company to be successful. If we are to believe the Hollywood and fictional stereotypes, company men sit at their desks for decades, in mortal fear of being asked a question, incapable of inspired thought—unless it is an embezzlement scheme in the twilight of their careers.

It should come as no surprise that these popular stereotypes are ridiculous, and that company men and women are precisely the kind of people one wants tasked with a significant deadline. They are less likely to look on a successful project as a feather in their cap and more likely to factor in the long-term interests of the company and of the customer (which are, in the long run, complementary). If Boeing's leadership had thought only of the immediate goal of delivering plane number one on time—and less of a management system for the next generation of Boeing leaders—it might never have implemented the new programs requiring countless hours of training. Similarly, the JPL *Odyssey* team—led by a forty-year "company man"—knew that a failed mission to Mars would not affect their careers, considering that the vast majority of Mars probes are unsuccessful. But each team member knew that another Mars failure would mean three "strikes" in a row for JPL and would certainly affect its relationship with NASA. The prospect of losing future planetary explorations to the competition was a tremendous motivation.

So, to whom does a newly born company, without tried and true employees, entrust its deadlines? With years in service not yet a factor, one has to identify the employees who seem sincerely interested in a career with the organization. Team players, who distinguish themselves by helping others without drawing attention to the fact, are prime candidates, as are those who have demonstrated a real concern for customer satisfaction. A manager must take a very active role with a team of fresh faces and must lead by personal example, in creating a sense of mission so compelling that the team will be carried in his or her wake.

This is not to suggest, however, that the dedication of veteran employees can be taken for granted. The wise manager assumes that the company's performers are always being courted by the competition and could, without proper attention, be gone in the blink of an eye. That cheerful, stalwart company icon, who has never given any indication of dissatisfaction, may already be composing a resignation letter. When he or she comes in with the bad news, it is too late to persuade that person to stay; commitments have already been made. As they leave, key customers may follow, as may loyal staff members. While it is true that everyone is "replaceable," the loss of a "company man" can wound the organization more deeply than management may care to admit. To paraphrase the Johnny Cash song "I Walk the Line," the manager who wishes to retain the organization's top performers must keep his or her eyes "wide open all the time."

FAMILY OUTREACH

It is quite natural for us to think in terms of "business" as distinct from other activities in our life, just as "work" is from play, worship, mowing the lawn, or driving the kids to school. We tend to put the family in the role of a beneficiary to the workplace—literally, in terms of retirement plans and accident insurance, and figuratively—doing "business" is the way families are fed, not the reverse.

The popular stereotype of an executive who sacrifices family for career is somewhat of a contradiction, because, clearly, business success is not sustainable without a strong emotional base. A hard-driving executive plagued by personal problems, distracted by divorce proceedings or custody battles, will not be able to focus on the job at hand and may even exacerbate his or her situation by finding a comfort of sorts in alcohol or drugs. This is not to suggest that family life is not without troubles, but the demands made from the "home front" can be powerfully motivating. The wise manager recognizes the importance of family and tries to find ways to symbolically involve the "other half" of the deadline team and to enlist their support in the pursuit of the deadline. By including a scroll bearing the signatures of the spouses and children of its team members into a spacecraft, and by inviting the family members to a presentation of the assembled 777 two years before the delivery date, both JPL and Boeing drew on resources not officially on the payroll, but crucial to the success of the deadline, nonetheless. Turner's gesture of opening up the stadium for the private enjoyment of the families of its construction workers weeks before the public opening was a tribute to the invisible foundation of support for the new stadium, manifested in steel and concrete. And Conoco took the concept of "family outreach" to its natural extension—first, by allowing the family members of its workforce to join in the volunteer effort, and second, by embracing the community itself.

MAKING IT EASY FOR THE CUSTOMER

Thinking in terms of the customer's deadline and of ways to facilitate their up-line obligations to yet another level of customers or end users was characteristic of all the companies in this book. By assuring Pat Bolin that the stadium would be delivered as promised, Turner made the Broncos owner comfortable enough to sell millions of dollars of tickets, advertising, and television rights for Game One. With its intelligent label, Airborne Express made it easy for the theater managers to keep pace with a cycle of deadlines that included a rapid return of films to Technicolor's distribution hub. JPL went against the objections of

NASA by launching its *Odyssey* orbiter with a "questionable" mechanical arm that beamed a radio transmitter toward Earth, while the science instruments were directed toward Mars—so that *its* customers, the scientific community, could receive an uninterrupted flow of information. Even FBI agents have their customer, the federal court, in mind and endeavor to make the prosecutor's job as easy as possible with well-documented case files. Boeing refused to celebrate the completion of its part of the bargain with United until it had helped the airline company meet its own deadline. Lastly, Conoco employees demonstrated great sensitivity to the needs of the "customer" by not steamrolling through each house in the massive cleanup effort, and by taking the time to help salvage irreplaceable mementos, letters, and photographs of each homeowner.

It is rather easy to imagine the reverse of these situations: Airborne, for example, insisting that the theaters take the time to fill out the return label like every other customer, or an acquiescent JPL abandoning the mechanical arm in question and instructing the orbiter to gather information, then turn to Earth to transmit, thereby cutting the flow of data to the scientific community by at least half. Perhaps the most frightening hypothetical would be that of a federal prosecutor's inability to convict a terrorist because of an agent's haphazard documentation. Fortunately, all of the organizations profiled here never lost sight of the big picture, which includes the customer meeting its own obligations. By making the customer's deadline its own, each company has developed a reputation as a dependable ally who will not let the customer fail.

WILLINGNESS TO RAMP UP

Just about all of the organizations discussed had to ramp up significantly in order to meet their deadlines. It wasn't as if they could meet these challenges "the way they were." Although the nation's largest builder, Turner does not ordinarily stockpile the huge steel and concrete forms required for its projects; it is much more cost effective simply to have them delivered to the job site the day they are needed.

But, in an effort to be independent of the local suppliers, and in reaction to anticipated shortages, it invested in the storage of colossal beams and risers that would eventually be used on the new Broncos stadium. In order to meet Technicolor's demands, Airborne had to build up its ground services and invent both a proactive monitoring system and an intelligent label. Technicolor, in turn, invested in two enormous distribution facilities. Jet Propulsion Labs—its timelines cut from the traditional ten-year project to less than three years—had to make great adjustments in order to launch its spacecraft on time. Even though Boeing could have built its new wide-body using the procedures that had served the company so well in the development of the 747, 767, 757, and 737, it chose to revolutionize the way planes were made at a price tag of tens of millions of dollars. Conoco's ramp up was no less impressive because of the short-term nature of its relief effort; in fact, it could be argued its logistical challenges were proportionately the most intense of all of the deadlines profiled.

The challenges these organizations had accepted, therefore, were further complicated by the steps that needed to be taken before each deadline could be earnestly addressed. That they were not intimidated by the deadlines, nor by the requirements to meet the deadlines, is quite remarkable. Surely one can imagine naysayers in each organization (other than the FBI) expressing opposition to the sudden demands on their infrastructure. But in all cases, the decisions of senior management to accept the challenges had very positive repercussions. It could be argued that the organizations profiled in this book were, in varying degrees, transformed by the requirements to meet challenges they had willingly accepted.

INDEX

239